Becoming a Di on Campus

MW01110063

Illuminating the emerging importance of the diversity leader on college campuses, this book offers perspectives and narratives from diversity leaders at institutions of higher education.

Becoming a Diversity Leader on Campus unpacks the tension of how diversity leadership is shaped by external factors and pressures that confront colleges and universities, as well as by the unique experiences and identities of the individuals appointed to diversity leadership positions. This book offers a better understanding of how diversity leaders make meaning and sense of their roles, desire, and passion for promoting diversity within their institutions. Chapter authors offer narratives that represent their realities regarding the concept of diversity leadership, how they came to be in their roles, and how diversity leaders do diversity work.

This important resource provides practical strategies and guides faculty and higher education professionals in navigating the situational, contextual, and relational constructs within the social and cultural contexts of college and university campuses.

Eugene T. Parker III is Associate Professor of Higher Education at the University of Kansas.

Becoming a Diversity Leader on Campus

Navigating Identity and Situational Pressures

Edited by
Eugene T. Parker III

Routledge
Taylor & Francis Group

NEW YORK AND LONDON

First published 2022
by Routledge
605 Third Avenue, New York, NY 10158

and by Routledge
2 Park Square, Milton Park, Abingdon, Oxon, OX14 4RN

Routledge is an imprint of the Taylor & Francis Group, an informa business

Library of Congress Cataloging-in-Publication Data
Names: Parker, Eugene T., III, editor.
Title: Becoming a diversity leader on campus : navigating identity and
situational pressures / Editedy by Eugene T. Parker III.
Description: New York, NY : Routledge, 2022. | Includes
bibliographical references and index.
Identifiers: LCCN 2021025667 (print) | LCCN 2021025668
(ebook) | ISBN 9780367441838 (hardback) | ISBN 9780367442491
(paperback) | ISBN 9781003008521 (ebook)
Subjects: LCSH: Minority college students—United States. |
Leadership—United States. | Identity (Psychology)—United States.
| Student affairs services—United States—Administration. |
Universities and colleges—Social aspects—United States.
Classification: LCC LC3731 .B42 2022 (print) | LCC LC3731
(ebook) | DDC 378.1/982—dc23
LC record available at https://lccn.loc.gov/2021025667
LC ebook record available at https://lccn.loc.gov/2021025668

ISBN: 978-0-367-44183-8 (hbk)
ISBN: 978-0-367-44249-1 (pbk)
ISBN: 978-1-003-00852-1 (ebk)

DOI: 10.4324/9781003008521

Typeset in Sabon
by codeMantra

Contents

Tables

Preface

The social, political, and cultural saliency of diversity in the United States continues to be a critical topic for our nation and institutions of higher education. Recently, our country has faced numerous social issues pertaining to anti-Black racism, sexism, misogyny, heterosexism, gender binarism and ableism. In the last five years, we have encountered a presidential election that has helped to promote a divisive nation. Political leaders have incited a riot on the nation's capital. The country has faced a historic pandemic and health crisis. Black men continue to be disproportionately brutalized and murdered by police officers. Hate crimes against Asian Americans are on the rise. Elected politicians are enacting voter suppression laws. Racial minorities continue to face inequitable policies and systemic barriers to community health, food security, homeownership, and education. While newer social movements, such as BlackLivesMatter, have ignited promise and hope for social justice in the United States, racial minorities in America must grapple with the present state of diversity and the continued fight for dignity, freedom, and justice.

Inherent in any discourse about diversity and social justice in our country is the need for change and transformation. When referring to the oppressed, Freire (1970) asserted:

> In order for the oppressed to be able to wage the struggle for their liberation, they must perceive the reality of oppression not as a closed world from which there is no exit, but as a limiting situation which they can transform. (p. 49)

Like most scholars in my field, I argue education, including postsecondary and advanced education, is the indispensable mechanism for transformation and social justice progress. Thus, discourse about racial and social justice in the United States ought to consider diversity, equity, inclusion, belonging, and social justice in the institutions of higher education in our nation.

Demographic projections show that our country is changing and will continue to change pertaining to racial and ethnic diversity. The national agencies have predicted that by 2060 the population of Blacks and Hispanics/Latinos in the citizenry will increase to 17.9 percent and 28.6 percent, respectively (Colby & Ortman, 2015). Similarly, the landscape of higher education continues to shift.

Accordingly, colleges and universities in the United States have increasingly become more diverse, particularly regarding race and ethnicity, since the 1960s (AAC&U, 2019). While this fact demonstrates progress toward equity and inclusion in higher education, undoubtedly, college campuses continue to embody persisting toxic and adverse college climates and environments for diverse institutional members, particularly students. During the past decade, there has been increased and heightened awareness and attention to the campus diversity and racial climate. With increasing diversity, colleges and universities have faced numerous campus issues about diversity, negative perceptions of the campus racial and diversity climate, and many campus crises centering on race, gender, ability, or sexual orientation (Eppolito, 2017; Everett, 2016; Jaschik, 2016; U.S. News, 2017). This is evidenced by increased student activism and social movements that center on their perceptions of adverse and unwelcoming campus environments (Chronicle of Higher Education [CHE], 2018; Inside Higher Ed [IHE], 2018). For example, in 2019, two students marched through campus at the University of Connecticut yelling racial slurs. Colleges and universities have yet to resolve how to create and maintain welcoming college environments for diverse individuals (Burke, 2019). Recently, in 2021, racist hate messages were posted in the newly opened multicultural center at Kansas State University (*Journal of Blacks in Higher Education* [JBHE], 2021). These campus incidents characterize how higher education, and particularly its leaders, have unsuccessfully disrupted persisting occurrences epitomizing anti-Black racism, and every -ism that supports unwelcoming campus climates for diverse students.

Considering these aforementioned issues at colleges and universities, college leadership emerges as a crucial matter for understanding how to promote more diverse and welcoming campus environments. Similarly, questions about how to effectively lead through a diversity-centered lens have continued to emerge in the higher education community. Numerous leadership theories have underscored the notion that diversity leadership is situational, relational, and contingent on internal and external environmental factors (Kezar, Carducci & Contreras-McGavin, 2006; Martin et al., 2016; Schriesheim, Castro & Cogliser, 1999). Yet, we know very little about effectual diversity leadership at colleges and universities, and particularly the experiences of diversity leaders.

Acknowledging the heightened awareness of the campus diversity and racial climate, broadly, there has been growing attention to diversity leadership and diversity leaders on college campuses. While there currently exists some form of a formal diversity leader at most higher education institutions, there continues to be inconsistent and vague conceptions of diversity leadership across higher education. This is exacerbated when referring to effective praxis. That is, diversity leadership and practice at one institution often looks much different than another institution. Diversity leadership is varied at higher education institutions and diversity leaders exist (either formally or informally) at all administrative ranks and levels. However, one structural response by institutions has been to inaugurate and appoint Senior or Chief Diversity Officers (Williams & Wade-Golden, 2013). These high-ranking senior administrators are charged with implementing and guiding their institution's diversity plans, goals, and initiatives.

The organizational structure, work environment, and climate for diversity leaders at American colleges and universities can be challenging. Many institutions have ill-conceived institutional structures coupled with underfunding diversity offices and units that impede diversity leaders' capacities to be efficacious leaders. The campus climate for diversity also presents a challenge for these individuals. Ahmed (2012) suggests the existence of a "brick wall." This represents the notion that diversity is commonly advocated and asserted; yet the work of diversity workers and leaders is impeded and obstructed. This paradigm makes the efforts of diversity leaders to promote transformation change particularly challenging at their institutions. Considering the dearth of information and scholarship about diversity leadership, this book provides knowledge about the experiences of present-day diversity leaders. This scholarly contribution offers personal narratives and perspectives of diversity leaders about their entry into diversity work, the importance of their work, and how they go about doing diversity work.

ORGANIZATION OF THE BOOK

The focus of this book is threefold. First, this resource helps readers to better understand the concept of diversity leadership and roles of diversity leaders at present-day higher education institutions. Second, this book describes how current diversity leaders came to be in their roles and their personal journeys. Third, this book focuses on what and how diversity leaders do diversity work.

The present text is a resource for administrators, faculty, students, and higher education professionals that offers perspectives, narratives, and personal accounts of diversity leaders that center on their current roles and diversity work in higher education. This book underscores the central theme that diversity leadership is a situational, contextual, and relational construct that is contingent on the social and cultural contexts of specific leaders and their respective institutional environments. Themes from the chapters epitomize the notion that present-day diversity leadership is shaped by the unique factors and environmental pressures that confront colleges and universities, but also by the unique experiences of the individual actors who are appointed to diversity leadership positions at colleges and universities. Considering the campus diversity and racial climate, this book uniquely illustrates the emerging importance of the diversity leader on college and university campuses.

As mentioned, the subject of diversity leadership at colleges and universities represents both senior diversity leaders and generally all diversity administrators who self-identify as a diversity leader. Thus, this book offers thoughtful attention to both positional and structural aspects of diversity leadership. This book offers a better understanding of how diversity leaders make meaning and sense of their roles, desire, and passion for promoting diversity within their institutions. The authors offer narratives that represent their realities regarding how they came to be in their roles and perform the critical work they do. Through their lens, the authors practice reflexivity and provide readers with knowledge about how they exist in their relative spaces. Authors grapple with current processes and practices for promoting and maintaining welcoming, equitable, and inclusive college environments for students, faculty, and staff in 21st-century institutions of higher education. Additionally, authors offer recommendations about doing diversity work and being change agents.

It is worth noting that this book juxtaposes two essential domains of diversity scholarship. In the beginning chapters, my aim is to foreground the subsequent chapters with information, theories, and concepts about institutional diversity and the structural aspect of diversity and diversity leadership in higher education. Reflective and reflexive accounts help us to understand how professionals and practitioners make sense of the world (Bolton, 2010). Aligning with the premise of this book, these stories and narratives describe individual's lived experiences, how they learn from those experiences, and individual's worldviews. The remaining chapters provide narratives and personal journeys of present-day diversity leaders to explicate present-day diversity leadership through the perspectives of diversity agents. That is, the early chapters help to situate the structural aspect of institutional diversity into the described lived experiences and reality of current diversity leaders.

Collectively, this book is delineated into three parts: *Understanding, Becoming,* and *Doing.* Part One, *Understanding,* provides background, conceptual and theoretical considerations for understanding diversity leadership in higher education. For the first chapter, I explicate the important theories of leadership and diversity that help to inform best practices in higher education. This chapter focuses on the foundational knowledge that will help to understand the state of diversity at institutions of higher education and foregrounds the subsequent chapters in the book. The next chapter of Part One centers on the Senior or Chief Diversity Officer at higher education institutions in the United States. The author, Raul A. Leon, provides a synthesis of what we have learned about the Chief Diversity Officer's (CDO) role in higher education in the past decade. Further, this chapter aims to identify, discuss, and situate the work of the CDO in the context of their role, focusing on connecting the work of the CDO to the work of other diversity leaders on campus.

Part Two represents the notion of *Becoming* a diversity leader in higher education. This section incorporates personal accounts and narratives that illuminate our understanding of how and why individuals come to engage in the work. In Chapter Three, Brighid Dwyer and LaTanya N. Buck describe their initial motivations for choosing to enter the diversity field and how those motivations have changed throughout their careers due to institutional transitions, personal, national, and international contexts about identity, and perspective-taking. The authors delve into what it means to reconcile their personal and professional experiences as they negotiate between critiquing institutional culture and being "of the institution." In the next chapter, steven p. bryant describes the journey of a White male becoming a leader within the diversity and inclusion field. The author shares his experience of becoming a leader through doing critical self-work and utilizing privilege to work toward eradicating systemic racism intentionally, and other forms of oppression, from our institutions. In the final chapter of Part Two, Kelli A. Perkins and Rafael A. Rodriguez argue that the intersection of leadership and social justice self-actualization hinges on substantive self-work and a critical examination of intersecting dominant and subordinate identities juxtaposed against situational power. This chapter captures the individual and collective narratives of a senior-level supervisor and mid-level supervisee and how they have approached self-work for diversity leadership in higher education when race, class, gender, and positional power are at play.

Part Three of this book focuses on *Doing* the work. This section concentrates on practice and how current diversity leaders employ their respective strategies to promote diversity initiatives. Grounded in institutional and transformative change, this section comprises personal accounts and narratives that embody doing diversity work considering the current campus racial and diversity climate. In Chapter Six, Jennifer Hamer and colleagues describe the practice of "doing diversity and equity leadership" on a large Midwestern university campus. The authors discuss the structure that they developed to lead and manage their office and the strategies implemented to address longstanding issues of diversity and equity for faculty, staff, and students. Primarily, the authors argue that this central diversity and equity leadership office effectively and swiftly established the foundations for transformational change following recent campus disruptions. However, a more significant movement forward is limited by how it is situated in the organization, its budgetary and human capacity, and the pervasiveness of resistance to diversity matters.

In Chapter Seven, Bennyce E. Hamilton and Kelley C. Kimple examine the convergence of their lived experiences, exemplified through their identities, social location, and praxis as a prelude to becoming transformative higher education administrators. The following chapter, written by Allison C. Roman and colleagues, explores the challenges that women of color experience in leadership positions, with particular attention to those who lead diversity and inclusion initiatives within their institutions. The authors outline the unique ways they engage in diversity leadership and how our leadership, as women of color administrators, is different from that of our other colleagues. The final chapter offers a contribution from Tony Tyler and Erin Lain. This chapter focuses on the nature of call-out culture toward diversity leaders, the effects of this culture on diversity leaders, and how the diversity leader can both respond with methods and best practices informed by various theories to transform the culture and maintain their own personal well-being.

REFERENCES

Ahmed, S. (2012). *On Being Included: Racism and Diversity in Institutional Life*. Duke University Press.

Association of American Colleges & Universities. (2019). *Facts & Figures: College Students Are More Diverse Than Ever. Faculty and*

Administrators Are Not. AACU, March Newsletter. https://www.aacu.org/aacu-news/newsletter/2019/march/facts-figures

Bolton, G. (2010). *Reflective Practice: Writing and Professional Development.* Sage Publications.

Burke, L. (2019). *UConn Criticized From All Sides in Racial Incident.* https://www.insidehighered.com/news/2019/10/25/uconn-satisfies-no-one-punishments-students-who-used-racial-slurs

Chronicle of Higher Education. (2018). *Students in Charge.* https://www.chronicle.com/article/Who-s-in-Charge-on-College/242656

Colby, S., & Ortman, J. (2015). *Projections of the Size and Composition of the U.S. Population: 2014–2060.* U.S. Census. https://www.census.gov/content/dam/Census/library/publications/2015/demo/p25-1143.pdf

Eppolito, S. (2017). *BC Students, Staff Protest Racial Incidents.* https://www.bostonglobe.com/metro/2017/10/20/boston-college-students-and-staff-march-protest-racial-incidents/WhXrJyQKLG-3pIosdgqH53J/story.html

Everett, G. (2016). *R.I. College Students Demand Expanded Diversity Initiatives.* http://www.browndailyherald.com/2016/04/20/r-i-college-students-demand-expanded-diversity-initiatives/

Freire, P. (1970, 2018). *Pedagogy of the Oppressed.* Bloomsbury Publishing USA.

Inside Higher Ed. (2018). *Patterns of Student Protest.* https://www.insidehighered.com/news/2019/01/03/student-activists-biggest-obstacle-often-rhythms-college-activism-itself

Jaschik, S. (2016). *As Protests Increase, Student Demands Get More Ambitious.* http://news.emory.edu/stories/2015/12/upress_response_to_student_concerns/index.html

Journal of Blacks in Higher Education [JBHE]. (2021). *Racist Hate Message Found on the Campus of Kansas State University.* https://www.jbhe.com/2021/03/racist-hate-message-found-on-the-campus-of-kansas-state-university/

Kezar, A., Carducci, R., & Contreras-McGavin, M. (2006). *Rethinking the "L" Word in Higher Education.* The Revolution of Research on Leadership: ASHE Higher Education Report. John Wiley & Sons.

Martin, R., Guillaume, Y., Thomas, G., Lee, A., & Epitropaki, O. (2016). Leader–Member Exchange (LMX) and Performance: A Meta-Analytic Review. *Personnel Psychology,* 69(1), 67–121.

Schriesheim, C. A., Castro, S. L., & Cogliser, C. C. (1999). Leader-Member Exchange (LMX) Research: A Comprehensive Review of Theory, Measurement, and Data-Analytic Practices. *The Leadership Quarterly*, *10*(1), 63–113.

U.S. News. (2017). *Black Students Voice Concerns after K-State Racist Incidents*. https://www.usnews.com/news/best-states/kansas/articles/2017-11-01/police-investigating-racist-graffiti-threat-on-vehicle

Williams, D. A., & Wade-Golden, K. C. (2013). *The Chief Diversity Officer*. Stylus Publishing, LLC.

Part One

Understanding

Chapter One

Diversity Leadership in Higher Education

Theoretical and Conceptual Considerations

Eugene T. Parker III

The growing body of scholarship and knowledge about diversity in higher education is robust. We have learned much about structural diversity, identity, institutional contexts, campus climates, student development, and psychosocial outcomes. This includes my own research and scholarship that have demonstrated the positive associations between diversity experiences on college student outcomes, such as academic, cognitive, moral development, and broader college success. To ground the topics discussed in this chapter, I offer a brief overview of some of the conceptual and theoretical perspectives regarding diversity and leadership through an institutional lens.

With any discussion about diversity leadership in higher education, one must begin with the fundamental question: *What is diversity at colleges and universities*? Unfortunately, my experience has shown there is no simple answer to that question. There is little consistency regarding the meaning of diversity in organizations (Harrison & Klein, 2007; Harrison & Sin, 2006). Diversity has varying meanings and definitions in present-day higher education. Diversity often represents structural or compositional diversity, i.e., the numbers or counting of diverse individuals and populations. Harrison and Klein (2007) asserted diversity as "the distribution of differences among the members of a unit with respect to a common attribute, X, such as tenure, ethnicity, conscientiousness, task attitude, or pay" (p. 1200). Other scholars have contended that diversity characterizes the social differences and differentiations of individuals and populations, such as education, wealth, and identity (Blau, 1977; Harrison & Sin, 2006).

DOI: 10.4324/9781003008521-2

3

Diversity has also been associated with multiculturalism, college access, and recruitment. Diversity is associated with campus climate, particularly the campus racial climate. Some higher education scholars contend diversity in higher education institution's racial environment, including educational outcomes, institutional programs, and practices that promote or impede diversity equity and inclusion (Milem et al., 2005). While we have furthered our understanding of diversity in higher education through research and best practices, these varying conceptions of diversity have exacerbated how we have attended to the issue. However, taken together, these different notions of diversity provide an overview of how diversity is conceived at colleges and universities and grounds the perspectives in this book.

As a preface for the subsequent chapters in this edited volume, this opening chapter begins with an explication of the concept of diversity in higher education. The literature and scholarship on diversity at colleges and universities are quite robust, expansive, and beyond the scope of this chapter; therefore, I offer a brief description of what we know about diversity as a means to ground the ensuing chapters in this book. Then, I discuss diversity leadership at institutions of higher education and the varying notions of the construct. Next, I focus on the specific roles and responsibilities of diversity leaders, including the senior diversity officer. Finally, I offer my reflections and considerations for 21st-century diversity leadership, representing my insight into the future of diversity leadership at colleges and universities.

INSTITUTIONAL DIVERSITY AND CAMPUS CLIMATE

I contend diversity leaders at colleges and universities primarily direct their attention to two main facets of diversity on campus: institutional/organizational diversity and campus climate. For the purposes of this discussion, institutional or organizational diversity refers to the diversity in organizational contexts, particularly administration and behavior. Diversity has often been purposely associated with the diversity work of institutional members. However, Smith (2015) developed a framework that shifts the focus of diversity in higher education from individuals to institutions. The premise of the framework is to "provide a way for understanding what institutional capacity or diversity might mean and what it might look like" (Smith, 2015, p. 64). Tenets of the model embody concepts, such as intergroup relations, institutional viability, access for underrepresented populations, and provide links between diversity, culture, institutional practice, and organizational change at colleges and universities. These conceptual underpinnings direct our attention to the diversity that grounds institutional administration and behavior, and particularly institutional decision-making processes.

Discourse pertaining to diversity leadership also focuses on campus climates and environments. Campus climate generally refers to the attitudes, beliefs, and practices of institutional members at colleges and universities (Rankin & Reason, 2008). National and professional associations, such as the American Council on Education (see ACE, 2016), have contended that understanding the campus climate is critical for colleges and universities. For the past decade, colleges and universities have faced heightened attention to the matter of campus climates, precisely the campus diversity and racial climate. This is evidenced by emerging social movements (e.g., Black Lives Matter) and student mobilization and activism which epitomize students' perceptions about persisting campus racism, inequity, and unwelcoming institutional climates (Milkman, 2017). Further, research has shown that unwelcoming campus climates adversely affect students of color, particularly regarding cognitive gains, mental health, and other academic, social, and psychosocial outcomes (Rankin, 2006; Rankin & Reason, 2008).

Prior research and theoretical perspectives (see Hurtado et al., 1998) have concentrated on the climates and environments that promote or impede progress toward equitable institutions of higher education. Hurtado et al. (1998) provided the higher education community with a deeper understanding of the significance of context, specifically when acknowledging institutions' historical legacy of inclusion/exclusion. Further, they contend the campus climate is associated with external and internal influences. External contexts embody environmental influences, such as socio-historical influences and regulative policies that impact institutional activities and decision-making. The internal influences represent the structural diversity, psychological, and behavioral aspects of college environments (Hurtado et al., 1998).

Similarly, Smith (1995) theorizes that the campus climate embodies several dimensions: representation, response to intolerance climate, educational and scholarly mission, and organizational and intellectual transformation. The *representation* dimension focuses on how higher education institutions grapple with (under)representation of student populations on campus, particularly regarding racial identity. *Climate and response to intolerance* epitomize how colleges and universities attend and respond to racism, discrimination on campus, climate, and responses to intolerance. *Educational and scholarly mission* represents the curricular and pedagogical aspects of diversity and campus climate, such as the

5

implementation of ethnic and/or gender studies programs. Finally, *organizational and intellectual transformation* symbolizes how colleges and universities have embraced transformational change to their entrenched and institutionalized processes and practices (Smith, 1995). These tenets center on the association between diversity, campus climate, and organizational context.

As mentioned, campus climate has been linked to college student outcomes (Rankin & Reason, 2008). Scholars have maintained that institutions must create diverse and supportive college environments (Hurtado & Carter, 1997; Museus, 2014) to promote students' perceptions of belonging and acceptance. Considering this, the campus diversity climate continues to be a significant matter in higher education and for diversity leaders.

CONCEPTUAL PERSPECTIVES OF DIVERSITY LEADERSHIP

During the past decade, we have benefitted from emerging and growing conceptual evaluations of diversity leadership in higher education institutions (Leon, 2014; Parker, 2015; Williams & Wade-Golden, 2013; Worthington et al., 2014). Perspectives about inclusive leadership, culturally responsive leadership (CRL), and transformative leadership have broadened our understanding of the experiences of diversity leaders, how they make sense and meaning of those experiences, and ultimately how they do diversity work at colleges and universities.

Concepts, such as inclusive excellence, underscore the call for higher education institutions to align better their organizations' actions and institutional pillars, namely research, teaching, and service, with inclusive practices and behaviors (AAC&U, 2021). Thus, present-day diversity leadership encompasses the matter of inclusive leadership. While the perspective that leaders should be inclusive is not new and has an extensive background in the literature, specific references about inclusive leadership in educational institutions emerged in the last few decades (Ryan, 2005). Inclusive leadership focuses on managing diversity but with attention to inclusion, and particularly full participation of traditionally underrepresented and minoritized individuals (Booysen, 2014). It allows for individuals to be themselves and affords them the opportunity to engage with institutional activities fully. Inclusive leadership prioritizes full participation. Diversity primarily represents the composition and representation of individuals in higher education, whereas inclusion and inclusive leadership focus on ensuring those individuals can fully participate (Ferdman, 2021).

Ferdman (2021) provides a framework for understanding the complexity and necessity of inclusion in organizations. The model proposes that inclusion occurs at multiple layers ranging from the micro-level (i.e., individuals) to the macro-level (i.e., society). Inclusion ought to be inherent and ingrained in varying aspects of systems, processes, and organizational behaviors and is a necessary practice at all levels in institutions. Ferdman (2021) asserts, "A complete view of inclusive leadership needs to consider how change happens at each level of analysis—individual, interpersonal, group, organizational, and societal—and the influence processes, competencies, and interventions that foster more inclusion both within and across levels" (p. 10). Therefore, diversity leaders may employ inclusive leadership to disperse, maintain, and advance diversity initiatives and goals throughout institutions of higher education while seeking inclusive practices to promote institutional change.

Another relevant perspective on diversity leadership is CRL. While in the past, this concept has primarily been applied to educational administration in the K–12 sector, there is an emerging body of literature that applies this concept to institutions of higher education. CRL generally represents conceptual perspectives about the link pertaining to educational institutions, race, culture, and diversity. CRL epitomizes "theory and educational leadership practices...that take into consideration race, ethnicity, language, culture, and gender. These include the emphasis on high expectations for academic achievement, pedagogical and social inclusion of students' history, core values, community and cultural knowledge..." (Santamaría & Santamaría, 2015, p. 4). Aligning with the overarching concept of CRL is applied critical leadership (ACL). ACL draws from the tenets of critical responsive leadership and critical race theory to bring together perspectives about educational leadership, equity, social justice, and transformative leadership (Santamaría & Santamaría, 2015). CRL and ACL provide conceptual perspectives that illuminate how equity-centered and inclusive leadership may manifest in the work and practices of diversity leaders.

Finally, transformative leadership is a vital element of diversity leadership. Transformative leadership characterizes leadership practices that seek to affect change in organizations while interrogating, disrupting, and challenging power, structures, and systems that continue to oppress and marginalize diverse individuals (Hewitt et al., 2014). Associated with the aforementioned concepts (e.g., inclusive leadership), transformative leadership helps us to understand how diversity leaders seek to promote transformational change at colleges and universities through critical work and practices that confront deep-rooted institutional equities.

THE DIVERSITY LEADER IN HIGHER EDUCATION

Considering the conceptions mentioned above about diversity on college campuses, I now turn my attention to the stewards who are principally leading diversity initiatives and maintaining diversity missions at institutions of higher education. Through my previous scholarly work with diversity leaders and senior diversity officers, I affirm doing the job can be taxing. Ahmed (2012) describes the institutionalization of diversity as *conditional hospitality*. This perspective suggests the institution and its entrenched and unrelenting structure and systems is the host while diversity (and diversity advocates) is the guest. The diverse guest is welcomed only with conditions (i.e., giving something back in return). Hospitality is granted to diverse guests with the condition they return the favor by integrating into (and accepting) the dominant/host organization. This reinforces the institution's proclamation to internal and external stakeholders and constituents of being a "diverse" college or university. Diversity leaders are then left to navigate this dynamic and the associated challenges. Despite this assertion, diversity leaders predominately espouse the skills, competencies, and passion for doing the work while facing these challenges. The ensuing discussion of diversity leadership broadly captures institutional members, e.g. administrators, staff, and faculty, with administrative leadership roles pertaining to diversity, equity, and inclusion.

Emergence of Diversity Leadership in Higher Education

Little is known about the historical formation and evolution of diversity offices, units, and diversity leaders at colleges and universities. While generally the concept of diversity certainly embodies varying aspects of diversity and difference (e.g., race, gender identification, social class), much of the conventional literature has mainly focused on racial diversity and particularly the experiences of Black students. An exhaustive review of the historical emergence of the diversity office (and leader) is beyond the scope of this discussion; however, for the purposes of this text, it is important to preface the ensuing narratives with background information about the structural rise of diversity officers and leaders.

Though in few numbers, Black students were admitted into institutions of higher education, both Predominately White Institutions (PWIs) and Historically Black Colleges and Universities, since as early as the late 19th century (Thelin, 2011). Key historical events in higher education prompted an increase in the participation of Black students at American colleges and universities. Federal policies, such as the Morrill Acts, GI Bill and Higher Education Act of 1965, and responses to the civil rights social movements during the 1960s, ushered in an era when greater numbers of Black students were enrolling at institutions of higher education (Allen, 1988; Thelin, 2011). Specifically, Black students (to a greater extent) were admitted to and ultimately diversified to PWIs.

Responding to federal policies and the civil rights movement, colleges and universities mainly focused on compositional diversity and getting students on campus (Thelin, 2011). With increasing numbers of Black students, colleges and universities then had to grapple with college environments that were unwelcome to diverse students' increasing population. Institutions had to grapple with how to respond to cultural and social issues at the national and institutional levels. As such, institutions began to delegate diversity labor to any and all diverse persons and varying departments on campus (Chang et al., 2003). Similarly, during the 1960s, the advent of offices of Minority Affairs emerged (Gose, 2013). These early institutional units primarily worked to increase the compositional diversity of underrepresented racial minority students, mainly through recruitment and admissions initiatives and practices. These offices were also charged with handling and managing diversity. Arguably, this intrinsically represented the undertaking of working with all the Black students on campus through programmatic initiatives and promoting facets of the college environment.

Considering the early directives of these offices to increase structural diversity (i.e., recruitment and admissions), the inaugural diversity officers and leaders implemented and developed recruitment strategies and focused on institutional equity and policy for employees (Gose, 2013). Eventually, the aim for these early offices was to oversee diversity. These units represented the institutions' emblematic (and mostly superficial) objectives and commitment to diversity. Accordingly, individuals were appointed to administrative positions to lead these offices. Again, diversity has and continues to be charged to any and all diverse peoples. Thus, the term *diversity leader* is hazy when referencing the emergence of the role. However, the early directors and coordinators of Minority Affairs offices, cultural centers, and multicultural programs were the antecedents of present-day diversity leaders who hold formalized diversity titles. Notably, during the early beginnings of diversity offices, diversity leaders were any and all diverse persons, and mainly Black staff members were considered diversity leaders. This designation was based on both self-identification but often imposed on individuals.

Varying Aspects of Diversity Leadership in Higher Education

Presently, diversity leadership is exhibited at colleges and universities in several ways. There exist leaders who have formalized diversity leadership roles at the institution. These individuals have typically had administrative positions that are formally structured on the organizational chart. These individuals have specific job roles and duties that center on diversity initiatives, such as the director of the Multicultural Affairs office, the coordinator of diversity programs for the business school, or the person charged with diversity recruiting for the Admissions office. There are also institutional members with formal non-diversity roles who are considered to be diversity leaders. For instance, a Black Professor in the School of Engineering may be considered (intentionally or unintentionally) a diversity leader. Some institutional members informally do the work and labor. These are also community members who simply are dedicated and passionate about diversity at the institution. However, it is worth noting, this book primarily focuses on individuals with formal diversity roles.

One emerging facet of present-day formalized diversity leadership is the growing presence and professionalization of the senior/executive diversity officer at colleges and universities. During the past few decades, there has been an increasing trend in higher education to appoint diversity leaders to senior- or executive-level administrative positions (Williams & Wade-Golden, 2013). With the institutionalized and common job title, Chief Diversity Officer, these positions represent the highest-ranking administrator who is charged with advancing diversity initiatives and maintaining the diversity mission and strategies. There is also greater attention to professionalization of the role in higher education (Worthington et al., 2014). While sometimes considered to be a symbolic representation and face of the institution (see Parker, 2020; Williams & Wade-Golden, 2013), the position is essential for colleges and universities as it conveys to internal and external stakeholders the institution's commitment to diversity, attends to diversity in organizational structure, and promotes the capacity for a foremost campus leader to coordinate and advance the institution's diversity goals and initiatives.

It is worth noting the terms associated with the Chief Diversity Officer are not without criticism. Observers have questioned the use of the term "chief" in the widely utilized title. Besides apparent culturally insensitive aspects of the term, these critics have asserted that diversity should not be limited to just one individual or institutional leader. If diversity is valued at the institution, the responsibility ought to be dispersed and maintained by several leaders. That is, maintaining diversity and a welcoming campus environment is the job of every institutional leader. The growing consensus among many diverse stakeholders and experts is that "senior diversity leader" is the preferable reference. Nonetheless, Chief Diversity Officer continues to be the predominant title utilized at present-day institutions of higher education.

Considering the varying roles and formalized (and informal) diversity-related administrative positions at colleges and universities, this book offers broad, all-encompassing attention to the subject matter. The narratives offered in this chapter center on the experiences of both senior-level administrators with formal diversity job titles and other institutional members who can be characterized as diversity leaders on their respective campuses. This all-encompassing conception of diversity leadership provides a rich and deep understanding of the experiences and reality of these leaders.

Diversity, Institutional, and Transformational Change

Grounded in any discourse about how diversity leadership impacts institutional environments is the matter of change. Sweeney and Bothwick (2016) suggest several traits of change agents, such as trust, communication skills, and future-focused. For diversity leadership, I draw from and apply several of their perspectives about change agents. Diversity leaders are resilient as they tend to navigate spaces with unrelenting and tenacious systems and processes that are not conducive to transformational change. These individuals engender trust. They build effective relationships with internal and external members and stakeholders to promote change. Diversity leaders ought to have exceptional communication and active listening skills. Additionally, these individuals must have a love for learning, life-long learning, professional and personal development. Finally, diversity leaders are future-focused. These leaders have a clear vision for the organization and how best to achieve the institution's diversity goals and initiatives. These traits help diversity leaders to enact the transformational change required for change.

Unfortunately, enacting change has arguably been challenging for diversity leaders, given the organizational (and bureaucratic) structures that long existed at higher education institutions for hundreds of years. I have often argued that higher education maintains some of the most stubborn institutions in American society. Diversity leaders often have unclear, unstructured, and ill-defined job descriptions and are problematic for the role of diversity leaders (Smith, 2015; Williams & Wade-Golden, 2013). Agency for diversity leaders to promote and enact transformation change is directly linked to how and why the positions are created. Diversity leaders can sometimes be thrust into challenging circumstances because of unclear role responsibilities and expectations. Ultimately, this affects their capacity and efficacy to be change agents.

Diversity Leaders as Relational Leaders

Leadership scholars contend leadership is a relational construct (Fletcher, 2012). Leadership is relational and is a relational process (Ospina & Uhl-Bien, 2012). Komives et al. (2009) asserted that "relational leadership is purposeful, inclusive, empowering, ethical and about process" (p. 113). Individuals who value and employ relational leadership center their practice on developing and maintaining effective relationships to promote institutional change. Similarly, relationships and effective relationship-building are vital for diversity leaders at colleges and universities.

Some leadership models that focus on leadership relationships highlight perspectives representing two primary conceptual domains: *entity perspectives* and *constructionist perspectives* (Dugan, 2017; Ospina & Uhl-Bien, 2012; Uhl-Bien, 2011). The entity perspective considers individual traits, behaviors, and relational leadership skills, while the constructionist perspective refers to the social construction, processes, and practices related to relational leadership and its outcomes (Ospina & Uhl-Bien, 2012). Scholars suggest leader-follower relationships may be grounded in relational constructionist philosophical views and relations are interdependent (or co-dependent) constructions of social realities (Day & Drath, 2012; Uhl-Bien, 2011). Constructionist perspectives emphasize that leadership "is a process that emerges from social relationships in which knowledge is co-constructed" (Dugan, 2017, p. 214). These perspectives embody the unique and distinct manner in which diversity is associated with leadership.

Relational leadership is particularly relevant when discussing diversity leadership in higher education. Komives et al.'s (2013) relational leadership model underscore the integral role of relationships and relationship-building for leadership. According to Komives et al. (2013), "relationships are the focal point of the leadership process" (p. 95). Further, it emphasizes the importance of groups, teams, and processes and highlights the saliency of relationships for effectiveness (Dugan, 2017).

Similarly, other perspectives about relational leadership illuminate five aspects of relational leadership (Dugan, 2017; Komives et al., 2013). Relational leadership is purposeful, inclusive, empowering, ethical, and process-oriented. I argue that diversity leaders tend to demonstrate these five tenets of relational leadership. Diversity leaders display purposeful leadership by clearly identifying goals and communicating a shared vision. Diversity leaders practice inclusive leadership. Inclusive leadership represents diversity leaders' inclination to consider diverse perspectives, experiences, and social identities on decision-making and actions. Diversity leaders tend to be empowered by working with various individuals to limit barriers and promote full participation and agency in followers and constituents. Diversity ought to display ethical leadership. Finally, diversity leadership is process-oriented. That is, these leaders have intentional and strategic processes to achieve goals and diversity initiatives. These tenets of relational leadership represent how diversity leaders aim to promote change at their respective institutions.

MOVING FORWARD: 21ST-CENTURY DIVERSITY LEADERSHIP

The prior sections provide a succinct overview of the conceptual and theoretical perspectives that guide what we know about leadership, with particular attention to diversity leadership. It is essential to apply these concepts to best practices and consider the implications for present-day higher education and student affairs. To this point, I offer considerations that represent my perspectives about the state of diversity leadership for 21st-century higher education.

Critical Approach to Leadership

We must continue to interrogate critical aspects of leadership. This includes understanding notions of power associated with leaders and maybe inherent in leadership positions. Dugan's (2017) conceptual perspectives on leadership, particularly critical leadership, suggest it is vital to understand power and leadership as power can sometimes be used to construct and maintain social systems and structures. Further, critical leadership acknowledges the assertion that the values, beliefs, and norms of dominant groups drive leadership behaviors and decisions.

Considering a Shift toward Anti-Racist Leadership

As the last few years have shown, it is not enough to be a diversity leader. The term "diversity" is often associated with pacifying the dominant group. Ahmed (2012) notes that diversity often epitomizes a positive concept. Diversity is utilized by diversity leaders and stakeholders to promote diversity issues and influence how stakeholders and constituents generally embrace diversity, inclusion, equity, and social justice. Put another way; it is a "happy" term. However, higher education leaders who are champions and advocates for social justice need to vigorously urge transformational change by being anti-racist leaders rather than diversity leaders. Scholars have described normalized institutional practices (see Ahmed, 2012; Squire et al., 2019), such as the issuance of diversity plans and statements, as non-performatives. These normal practices usually espouse the importance of diversity and the inclusion of diverse persons. Yet, they remain as ineffective artifacts that do not address and fulfill their stated purpose. Anti-Blackness racism and institutional structures encompassing whiteness and white supremacy continue to subsist at higher education institutions. Active leaders can utilize leadership skills, competencies, and prior experiences to disrupt racist processes, practices, and policies to promote a more diverse, equitable, and inclusive institution. Diversity leadership must shift to anti-racist leadership. Anti-racist leaders symbolize the social justice champions and advocates who help to disturb institutional cultures still seeping with oppressive, violent, and unwelcoming environments for diverse campus members. Anti-racist leaders should help to undo the usual performative rituals that do little to disrupt racism on campus. These leaders focus on identifying and disrupting anti-racist policies, structures, and systems that persist at higher education institutions.

Building Relationships for 21st-Century Higher Education

Diversity leaders must acknowledge and grapple with the changing context of institutions of higher education. As mentioned previously, diversity leaders are change agents who engender trust (Sweeney & Bothwick, 2016). Diversity leaders are relational leaders. Thus, these individuals must grapple with how to build and maintain relationships that support the increasing number of traditionally underrepresented social identities in American colleges and universities, such as race, gender, and low-income students, but also increasing enrollments of veteran and international students, students who identify with the LGBTQ community, and differently abled students. Diversity leaders must also confront the persisting policy-centered higher education issues, such as the disinvestment of public higher education and increasing neoliberal institutional strategies and activities. With state appropriations and funding continuing to decrease to record lows, to a greater extent, diversity leaders are challenged with how to do more with less. Viability for institutions of higher education and diversity offices will depend on adaptability in a changing world of higher education. From my perspective, institutional activities, symbolizing neoliberal strategies, are adversely affecting internal and external environments (such as community development and gentrification). Finally, online education is increasingly becoming a predominant facet of 21st-century higher education. As such, diversity leaders ought to consider ways to navigate the task of supporting diverse students and advancing diversity initiatives and programs in a virtual environment.

REFERENCES

AAC&U. (2021). Making excellence inclusive. https://www.aacu.org/making-excellence-inclusive

ACE. (2016). Ace survey finds increased focus among College Presidents on Campus Racial Climate. https://www.acenet.edu/News-Room/Pages/ACE-Survey-Finds-Increased-Focus-Among-College-Presidents-on-Campus-Racial-Climate.aspx

Ahmed, S. (2012). *On being included: Racism and diversity in institutional life.* Durham, NC: Duke University Press.

Allen, W. R. (1988). Black students in US higher education: Toward improved access, adjustment, and achievement. *The Urban Review, 20*(3), 165–188.

Blau, P. (1977). *Inequality and heterogeneity.* New York: Free Press.

Booysen, L. (2014). The development of inclusive leadership practice and processes. In Ferdman B.M. & Deane B.R., *Diversity at work: The practice of inclusion* (pp. 296–329). Jossey-Bass.

Chang, M. J., Witt, D., Jones, J., & Hakuta, K. (Eds.). (2003). *Compelling interest: Examining the evidence on racial dynamics in colleges and universities.* Stanford University Press.

Day, D., & Drath, W. (2012). A dialogues of theorizing relational leadership. In Uhl-Bien, M., & Ospina, S. (Eds.). *Advancing relational leadership research : A dialogue among perspectives* (pp. 83–106). Information Age Pub.

Dugan, J. P. (2017). *Leadership theory: Cultivating critical perspectives.* John Wiley & Sons.

Ferdman, B. M. (2021). Inclusive leadership: The fulcrum of inclusion. In Ferdman, B., Prime, J., & Riggio, R. (Eds.). *Inclusive leadership. Inclusive leadership: Transforming diverse lives, workplaces, and societies* (pp. 1–25). Taylor & Francis Group.

Fletcher, J. (2012). The relational practice of leadership. In Uhl-Bien, M., & Ospina, S. (Eds.). *Advancing relational leadership research : A dialogue among perspectives* (pp. 83–106). Information Age Pub.

Gose, B. (2013). Diversity offices aren't what they used to be. https://www.chronicle.com/article/diversity-offices-arent-what-they-used-to-be/

Harrison, D., & Klein, K. (2007). What's the difference? Diversity constructs as separation, variety, or disparity in organizations. *Academy of Management Review, 32*(4), 1199–1228.

Harrison, D., & Sin, H.-P. (2006). What is diversity and how should it be measured. In A. M. Konrad, P. Prasad, & J. K. Pringle (Eds.), *Handbook of workplace diversity* (pp. 191–216). Sage Publications, Inc.

Hewitt, K. K., Davis, A. W., & Lashley, C. (2014). Transformational and transformative leadership in a research-informed leadership preparation program. *Journal of Research on Leadership Education, 9*(3), 225–253.

Hurtado, S., Clayton-Pedersen, A., Allen, W., & Milem, J. (1998). Enhancing campus climates for racial/ethnic diversity: Educational policy and practice. *The Review of Higher Education, 21*(3), 279–302.

Hurtado, S., & Carter, D. (1997). Effects of college transition and perceptions of the campus racial climate on Latino college students' sense of belonging. *Sociology of Education, 70*, 324–345.

Hurtado, S., Carter, D. F., & Spuler, A. (1996). Latino student transition to college: Assessing difficulties and factors in successful college adjustment. *Research in Higher Education, 37*(2), 135–157.

Komives, S. R., Lucas, N., & McMahon, T. R. (2013). *Exploring leadership: For college students who want to make a difference.* John Wiley & Sons.

Leon, R. A. (2014). The chief diversity officer: An examination of CDO models and strategies. *Journal of Diversity in Higher Education, 7*(2), 77.

Milem, J., Chang, M., & Antonio, A. (2005). *Making diversity work on campus: A research-based perspective.* Washington, DC: Association American Colleges and Universities.

Milkman, R. (2017). A new political generation: Millennials and the post-2008 wave of protest. *American Sociological Review, 82*(1), 1–31.

Museus, S. D. (2014). The culturally engaging campus environments (CECE) model: A new theory of college success among racially diverse student populations. In *Higher education: Handbook of theory and research* (Vol. 29, pp. 189–227). https://doi.org/10.1007/978-94-017-8005-6

Ospina, S., & Uhl-Bien, M. (2012). Convergence and divergence around relational leadership. In Uhl-Bien, M., & Ospina, S. (Eds.). *Advancing relational leadership research : A dialogue among perspectives* (pp. 83–106). Information Age Pub.

Parker, E. (2020). Do colleges need a chief diversity officer? https://www.insidehighered.com/views/2020/08/20/chief-diversity-officers-play-vital-role-if-appropriately-positioned-and-supported#:~:text=Do%20higher%20education%20institutions%20need, and%20universities%20have%20grown%20significantly

Parker, E. T. (2015). *Exploring the establishment of the office of the chief diversity officer in higher education: A multisite case study* (Publication No. 10016542) [Doctoral dissertation, University of Iowa], ProQuest Dissertation Publishing.

Rankin, S. R. (2006). LGBTQA students on campus: Is higher education making the grade? *Journal of Gay & Lesbian Issues in Education, 3*(2), 111–117.

Rankin, S., & Reason. (2008). Transformational tapestry model: A comprehensive approach to transforming campus climate. *Journal of Diversity in Higher Education, 1*(4), 262–274.

Ryan, J. (2006). *Inclusive leadership* (Vol. 2). San Francisco, CA: Jossey-Bass.

Santamaría, L., & Santamaría, A. (Eds.). (2015). *Culturally responsive leadership in higher education: Promoting access, equity, and improvement.* Routledge.

Smith, D. (1995). Organizational implications of diversity in higher education. In Chemers, M., Oskamp, S., & Constanzo, M. (Eds.). *Diversity in organizations: New perspectives for a changing workplace* (Vol. 8, pp. 220–244). Sage.

Smith, D. G. (2015). *Diversity's promise for higher education: Making it work.* JHU Press.

Squire, D., Nicolazzo, Z., & Perez, R. J. (2019). Institutional response as nonperformative: What university communications (don't) say about movements toward justice. *The Review of Higher Education, 42*(5), 109–133.

Sweeney, C., & Bothwick, F. (2016). *Inclusive leadership: The definitive guide to developing and executing an impactful diversity and inclusion strategy:-Locally and globally.* Pearson UK.

Thelin, J. R. (2011). *A history of American higher education.* JHU Press.

Uhl-Bien, M. (2011). Relational leadership theory: Exploring the social processes of leadership and organizing. In Werhane P.H. & Painter-Morland M. (Eds), *Leadership, gender, and organization* (pp. 75–108). Springer.

Williams, D. A., & Wade-Golden, K. C. (2013). *The chief diversity officer.* Stylus Publishing, LLC.

Worthington, R. L., Stanley, C. A., & Lewis Sr, W. T. (2014). National Association of Diversity Officers in Higher Education standards of professional practice for chief diversity officers. *Journal of Diversity in Higher Education, 7*(4), 227.

Chapter Two

Empowering Diversity Leaders

Reflecting on the Chief Diversity Officer Role

Raul A. Leon

Chief Diversity Officers (CDOs) have been described as important players in guiding a new era of diversity leadership. A review of the landscape in higher education indicates that CDO positions have continued to be created or redesigned in a number of colleges and universities. CDOs today operate across distinct institutional types, are found in different regions across the country, have different configurations, report various degrees of budgetary support, and continue to be challenged to address the needs of their institutions and communities.

Captivated by the work of the CDOs and the expectations surrounding their appointment, scholars have made a number of contributions focused on this executive-level diversity role. This chapter will synthesize what we have learned about the CDO in higher education; will revisit organizational models defining the structure of the CDO; and will discuss the roles that CDOs can adopt to create, coordinate, and support a diversity infrastructure. To conclude, the chapter will offer a reflection focused on the future of the CDO, addressing relational, situational, and contextual aspects that shape the work of CDOs as campus diversity leaders.

RESEARCHING THE CDO ROLE

At the start of the year 2000, there were few CDO positions in higher education that existed and had operated for longer than a decade (e.g., University of Michigan, the University of Washington, the University of Connecticut, the University of Denver, and Brown University). Banerji (2005) noted that interest in the CDO role peaked when, in the mid-2000s,

DOI: 10.4324/9781003008521-3

over 40 institutions appointed their first CDO (Banerji, 2005). Articles published in major higher education media outlets (i.e., Diverse Issues in Higher Education, Inside Higher Ed, Chronicle of Higher Education) documented this phenomenon and provided a basic context to the public to familiarize people with the work and responsibilities of this diversity leader. Yet, as interest grew, it was clear that as a field, higher education had little knowledge about the CDO role and only a few scholarly contributions guided our understanding (Banerji, 2005; Barcelo, 2007; Williams, Berger, & McClendon, 2005). In fact, questions such as how to design a CDO role, how to identify the right individual, or how to support this leader were still largely unanswered.

Described as a seminal contribution to the field, Williams and Wade-Golden (2007) conducted the first national study in higher education, interviewing 110 CDOs and collecting data from over 700 CDOs nationally. This was largely an exploratory study, considering that 72 percent of all CDOs who took part in this study had been in their role for less than five years.

In 2013, Williams and Wade-Golden made an additional contribution to the field, expanding and refining their research with a publication titled *The Chief Diversity Officer: Strategy, Structure, and Change Management.* This work became a major reference text in the field for those interested in the CDO role. Stemming largely from the ideas expressed in this publication, administrators, current CDOs, faculty, and doctoral students followed in their steps and engaged in academic inquiries centered on the experiences of the CDO. A brief summary of this body of work indicates that academic inquiries have ranged from analyzing the creation of the first CDO position at a single institution (Arnold & Kowalski-Brown, 2011) to documenting the stories, narratives, and experiences of CDOs across several institutions (Davalos, 2014; Parker, 2015; Wilson, 2013; Woodard, 2014). Other topics explored included how race, gender, or serving at a particular type of institution may affect the work of the CDO (Greenfield, 2015; Johnson, 2010; Nixon, 2013; Pittard, 2010); how the structural configuration of the CDO position impacts the work of this leader (Leon, 2014; Marshall, 2019; Woodard, 2014); and on the relationship between the role of the CDO and an increase in student and faculty diversity (Gichuru, 2010; Green, 2008).

DEFINING THE CDO ROLE

When examining the roots of the CDO position, researchers have noted that as far back as the 1970s, the CDO role has deep connections to

19

diversity leadership roles. These roles are considered to some extent the predecessors of the CDO today, including positions such as minority affairs officers, equal opportunity officers, and affirmative action officers (Banerji, 2005; Williams & Wade-Golden, 2007). Williams and Wade-Golden (2007) described three particular characteristics that can distinguish the CDO role from its predecessors. First, the work of the CDO is not confined to exclusively fulfilling the goals of affirmative action and compliance policies. Rather, CDOs can help institutions link diversity to their educational mission and practices, focusing on the process of creating better learning environments (Milem, Chang, & Antonio, 2005). Second, the CDO is positioned as an executive-level diversity administrator who directly reports to the president and/or provost. Operating at the executive level and having a direct reporting line to the president and/or provost is "a primary source of influence for chief diversity officers"[1] (Williams & Wade-Golden, 2007, p. 16). Lastly, the charge of the CDO is to manage, integrate, and coordinate campus diversity efforts. In essence, the CDO position has the responsibility of developing and synchronizing diversity initiatives and resources (Barcelo, 2007; Williams & Wade-Golden, 2007). To help CDOs accomplish this task, CDOs can coordinate resources and can supervise other senior diversity leaders and/or units. The presence of this organizational reporting structure helps the CDO to collaborate, coordinate, and maximize diversity resources.

DESIGNING THE CDO ROLE

Researchers have noted that institutions with a plan to hire a CDO should pay attention to the design of the CDO position (Leon, 2014; Parker, 2015). To provide some guidance for institutions contemplating creating a new CDO role or revamping an existing role, this section is organized across three subsections informing our understanding: (A) CDO role configurations, (B) budgetary and staff considerations, and (C) diversity leadership strategies.

CDO Role Configurations

Williams and Wade-Golden (2007) presented three main configurations or models describing CDO positions operating in higher education. While these models are not static and can evolve over time, they provide a framework to examine the CDO position. These CDO models are briefly revisited with consideration to the connection between the configuration of the CDO and span of authority to fulfill the responsibilities of this role.

Collaborative Officer CDO Model

This CDO model represents the least hierarchical CDO configuration and is characterized by a one-person office, which at times may have access to support staff (e.g., secretary, student employees, special assistant). In this model, the CDO has no formal authority over lower ranking diversity officers, units, or departments across campus. In this model, projects are typically completed through collaborative relationships and lateral coordination. Due to a limited budget and limited human resources, Collaborative Officers are usually limited to a narrow scope of priorities and are rarely involved in the direct implementation of initiatives. Researchers have noted that the presence of a Collaborative Officer CDO is often associated with more symbolic than material commitment (Leon, 2014; Williams & Wade-Golden, 2013)

Unit-Based CDO Model

The Unit-Based CDO is a model defined by a higher level of vertical authority when compared to the Collaborative Officer CDO. This might include supervision of full-time support staff, research professionals, program assistants, or technical assistants. Unit-Based CDOs can enjoy direct reporting relationships to other lower ranking diversity officers on campus. Collaboration and lateral coordination are still at the core of the responsibilities of the CDO. Individuals operating under this model are often collaborating and co-sponsoring programs and initiatives with units devoted to diversity work or units in other academic and administrative areas. Unit-Based CDOs have been engaged with initiatives such as student and faculty recruitment and retention, grant writing, community outreach, or cultural competency training (Leon, 2014; Williams & Wade-Golden, 2013).

Portfolio-Divisional CDO Model

The Portfolio-Divisional CDO model represents the most visible vertically integrated reporting structure of all CDO configurations. In this model, CDOs typically supervise lower ranking diversity officers and have direct reporting with entire units or departments. This model is often characterized as the most cost-intensive model, taking into account the monetary and staff commitment placed under the leadership of the CDO. Although the majority of CDOs operating within this model are found in large institutions (e.g., institutions with over 10,000 students), this model can also operate in other types of institutions (e.g. community colleges, small liberal arts colleges) if attention is given to how to scale the position to fit the institution's organizational structure (Williams & Wade-Golden, 2013).

21

Budgetary and Staff Considerations

Scholars have voiced their concerns that establishing an operational budget and hiring staff to support this role are aspects that will continue to impact the degree of autonomy, authority, and influence of any CDO (Arnold & Kowalski-Brown, 2011; Leon, 2014; Nixon, 2013). Williams and Wade-Golden (2013) argued that budget and reporting structures are what make a CDO position an executive-level role consistent with the responsibilities and influence of other senior-level administrators. Leon (2014) found that CDOs have used their budget and staff in a number of ways, including supporting student programming, sponsoring training and workshops, funding faculty research, partnering with departments to hire diverse faculty, creating student scholarships, leading recruitment and retention efforts, or advocating for community initiatives. In each case, the presence of a budget and/or staff made a distinguishable difference impacting how CDOs were involved with implementing diversity efforts, how often they were involved, and how the campus perceived their commitment to diversity leadership as they partnered with campus stakeholders. Leon (2014) found that CDOs intentionally build competency among their reporting staff and units to create a network of diversity advocates who can lead diversity efforts. CDOs utilized their budget and staff to amplify their reach across institutional silos, positioning staff and reporting units as active players across a number of campus spaces (e.g., orientations, training sessions, conferences, workshops, stakeholder meetings, or public events). Unfortunately, CDOs who operated under models with limited staff or budget faced the constraints of solely relying on their ability to build relationships to accomplish their work and often depended on senior leadership to enact programs or initiatives. As such, they had a reduced span of autonomy and authority, which hindered their ability to influence campus dynamics and in seeking to fulfill the expectations of the CDO role.

Diversity Leadership Strategies

CDOs have been appointed to help higher education institutions become more intentional about diversity work. Yet, they continue to encounter a lack of clarity in regard to their role, have difficulty fulfilling a number of responsibilities associated with their mandate, and are ill-positioned to become the diversity leader that institutions hoped for (Johnson, 2010; Nixon, 2013; Williams & Wade-Golden, 2013). According to the tenets of role theory, there is a greater potential for success in an organization when an individual encounters role clarity upon organizational entry.

Researchers have utilized role theory to examine administrative positions in higher education (e.g., president, senior student affairs officers, department chairs, and academic deans), focusing on the functions, characteristics, and behavior patterns of individuals operating in a selected role and within a particular context (Biddle, 1986; Cohen & March, 1974; Fowlkes, 1987; Jackson, 2006; Payne-Kirchmeier, 2009; Shaw & Costanzo, 1970). Understanding the work of CDOs from a role perspective could help institutions minimize the lack of congruence that often exists between institutional goals and diversity plans (Johnson, 2010; Leon, 2014; Nixon, 2013; Palmer, 2015; Williams & Wade-Golden, 2013). Researchers have identified a few key roles associated with the work of CDOs (Leon, 2014; Williams & Wade-Golden, 2013). The following section summarizes these roles.

Educator Role

One of the main roles of the CDO is to serve as a focal point for educating the campus. Broadly, the educator role can be divided into two important responsibilities: (a) educate the campus about the work and responsibilities of the CDO and (b) enhance diversity competencies for all stakeholders. As CDOs begin to work toward diversity goals, it is important for CDOs to create a campus culture where stakeholders understand the role of the CDO, where institutional priorities are connected to diversity goals, and where the entire campus is willing and prepared to actively engage in diversity work. As an educator, CDOs are expected to actively reach out to individuals, facilitate dialogue amongst groups, and create spaces where campus stakeholders can interact with the CDO. The literature indicates that CDOs spend a considerable amount of time forming these relationships, especially at the beginning of their journey, where one-on-one meetings, invitations, and other formal or informal interactions allow CDOs to engage campus stakeholders at all levels of the organization (e.g., provosts, deans, department heads, program directors, faculty, student groups, staff, community leaders). These interactions help CDOs to explore how stakeholders interpret diversity work in their spaces and created an opportunity to discuss how their work can be more closely aligned with a campus diversity vision (Leon, 2014).

In the educator role, CDOs are also responsible for enhancing the diversity competencies of the campus. CDOs can be at the forefront of creating, organizing, or facilitating these educational opportunities. This could include sponsoring training opportunities, facilitating workshops, bringing speakers to campus, or partnering with units to create forums or events focused on diversity priorities. CDOs can become a hub of diversity resources, information, and ideas, using their skills and ability to craft partnerships to infuse diversity across institutional boundaries. Reflecting upon the configuration of the CDO, Leon (2014) found that all CDOs can be directly involved with the educator role. However, CDOs, who had a reporting structure, leveraged staff and reporting units to become the face of these educational opportunities. In essence, CDOs with a reporting unit were at the center of a strategic process, discovering what educational opportunities the campus can benefit from, but their staff and units were in charge of the implementation, focusing on expanding opportunities for increased campus engagement with diverse educational opportunities.

Communicator Role

Establishing role clarity for a position is concerned with how CDOs connect with organizational insiders who will oversee and work along with this administrator (Biddle, 1986). In the communicator role, CDOs must create and maintain communication channels that support a unified diversity message. This diversity message needs to be clearly understood, widely shared, and supported by other leaders and campus stakeholders. CDOs can utilize a number of communication channels or spaces to share a diversity message (e.g., websites, annual reports, newsletters, speaking at public events, participating in leadership meetings, surveys, emails, town hall meetings). They can use communication channels as a tool to provide information to the campus about the status of current initiatives, new developments, diversity plans, or information pertaining to the work of the CDO (Pittard, 2010). CDOs must identify what communication channels will work best, considering the context of the institutions, the resources they have to implement communications plans, or other institutional circumstances or concerns (Green, 2008)

CDOs can also use communication channels to nurture relationships with individuals and groups across campus. If this is a goal, they need to pay attention to the frequency and quality of communications. Leon (2014) noted that CDOs viewed communicating their vision frequently and through many avenues as what sets the tone for campus interactions for other diversity leaders. In other words, CDOs must be aware that those who represent the CDO (staff or units reporting to the CDO) and the messages that they share can impact how stakeholders on campus view diversity work. In his research, Leon (2014) found that staff or units reporting to the CDO were aware that they represented the CDO in every space and interaction they encountered. Therefore, the clarity of messages shared and the quality of interactions were essential in strengthening a diversity vision and were crucial in forming new partnerships. As a communicator, CDOs must also become skilled public relations managers. Because CDOs are visible diversity leaders, they must be aware that they are often expected to represent the voice of the institution with regards to diversity (Nixon, 2013). Pittard (2010) shared that establishing channels of bidirectional communication can help CDOs become effective public relations managers. In essence, it is not enough for CDOs to communicate their message, ideas, or vision to the campus. They must also provide opportunities for stakeholders to affirm their voice, ideas, interests, or concerns. CDOs who formalize communications channels can use the information or feedback gathered to strengthen relationships, to create institutional buy-in, and to continue to refine the work of the CDO (Pittard, 2010).

Symbolic Role

Williams and Wade-Golden (2013) affirmed that what distinguishes the CDO from other diversity roles is that this leader has access and a direct reporting relationship at the highest level of the institutional hierarchy. This presence can elevate the visibility of diversity work and provide an opportunity for the CDO to establish a compelling narrative which situates diversity as an institutional priority. This is particularly important, considering that the presence of a leader in key spaces can help the institution construct a shared meaning (Bolman & Deal, 2003). Taking advantage of their positionality at the institution, CDOs can participate in conversations, events, campus rituals, or ceremonies where diversity can be reframed as a compelling campus interest. Woodward (2014) noted that in theory, this presence at the top of the institutional hierarchy should provide the CDO with "substantial power towards getting other campus constituents to cooperate, or at least comply" (p. 190). However, it does not necessarily create a campus-wide sense of ownership for diversity work. Green (2008) reflected upon this, asserting that, in many ways, CDOs assume the role of a "persuader" on campus, actively and tirelessly seeking to "transform the existing attitudes, beliefs, and practices" (p. 131). Consequently, it is not uncommon for CDOs to find themselves as leaders whose task includes convincing campus stakeholders to engage with diversity priorities.

Chubin (2009) noted that CDOs must convince stakeholders to collaborate and partner, while also assuring that said stakeholders do not interpret the arrival of the CDO as the end of collective responsibility to address campus diversity issues. Woodard (2014) found that this propensity to disengage from diversity responsibilities once a CDO is appointed can become a major obstacle, in particular when CDOs serve in institutions experiencing a change in top leadership (e.g., presidential or provost search). Symbolically, a transition in leadership can open or close doors for how diversity plans are enacted on campus. That is why it is important to think about the work of the CDO as work that must be organized in ways that will continue beyond the person holding the role of the CDO. Woodward (2014) revealed that transitions can create spaces, where CDOs might encounter "changes in resources, support, priorities, and roles and responsibilities," as presidents arrive or depart an institution more frequently (Woodard, 2014, p. 191). Consequently, institutions need to pay attention to the creation of succession plans for a new wave of diversity leaders (Leske & Tomlin, 2014), understanding that the appointment of new CDOs, the creation of new roles, or the revamping of existing responsibilities can enhance a sense of vulnerability for everyone involved in enacting institutional diversity priorities.

Strategic Planner Role

Many higher education institutions continue to grapple with the development of a diversity vision, have little guidance on how to transform this vision into a plan, and often lack basic and common language to describe what diversity means to the institution (Chun & Evans, 2008; Leon & Williams, 2013). CDOs can guide institutions to reach a better understanding of diversity and to examine how this will be translated into a plan. CDOs can help stakeholders come together to examine their commitment, create spaces where the campus determines how to engage with strategic diversity goals, and facilitate a process where units or departments make sense of diversity goals, considering their own strengths and limitations

In the role of strategic planner, CDOs understand that their work must be guided by an intentional and strategic approach. One of the main obstacles when engaging with strategic planning is the lack of collaboration of key individuals and groups (Eckel & Kezar, 2003). An important lesson for CDOs in confronting this reality is that they must become collaborators who are always thinking about how to galvanize the support and buy-in from campus stakeholders. More specifically, CDOs must understand the flow of institutional dynamics, where either proposals to implement changes, or change itself, can be supported or opposed based on the execution of plans at the right time, at the right place, and with the right people behind this change. To succeed as diversity leaders, CDOs must have expertise leading institutional change efforts. This entails constantly adapting to centralized or decentralized campus environments, confronting institutional politics, and, early in their journey, becoming fully aware that institutions will continue to place high expectations and demands CDOs, while too often ignoring how to appropriately support them in these roles (Jackson, 2020; Leon, 2014; Williams & Wade-Golden, 2013).

Collaborator Role

A major aspect of the work of each CDO is to collaborate with individuals, units, and departments across the campus. In fact, these diversity leaders will often find themselves developing personal relationships on campus, offering expertise and guidance, and crafting partnerships to support diversity work. Researchers who have examined the configuration of the CDO have stated that the presence of staff and units reporting to the CDO can play a significant role in enhancing the ability of the CDO position to become an active collaborator (Leon, 2014; Woodward, 2014). CDOs with more vertically integrated structures have leveraged their staff to lead or take part in a variety of programs, events, or initiatives. Through these interactions, CDOs have become a resource for advice, expertise, and guidance to link people beyond institutional silos. The rationale behind this is that "diversity does not fit into the traditional administrative box, and these officers [CDOs] span the boundaries of their institution" (Williams & Wade-Golden, 2007, p. 12).

To be an effective collaborative leader, a CDO must have a deep understanding of the status of diversity work and progress across the entire campus. This knowledge and awareness will help CDOs to think about diversity as a big picture issue, while also considering the context for each individual, department, unit, or college immersed in diversity work. If CDOs expect to create organizational environments where everyone shares a responsibility for diversity work, they must become collaborators, advocates, and partners across institutional silos. This collaboration can range from providing feedback and expertise when developing new diversity capabilities, refining how current diversity work is enacted, or thinking about the organizational redesign of diversity resources to position individuals and units under the direction of the CDO.

Entrepreneur Role

The CDO can directly impact diversity initiatives by creating, providing, or securing financial incentives to support a diversity plan. Positioning the

CDO as an administrator with the capacity to use and allocate funds can reassure campus stakeholders that diversity is an institutional commitment. In an entrepreneur role, CDOs can utilize monetary resources to engage in initiatives with a number of campus stakeholders. Williams and Wade-Golden (2013) recommended that prior to the creation of a CDO position, campus leaders must develop at minimum "a first-year budget" (p. 34). Unfortunately, for many CDOs, they will step into positions with little knowledge or reassurance about the resources allocated to support their work (Greenfield, 2015). Defining a specific budget for a CDO must take into consideration institutional size, diversity goals, existing diversity resources, institutional finances, and how the CDO will be positioned in regard to this budget. Williams and Wade-Golden (2013) noted that budgetary commitments to CDO positions can vary widely among institutions, ranging from less than $50,000 to over $1 million. For example, in the category of Portfolio Divisional CDOs operating at large institutions (more than 20,000 students), over 50 percent of these officers had a budget of over $500,000. In contrast, only 16 percent of CDOs at small institutions (less than 5,000 students) and 13 percent of CDOs at medium institutions (less than 10,000 students) had access to this level of funding.

Researchers have noted that budgets can influence both how stakeholders view the CDO position and how CDOs engage with diversity work. Feelings of dismay, distrust, consternation, and doubt can undermine the efforts of any CDO if stakeholders believe the CDO position and diversity work is underfunded (Leon, 2014). For many stakeholders, the lack of a suitable budget can be translated into interpreting the work of the CDO as only "diversity talk" which rarely becomes a strategic plan and is even less likely to be enacted or implemented (Leon, 2014; Williams, 2013). Researchers have found that monetary support (commitment?) can determine the breadth and depth of initiatives in which CDOs engage (Arnold & Kowalski-Brown, 2011; Leon, 2014; Nixon, 2013). The lack of an adequate budget can impact how a CDO is able to respond to requests to sponsor events, implement programs, create initiatives, or provide financial incentives to ideas supporting diversity goals. In times of economic distress, campus stakeholders have too often experienced the consequences of fiscal decisions that have resulted in cutting staff, programs, or initiatives. Leon (2014) revealed that many diversity leaders know that financial distress disproportionately impacts funds dedicated to diversity work. This can reduce CDOs to campus administrators who solely rely on their ability to collaborate, coordinate, and build relationships, knowing that financial resources will not be supporting their efforts or vision.

Recruiter Role

Reflecting upon the existing administrative roles on campus prior to the CDO (e.g., minority affairs, multicultural affairs, or affirmative action officers), it is clear that the recruitment of students and minoritized faculty and staff, in particular to fulfill employment equity mandates, occupied a central space (Gose, 2013). Nixon (2013) noted that in many cases, CDOs bring with them a professional background that includes recruiting or retaining minoritized populations. In fact, institutions value CDOs who bring this expertise, hoping that this "will effectively influence the recruitment and retention of minority students at the undergraduate and graduate levels, [and] promote the recruitment of minority faculty," (Parker, 2015, p. 150). Today, while the CDO role does not solely focus on these responsibilities, many CDOs are directly or indirectly involved with this type of work (Green, 2008; Leon, 2014; Palmer, 2015). One aspect worth discussing is that many CDOs identify themselves as members of a minoritized group or groups. For example, Williams and Wade-Golden (2013) reported that 70 percent of all CDOs nationally are African American. That is why it is not uncommon for CDOs to rely upon their own networks to carry out their work. As such, CDOs can be a significant force outreaching to groups and organizations representing diverse staff, faculty, or students, helping institutions create recruitment pipelines for underrepresented groups in higher education.

Research and Assessment Role

Campuses and their diversity leaders have been criticized because of a perceived lack of assessment or evaluations focused on diversity goals (Gose, 2013). That is why it is important for CDOs to establish baselines, metrics, and goals that can help the campus understand how a CDO can help move the diversity conversation forward. One approach to fulfill this responsibility can include establishing priorities to help the campus collect, understand, and utilize data, determining where the campus stands in regard to diversity and offering recommendations for future steps. In a research and assessment role, CDOs can be directly involved with managing an internal diversity audit, mapping campus diversity resources, or sponsoring research studies (e.g., climate, demographic, retention, salary equity). These tools can help the CDO visualize where opportunities for collaboration, supervision, or partnership exist. Williams and Wade-Golden (2013) noted that research and assessment work is how CDOs help institutions reimagine how diversity resources can be organized. CDOs who embrace the research and assessment role are better informed to make sound recommendations regarding diversity strategic planning. However, their work creating a sense of accountability should not be interpreted as a responsibility to become a diversity watchdog. Rather, CDOs must engage with research and assessment to identify opportunities to celebrate diversity milestones and progress, which can help the campus create a sense of shared accountability. However, researchers have reminded us that creating a sense of accountability for diversity work on campus has been a major challenge and source of frustration for many CDOs, particularly when it appears that repercussions or consequence do not exist for individuals or units on campus not fulfilling or aligning their work with diversity plans (Green, 2008; Nixon, 2013).

To clarify, CDOs must be prepared for institutional cultures where sophisticated research or assessment instruments might have been in place tracking diversity progress, but no accountability exists if individuals or campus units do not reach these diversity markers (Green, 2008). Leon (2014) found that CDOs who enjoyed a configuration with a reporting structure might set an example of accountability for institutions when they organize and lead their units to participate in research and self-assessment efforts. In one case, Leon (2014) found that having staff and units reporting to the CDO participate in the same external campus climate assessment sent a message to the institution that accountability is a responsibility for everyone involved in the journey of diversity work. This finding provides hope for campuses attempting to create a culture of accountability where the responsibility for fulfilling diversity goals extends beyond a few institutional pockets.

THE FUTURE OF CDOS

CDOs have continued to be appointed across a number of institutions where they have gained stature as higher education administrators, whose expertise can help campuses organize diversity resources and lead strategic diversity efforts. Unfortunately, their journey has not been one without challenges, concerns, setbacks; at times, they have met with frustration and hopelessness from campus stakeholders who have heard the promises of diversity one too many times, but still await for visible and sustainable commitments. What is different in the higher education landscape pertaining to the journey for CDOs today? One important aspect is that institutions today can look at the past 15–20 years and seek to understand the experiences of diversity leaders across the country who were appointed and served as the first CDOs at many institutions. Institutions can reflect upon their success and shortcomings, and in fact, institutions should carefully analyze the journey of CDOs hoping to continue to develop theoretical and practical recommendations that illuminate our understanding of contemporary diversity leadership. Taking into account the scholarly inquiries that have focused on the role, four major areas can guide the future work of administrators and scholars interested in the CDO role.

The Configuration and Positioning of the CDO

While we have a better understanding of the CDO position today, many CDOs still report that their configuration and positioning within their institution is still unsatisfactory. Considering that many institutions began to appoint their inaugural CDO in the early 2000s, there is an important message that must be restated: creating a CDO position is not a call for institutions to reorganize every aspect of diversity on campus under the supervision of the CDO. Rather, a CDO should only supervise individuals, units, or resources that can benefit from the leadership of this role. What does this entail? To begin, it is important to appoint a CDO with an executive-level administrative title, and to truly match other executive-level administrators, CDOs must also enjoy the benefit and responsibility of having a budget and reporting structure. Providing leadership and supervision to staff or units is central to being a key decision maker. Having a budget that matches those supervisory responsibilities is central to being able to enact a diversity strategic plan. Lacking either one, it is unlikely a CDO will have the authority or influence to enact any mandates. Thus, institutions will continue to sabotage their own plans to identify opportunities, partnerships, or benefit from the leadership of the CDO.

Institutions must create adequate conditions for the CDO to bring synergy to diversity work. At times, leaders must consider structural reorganizations as an opportunity to position diversity as part of broader goals, strategic plans, and at the core of making financial decisions. If diversity work is simply an afterthought, the work of the CDO and those who collaborate with this role will likely end up once again on a bookcase as a report for the next diversity committee to review. The fear that little will be accomplished or changed, even when appointing a CDO, is real, and it can greatly deter diversity advocates (Leon & Williams, 2016). For that reason, as institutions redefine current CDO roles or bring a new leader to an existing position, they have a responsibility to think about this role beyond the expectations created with the arrival of this leader. Institutions must pay attention to the idea of continuity and sustainability and developing a campus diversity infrastructure that extends beyond the person appointed as a CDO. Institutions truly have an opportunity to build CDO roles that are blended with the campus. This will increase the likelihood that initiatives, programs, or changes implemented by a CDO will remain in operation, especially when transition in leadership occurs.

Institutional Context and Situational Leadership

CDOs have been described as leaders whose roles rely on coordination, collaboration, and partnerships to lead campus diversity efforts. Several studies have noted that this is commonly how diversity work is understood and enacted in higher education (Arnold & Kowalski-Brown, 2011; Davalos, 2014; Green, 2008; Nixon, 2013; Parker, 2015; Wilson, 2013; Woodard, 2014). Unfortunately, the expectation for this role to be a collaborative leader and an integrator can be a double-edged sword. As CDOs actively seek to build partnerships, it is not uncommon to find themselves in spaces where diversity work has been described as a reactive work in times of crisis, and where CDOs are depicted as a leader who is entirely responsible for any and all diversity issues or efforts. This interpretation creates a false narrative where the hiring of a CDO can be used as a "way out" or "free-pass" for other campus leaders and stakeholders to be accountable for diversity progress. In a recent study, Bradley, Garven, Law, and West (2018) noted that the presence of CDOs had not contributed to enhanced faculty diversification efforts. This interpretation assumes the CDO role was, in fact, tasked with addressing faculty diversification efforts or had responsibility for creating a sense of shared accountability for this effort. If neither was explicitly the mandate of a given CDO, associating their role with this responsibility just continues to erode the credibility of this leader in higher education (Wood, Hilton, Leon, & Hatch-Tocaimaza, 2018). Combined with disjointed diversity conversations, a lack of clear diversity priorities, and profound institutional divisions and dissonance, this can become a major deterrent for any diversity leader. In an integrator role, CDOs can help foster a sense of collective responsibility and accountability. However, this can occur only if individuals and groups on campus truly become partners with the CDO. In essence, aligning individuals and groups under the umbrella of strategic diversity priorities is key to how the leadership of a CDO can contribute to an institution. This type of strategy can be examined from a situational leadership framework, where CDOs are leaders actively working on building relationships with other stakeholders in their organizations. More specifically, CDOs are invested in developing competence amongst stakeholders. As a framework, situational leadership reminds us of the constant back and forth that is needed between leaders and collabora-tors creating plans, goals, or timelines (directive behaviors), while also communicating and helping collaborators (supportive behaviors) to refine their own competencies (Northouse, 2016). What is the key take-away? CDOs often arrive at institutions with decades of systemic issues, histor-ical legacies of inequities, and environmental influences that have eroded the campus climate. Ignoring this reality is a serious mistake, particularly when institutions continue to frame the arrival of CDOs as a solution to tackle all these issues. CDOs, from the time of their appointment, must have the support of executive leaders to intentionally build competency around their role. Without a commitment to create intentional partner-ships that are supported (e.g., staff, resources, campus spaces, top-level leadership buy-in), CDOs will continue to be seen as the only role re-sponsible for diversity work. If that is the case, it is unlikely CDOs will reduce organizational dissonance, minimize the isolation of initiatives, or support stakeholders to embrace diversity as an institutional asset.

Selecting the Right CDO

Williams and Wade-Golden (2013) presented four major paths that have typically defined the professional trajectory of those appointed as CDOs. The first three paths include serving institutions in different roles both as faculty or administrators (*line leadership track*), managing functional areas where diversity resources were an important or central part of their role (*traditional leadership track*), and expertise on workforce compliance and employment law (*affirmative action and equal opportunity track*). The last and most recent path is described as the *strategic diversity lead-ership track*. This is an emerging path which includes individuals whose work has taken place in diversity units or divisions where a CDO already existed.

However, writing and reflecting upon the nature of the CDO requires a succinct focus on the individual at the center of the role, the person assum-ing the CDO responsibilities as well as on the identities that are brought to the table as a diversity leader. In fact, writing about the future of CDOs challenges scholars to position the examination of the CDO as a person who must navigate the role and to the organizational dynamics that will continue to help or hinder those who have stepped into this role. Several scholarly inquiries have focused on the importance of understanding the connection between the individual and the role of the CDO. Considering the demanding and politicized nature of the CDO role (Greenfield, 2015; Johnson, 2010; Nixon, 2013; Pittard, 2010; Williams & Wade-Golden,

2007), scholars have suggested that characteristics such as "emotional intelligence, charisma, and communication abilities" are instrumental to leverage the CDO position on campus (Williams & Wade-Golden, 2007, p. 5). However, one aspect that grants further attention is the exploration of the fluid, interlocking identities that CDOs possess and how they influence how diversity leadership is enacted within a particular organization context.

In short, we know that a large number of CDOs are members of underrepresented groups; many are frequently the only underrepresented voice in executive-level spaces; and many have experienced discrimination in the form of micro or macro aggressions in their journeys arriving to or while being in a CDO role (Johnson, 2010; Woodard, 2014). In her essay, "The Nearly Impossible Job of a Chief Diversity Officer (CDO)," Pratt-Clarke (2020) recently described the existence of a push and pull dynamic, where CDOs will be caught in the middle because of their own identities and the type of work they are engaged in. On one end, as individuals from underrepresented backgrounds, many aspiring diversity leaders are seen as a strong fit to lead diversity efforts because of their ability to navigate spaces and relate to the issues that impact underserved populations. On the other, these individuals must also wear an administrative hat (Nixon, 2013), representing the system and the many inequities that campus stakeholders hope to change. Pratt-Clarke (2020) discusses the ideas of loyalties, and how CDOs will find themselves in spaces where their loyalties to a particular group (e.g., underrepresented students, faculty of color, community, executive-leaders, board of trustees) or their beliefs (e.g., equity, access, inclusion) will be questioned. Considering current campus climate dynamics across many institutions, it is expected that the CDO will continue to be expected to rebuild and regain institutional trust. Unfortunately, they will have to accomplish this task while responding to institutional pressures to minimize disruptions to the day-to-day activities of the campus, and to be wary of stirring the diversity pot in ways that could potentially shine a negative light on institutional pockets where diversity, equity, and inclusion has not been a priority.

CONCLUSION

This chapter established a foundation to better understand and conceptualize diversity leadership with a focus on the executive-level position role of the CDO. The chapter revealed that the leadership of the CDO is shaped by context, which at the institutional level has historically created the CDO role as a response to a campus crisis or discontent with campus commitment to a diversity agenda. Today, environmental and institutional factors continue to shape the work of the CDO and, more than ever, have raised the stakes for CDOs to meet the expectations of institutions who hope these leaders will emerge as transformative forces for diversity, equity, and inclusion. As CDOs roles have been more widely established across institutions, we must learn about their experiences and identify lessons that will help institutions support this role and establish continuity for diversity plans. Establishing a CDO brings campuses the opportunity to organize strategic efforts focused on diversity. This chapter provided important considerations to continue to create, refine, and adapt these roles to the evolving landscape of colleges, universities, and our society.

Considering the nuances of fluid identities and the complexity of scenarios CDOs will continue to encounter, examining diversity leadership as praxis demands that we carry out inquiries that help us understand the individual, the role, and the context where CDOs operate (Greenfield, 2015). Without a doubt, CDOs and aspiring CDOs can rely upon a growing body of scholarship that has emerged on the topic. CDOs can utilize these scholarly contributions not only to enhance their day-to-day work, but also to be prepared to ask critical questions when exploring new job opportunities in diversity leadership, when providing feedback and input to refine existing diversity leadership roles, and especially when mentoring aspiring diversity leaders. While gaining familiarity with the journey of other CDOs in the field does not guarantee that the job will be less complex, it does offer an additional perspective that CDOs can use to refine their relational, situational, and contextual understanding of diversity leadership across colleges and universities.

REFERENCES

Arnold, J., & Kowalski-Brown, M. (2011). The journey to an inaugural chief diversity officer: Preparation, implementation and beyond. *Innovative Higher Education*, 37(1), 27–36. Springer Science and Business Media. doi: 10.1007/s10755-011-9185-9.

Banerji, S. (2005). Diversity officers—Coming to a campus near you? *Diverse Issues in Higher Education*, 22(20), 38–40.

Barcelo, N. (2007). Transforming our institutions for the twenty-first century: The role of the chief diversity officer. *Diversity Digest: Institutional Leadership*, 10(2), 7–8. Retrieved from http://www.diversityweb.org/digest/vol10no2/barcelo.cfm

Biddle, B. (1986). Recent development in role theory. *Annual Review of Sociology*, 12, 1267–1292.

Bolman, L. G., & Deal, T. E. (2003). *Reframing organizations: Artistry, choice, and leadership* (3rd ed.). San Francisco, CA: Jossey-Bass.

Bradley, S., Garven, J., Law, W., & West, J. (2018). The impact of chief diversity officers on diverse faculty hiring. Working paper series (National Bureau of Economic Research). doi: 10.3386/w24969.

Chubin, D. E. (2009). 'Visible' diversity and the university. *Diverse Issues in Higher Education, 26*(12), 28.

Chun, E. B., & Evans, A. (2008, March 3). Demythologizing diversity in higher education. Retrieved from http://www.diverseeducation.com/artman/publish/printer_10763.shtml

Cohen, M. D., & March, J. G. (1974). *Leadership and ambiguity: The American college president*. New York: McGraw-Hill.

Davalos, C. (2014). *The role of chief diversity officers in institutionalizing diversity and inclusion: A multiple case study of three exemplar universities* (Unpublished doctoral dissertation). University of San Diego.

Eckel, P. D., & Kezar, A. (2003). *Taking the reins: Institutional transformation in higher education*. Westport, CT: Praeger.

Fowlkes, M. R. (1987). Role combinations and role conflict: Introductory perspective. In F. J. Crosby (Ed.), *Spouse, parent, worker: On gender and multiple roles*. New Haven, CT: Yale University, 3–10.

Gichuru, M. (2010). *Post-affirmative action: A phenomenological study of admission initiatives by chief diversity officers to support diversity* (Doctoral dissertation). Retrieved from ProQuest Databases (3417884).

Gose, B. (2013). Diversity Offices aren't what they used to be. The Chronicle of Higher Education. Retrieved from https://chronicle.com/article/Diversity-Offices-Arent-What/139633/

Green, B. (2008). *Increasing faculty diversity in higher education: A case study of the evolving role of the chief diversity officer at three public universities in Texas* (Doctoral dissertation). Retrieved from https://ttu-ir.tdl.org/bitstream/handle/2346/10210/Green_Birgit_Diss.pdf?seqence=1

Greenfield, D. (2015). *White face, Black Space: My journey as a Chief Diversity Officer at an HBCU. Diss. U of Washington*. (Doctoral dissertation) Retrieved from https://digital.lib.washington.edu/researchworks/bitstream/handle/1773/33979/Greenfieldwashington_0250E_14497.pdf;sequence=1

Jackson, J. F. L. (2006). The nature of academic dean's work: Moving toward and academic executive behavioral model in higher education. *Journal of the Professoriate, 1*, 7–21.

Jackson, J. F. L. (2020). Chief Diversity Officers need more than a title to succeed. CU Management. Retrieved from https://www.cumanagement.com/articles/2020/01/diversity-insight-set-fail?fbclid=IwAR2p1C2wr_yaLRrDpI-W00mEyE3UQe1D4pqg9G1unnk5N_UQQ0Pif59ZMghg

Johnson, E. (2010). *Lifting as we climb: Experiences of black diversity officers at three predominantly white institutions in Kentucky* (Doctoral dissertation). Retrieved from https://uknowledge.uky.edu/gradschool_diss/82/

Leon, R. A. (2014). The chief diversity officer: An examination of CDO models and strategies. *Journal of Diversity in Higher Education, 7*(2), 77–91.

Leon, R. A., & Williams, D. A. (2016). Contingencies for success: Examining diversity committees in higher education. *Innovative Higher Education, 41,* 395–410.

Leske, L., & Tomlin, O. (2014). *Developing the next generation of chief diversity officers in higher education.* Oak Brook, IL: Witt/Kieffer.

Marshall, G. (2019). *Chief Diversity Officers (CDOs): The relationships between organizational structure, institutional commitment to inclusive excellence, and CDOs' perceptions of their performance in facilitating transformational change* (Doctoral dissertation). Retrieved from https://fisherpub.sjfc.edu/cgi/viewcontent.cgi?article=1404&context=education_etd

Milem, J. F., Chang, M. J., & Antonio, A. L. (2005). *Making diversity work on campus: A research-based perspective.* Washington, DC: Association of American Colleges and Universities.

Nixon, M. (2013). *Women of color chief diversity officers: Their positionality and agency in higher education institutions* (Doctoral dissertation). Retrieved from https://digital.lib.washington.edu/researchworks/handle/1773/23632

Northouse, P. G. (2016). *Leadership: Theory and practice* (7th ed.). Thousand Oaks, CA: Sage.

Parker, E. T. (2015). *Exploring the establishment of the office of the chief diversity officer in higher education: A multisite case study* (Doctoral dissertation). Retrieved from https://doi.org/10.17077/etd.irgq8poj

Payne-Kirchmeier, J. (2009). *Women administrators's perceptions of the senior student affairs officer job search process* (Doctoral dissertation). Retrieved from ProQuest (UMI No. 3394724).

Pittard, L. A. (2010). *Select higher education chief diversity officers: Roles, realities, and reflections* (Doctoral dissertation). Retrieved from ProQuest (UMI No. 3446403)

Pratt-Clarke, M. (2020, July 2). The Nearly Impossible Job of a Chief Diversity Officer. Menah Pratt-Clarke Empowering the Powerless. http://menahprattclarke.com/2020/07/02/the-nearly-impossible-job-of-a-chief-diversity-officer/

Shaw, M., & Costanzo, P. (1970). *Theories of social psychology.* New York: McGraw-Hill.

Williams, D., Berger, J., & McClendon, S. (2005). *Toward a model of inclusive excellence and change in higher education.* Washington, DC: Association of American Colleges and Universities.

37

Williams, D. A. (2013). *Strategic diversity leadership: Activating change and transformation in higher education.* Fairfax, VA: Stylus Publishing Press.

Williams, D. A., & Wade-Golden, K. (2007). *The chief diversity officer: A primer for college and university presidents.* Washington, DC: American Council on Education.

Williams, D. A., & Wade-Golden, K. (2013). *The chief diversity officer: Strategy, structure, and change management.* Fairfax, VA: Stylus Publishing Press.

Wilson, J. L. (2013). Emerging trend: The chief diversity officer phenomenon within higher education. *The Journal of Negro Education, 82*(4), 433–445.

Wood, L. Hilton, A., Leon, R., & Hatch-Tocaimaza, D. (2018). Research design flaws identified in study suggesting that Chief Diversity Officers "Hurt" Diversity. Diverse Issues in Higher Education. Retrieved from https://diverseeducation.com/article/126144/

Woodard, Q. (2014). *Understanding the implications of organizational culture and organizational structure for the role of the Chief Diversity Officer in higher education* (Doctoral dissertation). Retrieved from https://pdfs.semanticscholar.org/dfd3/74e19a2cc7ec69058a13c92b0ff7ecb223f6.pdf

Part Two

Becoming

Chapter Three

Becoming a Senior Diversity Administrator

You Don't Get To Have All of Me

Brighid Dwyer and LaTanya N. Buck

Diversity leadership is based on context, history, and relationships. A strong diversity leader is one who knows their own talents and uses them appropriately within the changing contexts of higher education. A diversity leader reflects on the institutional mission and the institutional, local, national, and sometimes even the global contexts that shape the reality of higher education in the moment in which the leader finds themselves.

Within this chapter, we, the authors, discuss our personal narratives that ground us in the work we do and allow us to approach complex diversity, equity, and inclusion challenges that we face today with authenticity. This chapter details our initial motivations behind our choosing to enter the diversity field and how those motivations have changed over the course of our careers due to institutional transitions, personal, national, and international contexts about identity, and perspective taking. We delve into what it means to reconcile our personal and professional experiences as we negotiate between critiquing institutional culture and being "of the institution." Finally, we explore the complexities and complications of *becoming*, and the possibility of what emerges beyond in the field of equity, diversity, and inclusion.

This exploration of becoming takes the form of a transcript of a conversational interview we had with one another about what it means to *become* a senior-level diversity administrator.

DOI: 10.4324/9781003008521-5   **41**

BECOMING AN EARLY CAREER DIVERSITY ADMINISTRATOR: WHY WE INITIALLY ENTERED INTO THE WORK

As a result of our previous diversity, equity, and inclusion (DEI) work, we have learned the importance of personal stories and narratives in understanding how and why people approach DEI in higher education in particular ways. DEI work is often incredibly personal, complex, and emotional. Understanding personal approaches is critically important in forming a well-functioning and highly effective team. Felts (1992) found that by developing reciprocal relationships, communication is enhanced within organizations. By getting to know more about the backgrounds and approaches of your colleagues, their approaches to decision-making become clearer and communication challenges can be minimized.

To be an effective senior-level diversity leader, communication is key. In this section we share perspectives from our personal backgrounds and how they are connected to how we approach our diversity and inclusion roles.

LATANYA: So, Brighid, tell me how your upbringing informed your interest and connection to higher education and diversity and inclusion work.

BRIGHID: There has always been a strong connection to education in my family. My mom taught art to adults with disabilities, my godmother was a continuing education teacher, and my god sister taught in an ESL preschool. So, growing up I was always around conversations about education for some of the most vulnerable populations. I grew up in Oakland, California, and talking about diversity was the fabric of our life; and I don't mean conversations just about race. We talked a lot about race, but we were also talking about the pervasiveness of stereotypes, we talked about the importance of language and not using demeaning words like the "R-word," and we talked about what it meant to be gay.

I am multiracial and I grew up with a lot of multiracial kids. And that was really intentional. My mom was white but really wanted to make sure I was in a community where there were a lot of people who looked like me. And people who didn't. So, through her I learned the importance of surrounding myself with people who are different from me and learning about other people's perspectives.

As far as a career in higher education and DEI work, as a kid I didn't know higher education was even a career. I initially thought I would go into K-12 teaching and become an elementary school teacher. But in college I talked to my professors and some administrators I was close to who let me know this was a career possibility. Talking to other people about what they did really opened up opportunities for me.

LATANYA: It sounds like our experiences are pretty similar as it relates to our mothers. I grew up in St. Louis in a single parent household; I lived with my mom, but my dad and I were close. As a young child, my mom went to community college and then she transferred to a local four-year institution. I used to go with her to classes, and she was also a student activist. She was very involved in student organizations like the All-African People's Revolutionary Party; I would go to marches and travel out of town with her. It was really cool to see her as a young person and as a non-traditional student engaged in that way.

So early on I had exposure to higher education classes and co-curricular life. My mom was a certified K-12 special education teacher. Her path influenced me, and I planned on being a teacher. When it was time for me to go to college, I spent one year at the community college before I transferred into a four-year institution. I wanted to teach African American literature in high school, so I was planning to major in secondary education with an emphasis on English. But, once I got into school I did not like the observational experience, so I was like "I don't know if this is for me." I changed my major several times, but landed on public relations.

I often joke that I majored in student activities because I spent so much time engaged outside the classroom. So, I started asking administrators, "what do I have to do, to have a job like yours?" I had never heard of higher education administration, so I started looking into it and went to grad school for College Student Personnel Administration. I knew I wanted to with students who had similar experiences as mine…students from low-income backgrounds, students of color, students who were on the margins. I went to a predominantly white institution and so I was initially looking a lot at race and students of color when I thought of the population that I wanted to serve. At that time, my dream job was to become the director of a cultural center – that was the job for me.

BRIGHID: And you did that!

Hirschy et al. (2015) define professional identity as containing "a strong connection to the profession, alignment between one's own and the field's values, and ongoing professional development" (p. 787). We, the authors, have found this to be true for us. We began in the field of multicultural student affairs because of the ways in which our own experiences and values aligned with the professional development opportunities we sought, and because our early career aspirations related to diversity and higher education were fulfilled in this field. Our interests in working as higher education diversity administrators were driven in large part by our passions, our upbringings, our personal experiences, and our own identities. Yet, over time we have become more knowledgeable and we understand that being an effective DEI leader necessitates that we expand the scope of the work and those included in it.

BECOMING MORE KNOWLEDGEABLE: HOW (OUR VIEWS OF) THIS WORK HAS EXPANDED OVER TIME

As we became mid-level administrators, we recognized that serving as an effective higher education diversity practitioner was so much more than one's personal interest. Being an effective administrator depends deeply on one's ability to bring others on board, engender empathy beyond one's own identities, and cultivate courageous acts of humility within yourself and among others.

Within this context, conversations about diversity and inclusion have changed significantly over time. We too have grown as higher education professionals and our actions and decision-making have changed to reflect the new needs within the field and the type of leadership required to accomplish newly emerging goals. Here we explore the question "How have you seen the need for and focus on diversity and inclusion work change during your time as a professional?"

LATANYA: I started my professional career in higher education diversity and inclusion in 2004 as a coordinator of student multicultural services at a medium-sized school in Kentucky. At that time a lot of my work was specifically focused on serving and engaging students of color. That did not really change for me until maybe 2009, when I accepted a role as the director of a cultural center that served more than just students of color.

At this cultural center, we also focused efforts on religious, sexual, and gender identities. Working with a wider variety of communities broadened my perspective so much. It influenced how I thought about the work and who I was there to serve.

Starting off I did not see serving *all* students as my job; I saw my job as serving students of color. But then I had several experiences when I saw how important it was to engage all students and there was a shift of how I saw the work of diversity and inclusion.

BRIGHID: For me, the scope of the work has always been very broad. Throughout my career I have been aware of how place and location play a role in who people are and how they see the world. The experiences I had growing up in a diverse community in Oakland really shaped who I am. I thought everyone had friends from different racial and ethnic backgrounds and most people had been to a bar or bat mitzvah. These were the assumptions I had.

But a year after 9/11, I moved to Indiana for a job and found myself confronted with a whole new reality. I had a coworker who was in her 50s and had a son who was deployed in Afghanistan. She lived in Indiana her whole life and she was very focused on issues locally and on supporting veterans. I doubt she interacted with many people of color outside of work. She and I came from such different worlds. She was viewing 9/11 from a perspective of supporting the military and from a place of deep concern for her son. I, however, was coming from living in Los Angeles and seeing friends and classmates being profiled and questioned as they went about their daily lives.

For me, the entire year I spent in Indiana was this huge "aha" moment. I realized that until that point in my life I had mostly interacted with Californians and that one's location really mattered in terms of how people see and approach the world. I realized that I didn't see the world the way my colleague did and she didn't see it the way I did.

This work experience really changed me. My younger, more immature self, thought that I could ignore or dismiss people who didn't agree with me, but during my time in Indiana I realized I couldn't discount other people's opinions. I needed to listen and understand perspectives different from my own, even if I didn't agree with them.

LATANYA: I hear you. There are these moments that really shape and change us. For me, I had a specific situation happen that sparked that shift; this was my "Aha" moment.

I was working as a director in a cultural center and I received a report that there was a white male student who was drunk at 3 o'clock in the morning, and he had knocked on the door of one of our student athletes, who was a black woman. She had asked him to leave and he told her, "shut up, n*gg*r b***h or I will lynch you."

As you can imagine, it caused an uproar on campus. I was hearing about students' frustration, anger, and pain, all day every day, for weeks. Then, one of my colleagues from the Student Conduct Office reached out to me and asked that I be the person to work with the student – the perpetrator of the incident.

It was one of those situations where I wanted to say no, for two reasons – I was also personally impacted by the words that were used

45

and then I also knew first-hand the pain and the frustrations of the students. Working with the offending student sort of felt like a betrayal.

But I ended up working with him, and you know, it turned out that coaching him was very eye-opening for me. I really had to learn to get beyond myself, beyond how his words and actions hurt me personally. I had to look at myself as an educator and a student affairs practitioner who was there to engage all students.

BRIGHID: So, what was that like? How did you work with him?

LATANYA: Well, I started to meet with the student, and I felt like I was meeting with him in secrecy in my office [she laughs]. Of course, he was nervous. He didn't know what to expect and neither did I. I decided to give him books, I had him look up the history of lynching within the state where we resided. He had to explore the impact it had on the Black community. We talked about patriarchy, whiteness, and sexism, and I just had him do a lot of reading and writing assignments.

The culminating experience I created for him was to present his research findings to a faculty colleagues' African American Studies class, but when it came time to present, he was gone, and I couldn't find him for a while.

A semester or two later, it was time for him to graduate and a colleague reached out to me to see if he had completed his assignments, and I said "No, he still has one thing to complete." Ultimately, I was the one who had to determine whether or not he graduated.

In the end, the student did his presentation. The students in the class really challenged him and asked critical questions. I also saw the amount of grace the students gave him in that moment for being courageous enough to stand up in front of that class, answer questions, and discuss how much he learned.

I think he was genuinely apologetic for his actions and learned from it, and he wrote me this beautiful note right before he graduated.

This was one of the most pivotal moments in my career. It made me think about how we do this work. In that moment, I truly saw how our work is not just about engaging students of color or students who frequented the cultural center, but it really is about how to engage all students, and how to partner with faculty and staff colleagues to support students.

BRIGHID: You know, in hearing this story I see the influence of your upbringing. I remember you saying previously that your mom used to keep you in over the summer when friends wanted to go outside and play. Your mom would have you write reports and when her friends came calling, but you were not allowed to go out until the reports were complete; however, friends were welcome to come in and write reports of their own, right? So, I see your mom's influence in the way you approached the situation.

LATANYA: Yes, that's right. I never made that connection, but absolutely! This was the first thing I thought of doing. I said to myself "he is going to learn today!"

As educators, scholars, practitioners, and leaders, we stand on the shoulders of those who come before us, even in ways we are not aware. We solve problems using instincts and research. Our instincts often come from the training and practice we had early on in our careers and lives. The situations described above demonstrate the impact our early experiences have had in our decision-making throughout our careers.

Wilson et al. (2016) state, "Midlevel professionals can be classified as middle-line managers on the organizational hierarchy between those who perform basic services and those who provide vision and direction for the organization" (p. 558). We, the authors, were finding ourselves in exactly this situation. As mid-career professionals, we were working directly with students, building cross-campus partnerships, and strategically cultivating awareness in ways that opened new doors and possibilities for others and for ourselves. As we considered the next steps in our careers and how we would be able to advance, we made sure to stay abreast of current trends and changes in the field. In the same ways that new professional experiences expanded our views, we also sought out new experiences through professional development.

LATANYA: When entering the field, I kept hearing, "don't get pigeonholed." But I wanted to stay in this field, so I had to be okay with the perception of DEI work—that this is the only thing that I can do. But it does become frustrating when people assume that I don't have many skills outside the areas of D&I. You know I *love* strategic planning! I like the visioning process, and I like to think about the big picture. I also love assessment and evaluation, and there are a lot of other skills that I have. But, I have been boxed into this sort of position, and I am usually tapped when people want a D&I presentation. I am not often asked to do other things, even though I am very capable and excel in strategic planning; but, people think diversity is the only lane I can be in.

BRIGHID: I resonate so much with what you are saying about being pigeonholed in the field of DEI. At a previous institution, I was seeing a lot of men, and specifically white men, being promoted into new positions and positions that were created for them. But women of color, and specifically women of color in diversity roles, with the same or more experience, and education were not promoted in the same ways and had to fight more for office space and appropriate titling.

I didn't want to be viewed this way, and so I really had to be strategic to position myself so people saw me as someone who could do more than diversity work. I remember there was a job opening for internal candidates only, and I wasn't even sure I wanted that job, but I specifically put in an application because I needed my senior colleagues reading the applications to know that I was capable of more than just DEI work. I was a finalist for the position, and I wondered if I was selected as a finalist so they could report that they had a finalist pool that wasn't entirely white. In the interview, people were asking these coded questions and making statements like "I don't know if you would be able to use all of your talents in this role," which I took to mean, "You know this isn't a 'diversity' role, right?" While I was more than capable of doing the work required for the position, I ended up pulling out because I would not have been happy in that role. I would have been the only person of color in that unit, and I would have been treated as a token. But those are the types of decisions I felt I have had to make to get respect and prevent that pigeonholing you discussed.

In her study about women of color chief diversity officers (CDOs), Nixon (2013) states that women of color serving in diversity roles at Predominantly White Institutions "further isolates these women of color CDOs, in particular because it is viewed as the expected purview of those with marginalized identities." She also draws on the work of Niemann (2012), noting that diversity work can be doubly marginalizing for women of color because "diversity work is sometimes seen as feminine work" (Nixon, 2013, p. 106). In fact, one of the participants in the study expresses some of her challenges in a way quite similar to LaTanya. One woman of color states, "This kind of job tends to pigeonhole a person in their career. And because people will see you only as a diversity expert, they won't see any of your other skill sets as quickly or ever" (p. 106).

As women of African descent working in the diversity field, we have experienced many micro-aggressions, double standards, and the need to advocate for ourselves, oftentimes feeling that others wouldn't.

LATANYA: I have been very aware of how my colleagues have perceived me over the years, and there was a lot I felt I had to do just to gain their respect. At another institution we had leadership team meetings, and on those days, I felt like I had to dress up. I wore pantsuits and dresses, and my white colleagues next to me would be more casual. I felt that I had to be more polished to be seen as equal and felt the need to prove myself because I am a Black woman. I can't show up in the same way without repercussions.

Cheeks (2018) writes that "being black and female in the workplace means constantly having to walk a tightrope, balancing your own emotions with the perceptions and intentions of others, making everyone feel comfortable, instead of nervous, in the process." Research about workplace impacts related to African Americans and skin color also finds that darker skin is tied to increased workplace bias (Harrison, Reynolds-Dobbs, & Thomas, 2008; Marira & Mitra, 2013), lower wages (Goldsmith, Hamilton, & Darity, 2007; Kreisman & Rangel, 2015), and other forms of discrimination (e.g., Monk, 2015; Sims, 2009). As a brown-skinned woman, LaTanya's feeling that she needed to dress up and prove her competencies were not unfounded.

BRIGHID: I can relate to feeling like you really have to prove yourself. It's been humbling to me to advance in my career and to move into mid- and senior-level positions. Sometimes I sit back in meetings and think, "wow, I have a seat at the table. I am really in a position to advocate for those whose voice is not usually heard." I am so proud of my hard work and I feel like I have accomplished so much, and then there will be people who will ask me a question in a way that makes me feel so small. These moments will spiral me back down, these little comments make me feel like that 17-year old who people said only got into college because of Affirmative Action. There are still those times and those people who can really undo all the work I have done. And that is crushing, really crushing.

Research on racial micro-aggressions (Sue, 2010) and racial battle fatigue (Smith, Allen, & Danley, 2007; Yosso, Smith, Ceja, & Solorzano, 2009) describe the psychological stress responses that come from being made to feel "out of place" on college campuses because of one's race. These and other researchers discuss the pain, frustration, alienation, disappointment, and more that may ensue from the racist othering that can occur.

We have both experienced these psychological effects and they have resulted in us needing to exert additional energy in managing how others perceive us. Giving additional time to these psychological needs takes time and energy away from the work we would like to accomplish in our professional roles and in our personal lives. It can leave us tired.

BECOMING TIRED: YOU DON'T GET TO HAVE ALL OF ME: BALANCING GIVING AND BURNOUT

In their exploration of student affairs capitalism, Lee and Helm (2013) discuss how early career professionals can experience a disconnect between what they learned as students in their academic programs and what they experience in the workplace. These differences can translate into young professionals experiencing the work environment as one that does not align with the values of the field in which they were trained. While we have experienced moments like this within our careers, as we advanced our expectations for the possibilities of higher education have become clearer. As such, we experience less frustration about some of the inherent contradictions within any higher education institution or position.

While our dissonance is lessened, it is not absent. Hirschy et al. (2015) state that "older professionals may be clearer about their values and be able to evaluate their congruence with the field's espoused values, particularly if they had prior career experience" (p. 298). While we followed our passions, we have learned that no job is perfect and life needs to be well balanced between finding meaning in work and in our personal lives. We have learned we can find *some* meaning in work, but not complete life fulfillment.

Throughout our careers we have expended so many of our emotional resources on supporting and engaging students and colleagues alike. This can be exhausting, and in doing so we have ignored our own needs as raced, gendered, and otherwise minoritized beings. Here we deepen the conversation about what it means to recognize our own social identities and how they are wrapped up in the work we do, how we have managed our mental, emotional, and physical energy, and the dissonance we face in tending to our own needs while supporting others. Finally, we talk about how we navigate others' perceptions, stereotype threat, the internalization of messaging, and the collective psychological toll these have on our lives.

BRIGHID: There have been a lot of times in my career when I have not been balanced or said "no." In previous jobs I have worn *way* too many hats. It has felt like people whispered the word diversity and a huge project would land on my desk. In one job, I served as an administrator and I was teaching. I absolutely loved teaching, but it took a lot of time and energy. When I think about this particular period of about 3–4 years, I realize how out of control things were. I had three kids under 7, I was working an average 10 hours/day 6 days/week, and multiple days each week I worked 12–13 hour days. I remember trying to find a time to meet with a student group and we were all busy throughout the day so I set a meeting with them at 10 pm after I worked a 9 hour day and then taught a three hour class. I would go to my kids' swim meets and I would pull out my computer and work during warm up and in between their races. My kids would watch TV or play outside and I would be working at the dining room table taking breaks to nurse my infant. There was absolutely no balance! I was doing it to support students, but now I think that I was doing a horrible job modeling balancing work and family life for the students and my kids; and now I think my own health is suffering because of all of those years of working so much.

LATANYA: Yes, finding balance is really important. I never want to be in a position or a role at an institution where I become so ambitious that I lose sight of what's most important to me, which are of course family and community. I have had to be more intentional about that. I was that kind of person who would take a lot of work home, and now I have instituted a new practice where I leave my laptop in the office a few nights out of the week so I can be more present at home and do the things that I enjoy – writing or having a good meal with my kid. This is about having boundaries between my professional life and my personal life, and being more mindful about how much I give, how much I keep private, and how much I go home with. This is particularly important for me living and working within such a small community. When I go to my son's sporting events, I don't want someone to ask me about work, I want to be at the game as a supportive mom, not a representative of the institution. So, I have been more guarded about what I share with some people so I can be more engaged in the ways that I would like, in all areas of my life.

BRIGHID: I am getting better at saying "no" and thinking about how my "no" allows me to say "yes" to other projects, opportunities, or other areas of my life. I am blocking more time on my calendar to think and plan, to delete e-mail, and organize my files. I am putting myself first and recognizing how I can be more present for others when I am organized and less overwhelmed.

Despite the energy and creativity we put forth to engage students and colleagues of all backgrounds in DEI work, it can become exhausting. Many other professionals also find it exhausting, as evidenced by the growing number of webinars offered about self-care for DEI administrators as well as workshop sessions and pre-conference offerings that discuss topics such as *Mindful Wellness for the CDO: A Personalized Self Care Experience* (NADOHE, 2020).

In a study of 94 CDOs, Jaschik (2011) found that 48 percent CDOs planned to leave their positions within three years. Approximately one-third planned to leave for another leadership role in the diversity field and 28 percent for another opportunity beyond the field. Moreover, many CDOs do not tend to remain in their positions for a long time. In another study, a third of CDOs served in their roles for less than two years, another third for three to five years, 17 percent for six to ten years, and 11 percent for more than ten years (Williams & Wade-Golden, 2007).

In her study of women CDOs, Nixon (2013) notes that CDOs can be the ones "blamed when others in the institution made diversity-related mistakes…This leaves them in the position of serving as a target" (p. 154).

BRIGHID: It has also been so frustrating to see the double standard being applied to DEI work. I feel like we are not given the space to be seen as leaders. There have been so many times in my career when I have been asked to run a program, or a process, by colleagues in another department to get their approval first. I am all for collaboration and I truly believe that we are smarter and we make better decisions when we work together. But I cringe when I am asked to run programs that I have developed, based on research in my field, by others who have **no** knowledge in the area of diversity, equity, and inclusion. Are they diversity experts? – No! Colleagues in the Technology or Communications departments aren't asked to check with external colleagues about their decisions or processes in the same ways. They are trusted, it is assumed that they are using their specialized expertise to make sound decisions for the betterment of the university. But diversity administrators are not given that same trust.

LATANYA: The reality is that these institutions have been around for centuries, and they have established philosophies, history, and deeply embedded cultures; and there is this awareness of having to understand that these cultures will not shift in a year or two or five or even during my experience here so I think this is an important thing to consider and reconcile.

So, for me it is about connecting with others, but then also thinking about my sphere of influence and where I can make change. It may not happen on the institutional level, but I think "what does it look like within our division or office?" I like to think about the small victories and consider how in combination they amount to sizable growth and change. We keep pushing, and that's part of our work, but broader change might not happen during our time here. We're working for future generations. It's difficult for students to hear that. Often, they want things to happen now. This institution has been here for 250 years, so it (the change you want) might not happen within your four years here, but let's think about the long game and future generations of students whose experiences will be so much better because of you.

We have both worked to create and maintain balance. However, this sense of balance oftentimes oscillates from its center and is dependent upon what is happening locally, nationally, and globally. Social and political events (e.g., police-involved murders of Black people, national political rhetoric, COVID-related xenophobia/anti-Asian discrimination) have an impact on the identities, experiences, and realities of student and broader community members. It is during these moments that diversity leaders are called upon. It has been increasingly difficult in recent years (including during the writing of this manuscript) to maintain balance as we are often front and center to conversations and initiatives and are providing broad support to campus communities. In addition to engaging "the institution," we, too, are challenged in ways that are similar to the experiences of members of the community. This becomes complex in our professional experiences, both as individuals *and* agents of "the institution," where there is an expectation to uphold institutional norms as an employee.

BECOMING THE SENIOR-LEVEL DIVERSITY ADMINISTRATOR

We, the authors, are now senior-level administrators at Princeton University. For us this is a surreal experience as women of color who took our first college credits at community colleges. However, the work environment at an Ivy League institution has been more welcoming and affirming from what we imagined it would be. The institutional resources available, community support, personal experiences, and the professional self-actualization, comfort, and maturity we have developed, all contribute to our positive experience as a senior-level administrator, but this was not always the case for us.

LATANYA: My interview here was probably one of the most comfortable interviews for me and there are multiple reasons behind that. One is that I was totally comfortable. I thought that this was a great opportunity for such an amazing position, and I enjoyed meeting many people.

My comfort was connected to previous interview experiences. A while back, I interviewed for an executive-level position that I didn't get, but I was one of the top two finalists. The search process was probably the worst I've ever experienced in terms of organization and communication. It was an institution that I was familiar with, so I was a little disappointed with the process. The interviews began in February and steps were added, including psychological testing, throughout the process.

BRIGHID: What?!

LATANYA: Yes! It was something else. And the last step was to interview with the president, to whom the position reported. But the process was so prolonged. I believed my interview took place in May or June…I had been waiting since February. I was finally scheduled for the interview with the president, but over the months I wanted to get my hair braided because I had planned to start exercising. I kept holding it off. I did not get it braided because I wanted to get this interview over with the president first. Both foolishly and strategically, I had made this decision solely based on my understanding of others' perceptions of natural and braided hairstyles in professional spaces.

I have the interview, hair straightened and realize the position was not a good fit. I was not selected for the job, and there was a bigger lesson there for me in that. I had compromised. I decided to "show up" in a way that I felt would be comfortable for others for this particular position, its counterparts, and the boss – a white man. This all played into it…identities, perceptions, positioning, etc. As trivial as it may sound, I said never again would I compromise in that way – in who I am and how I present at that moment.

During this experience, LaTanya was challenged with the notion of stereotype threat (Steele & Aronson, 1995), being viewed through the lens of negative stereotypes based on her social identities of race and gender. The stereotype threat she felt was grounded in her internalization of beliefs and judgments that others hold of Black women and the politicization of their natural hair. Casad and Bryant (2016) argue that stereotype threat is highly relevant in personnel selection. They note that members of stereotyped groups (e.g., women, racial minorities) can experience stereotype threat in evaluative situations.

LATANYA: The other experience was interviewing my former Vice President, Dr. White, at a previous institution; she, too, is a black woman. I was on the search committee for her position. I remember she walked into the room for her initial "airport" interview, and she was everything that everyone told me not to be or to not show up as. I've done women's leadership retreats; they tell you for interviews to wear navy blue and all black with small earrings... She walked in wearing this fire red blazer, high heels, and all of her personality! She rocked it, and I recall just being so mesmerized with her in this interview and thinking that she is totally herself. She showed up in all her colorful glory. It did not take away anything from her; in fact, it added to her. All I could focus on was her vast experience and the content and depth of all her responses. Needless to say, she was hired.

It was both Dr. White and that interview process that made me say "never again." So, when I visited Princeton to interview I decided, I'm going to be comfortable. Of course, I dressed up, but with colors that were comfortable for me and my personality, but I was comfortable in my skin.

BRIGHID: These are both powerful stories! I'm so glad there are more conversations happening on campus about what it means to be and look professional. There are different ways of being and coming into spaces whether it's the clothing you wear or the hairstyle you have; it has nothing to do with the effectiveness of your work. In fact, I might be more effective if I'm really comfortable in my clothing and I feel that I can be myself, and I hear that in what you shared here.

Self-actualization (Maslow, 1943) refers to the need for personal growth and discovery that is present throughout a person's life. This stage of self-actualization, the highest of Maslow's hierarchical model of five basic human needs, suggests pursuing and achieving one's potential. For Maslow, a person is always "becoming" and never remains static (McLeod, 2020). We understand Maslow's research in humanistic psychology and hierarchy of needs as one that does not consider the intersections of multiple identities, and it is not one that centers Black women and differing experiences. We use this term within a professional context to describe an aspirational freedom of being ones' self in truth, authenticity, and self-acceptance while navigating our work and responsibilities. In bell hooks' *Sisters of the Yam* (1993) about Black womanhood, sexism, and racism, she describes a linkage between self-recovery, political resistance, and individual efforts for self-actualization while remaining connected to a larger world of collective struggle.

LATANYA: I see my present role as having many tentacles within the campus community, but I would say that it's primarily focused to support student affairs. My role is not just to support and engage students in DEI issues; it is also about determining how we create capacity and bandwidth across the division of Campus Life and for the 300 professionals across the division. My role is not just direct student engagement, but also considering how colleagues can engage intentionally with students about diversity and inclusion. Although primarily focused on the student experience, we also want to be intentional about our colleagues' understanding. All of the diversity efforts cannot just be focused within the Office of Diversity and Inclusion, it is imperative to have institutional buy-in.

BRIGHID: I've always said that diversity work is done best when it is not just centralized with one diversity office – one office can act as a coordinator but not do all things for all people. It's not possible. My hope is that everybody on campus feels that this work is a part of their backbone. Our chief diversity officer has essentially deputized us to be able to say that the institutional mission and our job here is not only whatever the departmental duties are, but our work also lives outside of these responsibilities. I appreciate this model. We really are here to support one another. I very much see my role as one that bolsters the work of members of our team and colleagues across campus.

While we feel much more comfortable in our current roles, having become senior diversity practitioners, we are also continuing to evolve and learn. Our process of "becoming" is still not complete. Our personal and professional experiences have shaped us thus far and these, along with emerging trends in the field, will continue to shape where we envision ourselves in the future.

BEYOND BECOMING

The future of DEI work looks different from the past. We have discussed our own journeys to become senior-level diversity leaders, but this is not where our time as leaders or our journeys end. We must consider: generational differences in understandings, the importance of creating space for divergent viewpoints in advancing diversity and inclusion work, the notion of free speech and how it continues to challenge the work with regard to freedom of expression, institutional missions, and students' psychological safety. We discuss these here.

For the first time in history, there are five different generations at work. Along with age differences, research shows that each generation has a unique take on the very concept of work some view it as transactional for gaining resources and while others as meaning-making and impactful to society (Imtiaz, 2020). As diversity practitioners navigate the workplace, they must consider the ways in which different people (students, faculty, staff, etc.) have varying goals in relation to generational cultures and institutional culture and expectations.

LATANYA: What I appreciate about doing this work is that students today are coming in with such a level of awareness that is refreshing. I feel that we're starting at a different point than we would have ten or fifteen years ago because students are exposed to so much more before they get to college, and they challenge us.

BRIGHID: Students are supposed to push us in those ways and we're supposed to push the generation that's before us. Maybe that's a part of it. Students today are learning things we haven't learned because they're connecting into online communities. We are 20+ years removed from our undergraduate experience, we are not in the same online spaces as our students and sometimes we don't even know what they're learning.

Whether it's generational or valuing others' experiences, we both agree that differing perspectives within DEI work is essential to one's learning and development. Given that our students, community, and environment are not homogeneous, there is undoubtedly no expectation that everyone will understand, interpret, and/or receive knowledge similarly, nor should they. Moody (2020) writes that the interaction between students with different worldviews can help change minds or shape ideas.

As we think about what's ahead in the field, there is so much possibility. Right now, as we write this chapter, we are amidst a resurgence of the Black Lives Matter Movement after the lynching of Ahmaud Arbery, George Floyd, Breonna Taylor, Nina Pop, Daunte Wright, the attempted lynching of Jacob Blake, and so many others. Right now we also find ourselves amidst the COVID-19 pandemic which has highlighted racial health disparities and led to tremendous job loss. Amidst these two epidemics, higher education institutions are finding themselves simultaneously financially strapped and called to reckon with racial inequities embedded within their institutions. Many institutions are forming committees and asking what actions they can take to be an anti-racist institution. Along with other topics mentioned above, institutions need to consider how they are going to confront racial justice in an economical way, and these two don't usually go together. In doing so, colleges and universities, with the exception of some minority-serving institutions (MSIs) need to consider how they can transform the foundation upon which they were built. Many institutions were founded before 1900 and were not intended to be anti-racist; therefore considerable work needs to be done.

As we look ahead to the work of senior diversity practitioners, this is really where the work lies – in being the courageous transformational leaders. To this end, we see the following opportunities for senior DEI professionals to lead.

Senior DEI leaders can help their universities:

1. Consider suspending or permanently dissolving standardized testing. Instead, consider a holistic admission process.
2. Support pipeline programs, college preparation programs for students of color.
3. Make a commitment and action plan to recruit more students from Black, Latinx, South, and Southeast Asian students, and Native and Indigenous backgrounds.
4. Relatedly, provide additional staff support to provide support and enhance retention once these students are on-campus.
5. Create more STEM-based support systems and structures for students of color.
6. Undertake or continue to consider the racist histories that live on your campus. This might mean examining which statues are on your campus, the names of buildings, and/or the role of slavery in the formation of the campus.
7. Relatedly, rename campus buildings that have a connection to white supremacy and the legacy of slavery that makes. Present names of buildings may make Black students and other students of color feel like guests on campus instead of a part of the community.
8. Acknowledge Indigenous land and spaces through dedication of the space to local tribal nations.
9. Partner with local tribal communities, asking what they need and how the university can be of service.
10. Thank your student-activists for their hard-fought efforts to make your university a better place.
11. Issuing apologies where appropriate, to individuals, students, community members who have been wronged whether recently or in the past.
12. Publicly condemn racism/hate/discrimination.
13. Conduct an "audit" of when statements have been crafted or vigils have been held. Consider if there are any trends and aim for consistency. Are racist events likely to lead to statements being crafted? What about homophobic, xenophobic, anti-Semitic, or other incidents?
14. Develop opportunities for the campus community to talk with one another before engaging in cancel culture. This might mean developing

an intergroup dialogue program and it also might mean developing restorative justice practices.

15. Relatedly, examine demographic data on disciplinary infractions and make necessary changes, according to the results.

16. Revise the student handbook and policies that are more inclusive of anti-racist wording and initiatives.

17. Provide widespread education to the campus community about the impact of racial trauma. This can be done through interactive programming on websites and in-person/virtually during orientation.

18. Deepen the connection between faculty and student affairs practitioners through grant funding and partnerships that encourage staff-faculty collaborations (e.g., Community Building Grants, Faculty Affiliates). Many student life practitioners have extensive research and professional experience that could enhance the work of faculty and vice versa.

19. Relatedly, value student life and DEI professionals as experts and educators, not just programmers. This would mean proactively including staff members in institution-wide decision-making in areas related to their specific expertise, and including them as essential campus partners that must be included as thought leaders in DEI work. For example, revise committee structures to include faculty and staff/admins on committees. It is valuable to know more about the work of one another in order to build a more informed and equitable university.

20. Encourage all committees to approach and evaluate their charges through an anti-racist lens. Anti-racism as well as diversity and inclusion work should not just be relegated to the "diversity committee."

21. Hire more staff/faculty whose work focuses on social justice, critical (race, gender, queer) approaches, ethnic, and gender studies, and native and indigenous populations.

22. Utilize cluster hiring (APLU, 2020; Freeman, 2019) which has shown to increase retention among faculty (Flaherty, 2015).

23. Utilize your professional schools. Great knowledge is produced that can be immediately utilized by professional schools (e.g., Law, Education, Nursing). Of particular use would be programs in higher education. Higher education experts skilled in anti-racism on college campuses could help better develop the institution's own anti-racism framework. Law Schools may have civil rights scholars to draw upon, and nursing, public health, and medical schools can assist with work related to COVID-19 and health disparities.

24. Include anti-racism efforts as a part of annual performance review processes for staff and tenure review processes for faculty.

25. Pay students as employees who lead challenging conversations about race and identity on campus. This will help them feel valued and note the importance of their work to the college community.

26. Design paths for promotion and retention. In many offices across there are fixed titles and structures that don't allow for promotion. For example, some offices have Assistant Directors and Directors, but they do not have a path for assistant directors to be promoted to Senior Assistant Directors or Associate Directors. As such, talented employees may be leaving the institution to seek promotion.

27. Encourage institutional commitment to supplier diversity programs. For university business (hiring consultants, IT contracts, food suppliers, etc.) consider if businesses owned by women, LGBTQIA folks, and people of color will meet your needs. Depending on the services desired, local and state municipalities sometimes have lists of registered businesses.

As DEI professionals help our institutions to become more just organizations, it is important to consider what tools we are using to do so and what other tools may be available for faculty, staff, and students to engage in conversation and decision-making with one another. Our challenge moving forward will be to determine how we engage in the next iteration of this exciting and revolutionary work while maintaining balance. This list of current and future work for DEI practitioners is hefty, but it is this work that is transformational and will help our institutions become what we hope them to be.

REFERENCES

Association of Public Land-Grant Universities (APLU). (2020). Retrieved August 1, 2020 from https://www.aplu.org/members/commissions/urban-serving-universities/student-success/cluster.html

Casad, B. J. & Bryant, W. J. (2016, January 20). Addressing stereotype threat is critical to diversity and inclusion in organizational psychology. *Frontiers in Psychology*. Retrieved from https://www.frontiersin.org/articles/10.3389/fpsyg.2016.00008/full

Cheeks, M. (2018, January 16). The psychic stress of being the only black woman at work: The first step in making a more equal office is recognizing the unique problems women of color are facing. Lenny Letter. Retrieved from https://www.lennyletter.com/story/the-stress-of-being-the-only-black-woman-at-work

Felts, A.A. (1992). Organizational communication: A critical perspective. *Administration & Society, 23*(4), 495–513.

Flaherty, C. (2015). Cluster hiring and diversity. Retrieved August 1, 2020 from https://www.insidehighered.com/news/2015/05/01/new-report-says-cluster-hiring-can-lead-increased-faculty-diversity

Freeman, C (2019). The case for cluster hiring to diversify your faculty. Retrieved August 2, 2020 from https://www.chronicle.com/article/the-case-for-cluster-hiring-to-diversify-your-faculty/?cid=gen_sign_in&cid2=gen_login_refresh

Goldsmith, A. H., Hamilton, D., & Darity, W., Jr. (2007). From dark to light: Skin color and wages among African-Americans. *Journal of Human Resources, 42*, 701–738. doi:10.3368/jhr.XLII.4.701

Harrison, M. S., Reynolds-Dobbs, W., & Thomas, K. M. (2008). Skin color bias in the workplace: The media's role and implications toward preference. In R. E. Hall (Ed.), *Racism in the 21st Century: An empirical analysis of skin color* (pp. 47–62). New York: Springer.

Hirschy, A. S., Wilson, M. E., Liddell, D. L., Boyle, K. M., & Pasquesi, K. (2015). Socialization to student affairs: Early career experiences associated with professional identity development. *Journal of College Student Development, 56*(8), 777–793.

hooks, b. (1993). *Sisters of the Yam*. Boston, MA: South End Press.

Imtiaz, F. (2020, January 21). From millennials to boomers: Leading five generations in the workplace. Leadership and Organizational Development. Retrieved from http://www.engagetu.com/2020/01/21/from-millennials-to-boomers-leadingfive-generations-workplace/

Jaschik, S. (2011, August 12). Change for Chief Diversity Officers. Inside Higher Ed. Retrieved from www.insidehighered.com

Kreisman, D., & Rangel, M. A. (2015). On the blurring of the color line: Wages and employment for black males of different skin tones. *Review of Economics and Statistics, 97*, 1–13. doi: 10.1162/REST_a_00464

Lee, J. J., & Helm, M. (2013). Student affairs capitalism and early-career student affairs professionals. *Journal of Student Affairs Research and Practice, 50*(3), 290–307.

Marira, T. D., & Mitra, P. (2013). Colorism: Ubiquitous yet understudied. *Industrial & Organizational Psychology, 6*, 103–107. doi: 10.1111/iops.12018

Maslow, A. H. (1943). A theory of human motivation. *Psychological Review, 50*(4), 370–396.

McLeod, S. A. (2020, March 20). Maslow's hierarchy of needs. Simply Psychology. Retrieved from https://www.simplypsychology.org/maslow.html

Monk, E. P., Jr. (2015). The cost of color: Sink color, discrimination, and health among African-Americans. *American Journal of Sociology, 121*, 396–444. doi:10.1086/682162

Moody, J. (2020, March 31). Diversity in college and why it matters. U.S. News and World Report. Retrieved from https://www.usnews.com/education/best-colleges/articles/diversity-in-college-and-why-it-matters

National Association of Diversity Officers in Higher Education (NADOHE). (2020). NADOHE 2020 Conference Program. Located at https://nadohe.memberclicks.net/assets/2020conf/NADOHE_ConferenceGuide%20 2020_FINAL_Updated.pdf

Niemann, Y. F. (2012). Lessons from the experiences of women of color working in academia. In Gutiérrez y Muhs, G., Niemann, Y. F., González, C. G., & Harris, A. P. (Eds.), *Presumed incompetent: The intersections of race and class for women in academia* (pp. 446–499). Boulder: University Press of Colorado.

Nixon, M. (2013). *Women of color chief diversity officers: Their positionality and agency in higher education institutions* (Doctoral dissertation).

Sims, C. (2009). The impact of African American skin tone bias in the workplace: Implications for critical human resource development. *Online Journal for Workforce Education and Development, 3*(4), 1–17. Retrieved from http://opensiuc.lib.siu.edu/ojwed

Smith, W. A., Allen, W. R., & Danley, L. L. (2007). "Assume the position... you fit the description" psychosocial experiences and racial battle fatigue among African American male college students. *American Behavioral Scientist, 51*(4), 551–578.

Steele, C. M., & Aronson, J. (1995). Stereotype threat and the intellectual test performance of African Americans. *Journal of Personality and Social Psychology, 69*, 797–811. doi: 10.1037/0022–3514.69.5.797

Sue, D. W. (2010). *Microaggressions in everyday life: Race, gender, and sexual orientation.* New York, NY: John Wiley & Sons.

Williams, D. A., & Wade-Golden, K. C. (2007). *The Chief Diversity Officer: A primer for College and University Presidents.* Washington, DC: American Council on Education.

Wilson, M. E., Liddell, D. L., Hirschy, A. S., & Pasquesi, K. (2016). Professional identity, career commitment, and career entrenchment of midlevel student affairs professionals. *Journal of College Student Development, 57*(5), 557–572.

Yosso, T., Smith, W., Ceja, M., & Solórzano, D. (2009). Critical race theory, racial microaggressions, and campus racial climate for Latina/o undergraduates. *Harvard Educational Review, 79*(4), 659–691.

Chapter Four

Becoming a Diversity and Inclusion Leader Was Not the Original Plan

steven p bryant

MY JOURNEY IN BECOMING A DIVERSITY AND INCLUSION LEADER

The original plan in "growing up" was to become a secondary education teacher. Through several pivotal points, continued self-reflection, and much-needed self-growth, I unintentionally became a diversity and inclusion practitioner on a college campus. Serving two different institutions in this role over the past ten years, I have worked to utilize my White privilege to educate and develop White leaders while also challenging systems and structures that perpetuate inequities and injustices. I firmly believe more White people need to engage appropriately in antiracist work. For me, the journey of becoming a diversity and inclusion leader began on my elementary school playground.

Recess

When I lead development sessions today, one of the first questions I ask participants is, "think about the time you first noticed race?" I have asked this question countless times when conducting diversity and inclusion training and development over the past decade. Answers vary, depending on the race of the individual sharing their personal experience, but two main themes have emerged from this question. The common answers received from racially minoritized individuals have mostly centered on the experience of being told explicitly or implicitly that they did not belong

DOI: 10.4324/9781003008521-6

or they were made to feel their presence or existence was not welcome in a specific childhood interaction or conversation. When analyzing answers from White participants, the common theme that emerges typically involves an experience where they or another White person was engaging in othering a person of color. Jensen (2011) defines othering as "discursive processes by which powerful groups, who may or may not make up a numerical majority, define subordinate groups into existence in a reductionist way which ascribe problematic and/or inferior characteristics to these subordinate groups" (p. 65). In order to lead effectively as a diversity and inclusion professional, it is important that I continue to take the time to do my own self-work. As a White male, it is imperative that I explore my own answer to first noticing race. In order to move forward and continue to become the leader I want to be, I must own my story and my own socialization in a society that continues to devalue and dehumanize Black, Indigenous, and other people of color.

The first time I noticed race was in third grade. I was eight or nine years old, attending an elementary school in rural Michigan filled exclusively with all White students, faculty, and staff. There were three sections of third grade, and a new student would be joining our class along with his brother who was being placed in the class across the hall. I vividly remember the first time meeting the two new students, their full names, and two additional things about them. The first being they both had dark brown complexion, much darker than my pale white skin. The second, which sits with me in detail, is the experience of being on the playground during recess, a shared time between all third grade students.

Recess could be its own case study of othering: how we treated each other based upon perceived gender, size, athletic ability, other identity groups, and the inequities we created based upon these social identities. Looking back, I did not notice how racial dynamics and White supremacy was at play even when surrounded by all White students. It would not be until later in life, when I chose to lean into learning about diversity and inclusion, would I begin to learn the complexities and dynamics of the system designed for someone like me to navigate the world without having to notice. That is how privilege works. I have the choice to engage in race while Black, Indigenous, and people of color do not have that choice.

Like many playgrounds, we had several different groupings where we would clump ourselves based upon where we felt a sense of belonging. There were students who would ride the swings, those who played on the metal bars where many ended up breaking an arm, and the basketball group, the kickball group, and those of us who would play on the newest piece of equipment that had slides, rope ladders, and all sorts of poles and bars coming off it. We would play Baywatch (do not ask) and try to save those who fell or jumped off the sides because they were "drowning" in the fake waters around us. In our minds, our acting was so good that we would have won a Tony or an Emmy for such a great and dramatic performance. I am still waiting for that award. I do not remember the specifics of conversations or even who all played Baywatch with me, but I do remember vividly looking down on the basketball court one day.

On this day, looking out at the basketball court that was so close you could hear conversations, I remember seeing the two new students playing basketball on the same team. I cannot remember if they appeared to play well or who was on their team, but I do remember them speaking Spanish to each other. Later I learned their parents moved from Mexico and that Spanish was the language spoken in their home. As clear as if it were today, I remember looking over at the basketball court and not knowing the language spoken, but my initial assumption was that they were obviously speaking about "us." This is the first experience I can remember noticing race, and clearly participating in racist attitudes and assumptions. I would not choose to or have the skills to reflect upon this until much later in life. Notice privilege again. I also did not recognize how I was already creating power dynamics where "us" was White people and these two students, in my mind, were a subordinate "them." Dissecting the messages I learned growing up would become a critical reflection point later in life.

Fast forward to fifth grade and back to the playground at recess. The playground was the same, we were just two years older. At this point, I chose to play kickball not because I enjoyed it and not because I was actually good at it, but because I felt that I needed to fit in with the other guys. Notice more messages I learned (and actually, I was terrible at kickball). Baywatch was no longer a hot show and clearly not cool in my eyes as a way to show off my masculinity, another problem that I would deal with later and continue to pay attention to now. I tended to spend most of my time conversing with fellow female students and am sure looking back that riding the swings with them rather than playing kickball would have been much more enjoyable. Through our conversations, I learned of a group of male students who would run out to the playground with the goal of getting to the swings first. These students did not want to ride the swings; they simply wanted to take the opportunity away from someone else. This would be the first time I noticed injustice and wanted to do something about it.

After conversing with my female friends, we decided to approach the principal and let him know of the problem occurring on the playground. Prior to meeting with the principal, we created a plan to place sign-up sheets for the swings in each classroom and then would assign times to all who wanted this opportunity. I know what you are thinking – nerd alert; I own that membership card proudly. The principal liked our plan and this was the first time I created an excel spreadsheet as a sign-up sheet, a skill that became useful later on in my student affairs career. This was also the first time I ran a committee focused on inclusion and equity, another skill that would become valuable. We called ourselves the swing committee, a term that is innocent for children but has potential for a completely different meaning later in life without the necessary context. Eventually the swing committee dissolved, because those who solely wanted to take the opportunity away from others did not want to appear as if they wanted to ride. Those who wanted to ride the swings eventually learned to work together and share the time appropriately. Welcome to my first planning and implementation of an equity-based approach that resulted in great success.

These two stories are completely different, yet have similar underlying issues when we look at them from a diversity, equity, and inclusion lens. The first focuses on race and highlights my inability to notice my implicit bias and racist thoughts and attitudes. The second focuses on sex and my ability to notice injustice occurring in this specific instance and working to do something about it (I specifically label this as sex because today I do not know the gender of these individuals). These stories represent the worst and best of me in fostering inclusion within spaces, places, and people. In order to become a more effective diversity and inclusion leader, I have to own my story. I must own the good, the bad, and the ugly, and that is how I can become the leader I need to be to move forward successfully.

Undergraduate Experience Shaping My Future

Looking back to elementary school and my experience on the swing committee is the beginning of developing a passion for an equitable and inclusive society. This passion drove me to opportunities in college where I began to develop skillsets in diversity, equity, and inclusion. Northouse (2016) describes the importance of middle managers having technical, human, and conceptual skills, which are essential when striving to be an effective diversity and inclusion professional. Both the curricular and co-curricular learning environments in college laid the framework for my understanding and knowledge today. Like recess in elementary school, it would be many years, meetings with a therapist, and reading several great books before I would utilize the learning from my college experience.

While completing my undergraduate studies, I participated in several learning experiences that helped me become the diversity and inclusion leader I am today. I majored in public health education and health promotion, and was fortunate the faculty intentionally incorporated diversity, equity, and inclusion within the curriculum of most courses. From studying how health disparities within Black, Indigenous, and people of color communities stem from systemic racism to analyzing drug laws and their roots in policing communities of color, understanding diversity and inclusion at a group and system level was woven throughout my educational experiences. I deeply thank these faculty for embedding these critical conversations and concepts into our learning and will forever be grateful. This shows that no matter what our role is in the academy, we must embed diversity, equity, and inclusion – otherwise we are graduating students who may continue to perpetuate inequitable and unjust systems and structures. We have influence in each interaction we have with students and fellow colleagues.

The co-curricular experience also gave me multiple opportunities to gain diversity, equity, and inclusion skillsets. I served in multiple student employment positions, was a hall council president, resident assistant, and volunteered within our Volunteer Center where I attended multiple alternative breaks. Living on campus for five years gave me the opportunity to build strong connections and relationships with individuals who hold multiple different minoritized social identities in areas I hold privilege. I do not recall any specific instances of expecting these individuals to teach me about their life experiences, but I am sure I created microaggressions during my college career, much like when I played Baywatch at recess.

Being a resident assistant was a pivotal moment in my diversity, equity, and inclusion journey. I owe credit to both my hall director of three years and to the amazing team members I worked with for aiding in my growth and development. My hall director modeled being an inclusive and equitable leader in her supervision style. She ensured that we were connecting with all of the students on our floor and in the building, held students and us accountable for fostering inclusion, and implemented a programming model that centered on minoritized communities. Her leadership aided in my own development of supervising through an inclusive and equitable lens. She placed high priority on hiring a team that represented the diversity of our student body and specifically the students living in our residence hall. Being on a diverse team that valued each other for who we are and what we authentically bring to the role created an environment where we could all share our truths, experiences, and challenges based upon our identities and lived experiences. These moments could only occur due to our hall director's intentionality with hiring, training, and developing all of us through an equitable and inclusive lens.

The other pivotal moment in college that shaped my diversity, equity, and inclusion leadership today was being part of the alternative breaks program and serving as an AmeriCorps Service Scholar, doing volunteer infrastructure within our Volunteer Center. The leadership within our Volunteer Center intentionally designed all the programs and services to provide education on social justice issues prior to conducting service, and then reorienting volunteers upon completion. This approach ensured the incorporation of concepts of understanding the history, current context, and local context of various social justice issues, issues which were intentionally designed to be part of communities across our society. I owe credit to leaders in the Volunteer Center for not only equipping me with skills around various social justice issues, but also with the ability to look at these different issues as interconnected symptoms stemming from underlying inequities and injustices. Again, this learning only occurred because of the design of these leadership opportunities. I have seen plenty of volunteer experiences in other institutions that lack education and result in perpetuating a savior complex.

Having faculty and staff who modeled infusing diversity, equity, and inclusion into curriculum, supervision, policies, and processes, instead of taking an othering approach, positively influenced my ability to do this work today. My undergraduate experience gave me the opportunity to deconstruct my own biases and privilege and how they show up in relationships, institutions, and the system as a whole. Without this solid foundation, I can honestly say I most likely would not be doing this work intentionally today. The experiences we have in life, and who they are with, have great potential in shaping our futures. How we lead matters, not just who or where we are leading.

The Other Side, Working Full-Time in Higher Education

After thoroughly enjoying my undergraduate experience and not wanting to jump directly into working in the public health field, I decided to go to a housing job conference and accepted a position as a hall director in Missouri. I officially transitioned to the "other side" from where I was during my first college experience. In this role, I incorporated the principles of diversity, equity, and inclusion that I learned from the leaders I worked with during my undergraduate career. I ensured we hired a team that reflected the diversity of our student body, implemented practices within the hall focusing on equity and inclusion, and worked to develop my student team members to incorporate diversity, equity, and inclusion into our scope of influence. My goal was to help graduate leaders in preparing for our global society, along with ensuring we provided a living environment where all residents had the opportunity to be their authentic selves.

During my four years as a hall director, I worked closely with our one professional staff member on campus serving in the diversity and inclusion role. Together, we developed training opportunities, had multiple conversations, and she offered me support in advising one of our historically Black sororities on campus that approached me in being their on-campus advisor. During one of our conversations, she asked me if I would ever consider doing her role on a college campus. My immediate answer was, "No." Thinking back, I did not feel that I was equipped or knew enough to do her role. I did not feel I was enough. She was charged with supporting minoritized students on campus and leading all of our diversity and inclusion programming. There was no way in my mind that I would ever be able to take on that role. We spoke about my reasons, and I do not remember my exact answer, but I do know it centered on being a White male. In all the skills I developed, I still did not feel qualified enough to engage in this work even though I was incorporating most of it in my current role. Her response contained encouragement and challenged me to reconsider my answer. My fourth year as a hall director, she would leave the institution. I owe it to her reinforcement, along with the encouragement of another colleague, to my applying for her vacant position. I accepted that position and started at the end of the academic year.

Transition into a Diversity and Inclusion Role

The focus for my first year in a diversity and inclusion role was to build strong relationships and partnerships across campus. The most critical of these was connecting with racially minoritized students. Understanding how I show up in spaces as a White male became critical to building authentic relationships. Also critical was ensuring that I took the approach of supporting and empowering but not speaking directly for identity groups in which I did not hold membership. It is important we give credit as well as helping to create space for people to share their own stories and experiences. The countless number of students who welcomed me into their lives has forever shaped and continues to transform how I approach weaving diversity, equity, and inclusion practices in being a diversity and inclusion leader

The first time I participated in deep level of self-work was the summer after my first year in a diversity and inclusion role. I had applied, was accepted, and participated in the Social Justice Training Institute. The Social Justice Training Institute (2020) "is designed for social justice educators in all fields to enhance and refine their skills and competencies to create greater inclusion for all members of the community" (Social Justice Training Institute, 2020). Through five days of intensive dialogue within and across groups, I fully immersed myself in the deepest level of consistent self-reflection through a racial lens that I have had to this date. This experience transformed both my approach to being a diversity and inclusion leader and also how I continue to navigate all levels of our systems and structures within society. I highly recommend this experience for anyone wanting to dig deeper into their own self learning, reflection, and growth.

After returning from attending the Social Justice Training Institute, I went through a period of reorientation filled with anger, frustration, guilt, shame, and hope. Experiencing these emotions, along with diving deeper into learning frameworks, theories, and critical perspectives, has become a lifelong learning journey. Many years later, while completing my dissertation, I would realize the continuum of White Racial Identity Development I had been navigating since those early days of recess. Now I had the words and knowledge of what was happening inside of me, all changing the way I approached the world.

The first emotions I experienced in exploring my own self in this society built on power and privilege were anger and frustration. I was angry about the intentional White washing of history that I learned throughout my primary education. I was irritated that my entire life had lacked the ability to begin noticing how my own thoughts and actions upheld White supremacy. Even on those early days of being on the playground and noticing inequities around gender, I lacked the ability to see how these same concepts applied to race. Throughout all of this, I was angry with myself and the harm I had caused others since childhood. Again, I felt I was not equipped to be an effective diversity and inclusion leader.

Working through my anger, and finding ways to use it to move forward productively, was critical in my journey of being a diversity and inclusion leader. I spent the rest of that year reading diversity and inclusion literature and studies, and continued to build competency around understanding the systems and structures I have navigated, mostly unconsciously. Looking back, I was gaining competency in understanding the concepts of inequity and injustice, yet still felt inadequate and an imposter in doing this work. I then stumbled across Brené Brown's (2012) book *Daring Greatly: How the Courage to Be Vulnerable Transforms the Way We Live, Love, Parent, and Lead*. I can vividly remember reading the following and I was only on page two: "Rather than sitting on the sidelines and hurling judgment and advice, we must dare to show up and let ourselves be seen. This is vulnerability. This is daring greatly" (Brown, 2012, p. 2). Thankfully, I lived alone at the time because curse words immediately came out of my mouth as I swore that she must have known my life. This became my own permission slip to go see a therapist, which became extremely valuable even though it felt challenging at the time. In addition, I began working through my own issues of being enough, both personally and professionally, as a diversity and inclusion leader.

Moving from Self to Structures

It can become easy as a White person in a diversity and inclusion leadership role to begin feeling that you have earned a seat at the table with Black, Indigenous, and people of color. Robin DiAngelo (2018) explains the good/bad binary and how problematic this viewpoint is on our actions. DiAngelo (2018) describes applying this viewpoint can allow a White person to label themselves on the side of "not racist," implying no further action or growth is needed. As a White person in a role predominantly occupied by racially minoritized individuals, understanding the good/bad binary remains critical. I reflect on this concept daily as I prepare myself mentally for engaging in diversity and inclusion leadership. If I get to the point where I begin labeling myself as a "good White person," I will have failed drastically. As a White person doing this work, I must stay committed to analyzing how I am supporting White supremacy in my thoughts and to changing my actions to ensure equity and inclusion is possible. This is important in working toward antiracism within myself, role modeling to others when challenging bias and privilege, and in how we begin to tackle structural and systemic inequities.

Ibram X. Kendi (2019) describes being antiracist as "one who is supporting antiracist policy through their actions or expressing an antiracist idea" (p. 13). The two words that stand out to me in Kendi's (2019) definition are policy and actions. In becoming a diversity and inclusion leader, I had to learn not only how to change my own thinking, actions, and biases, but also how to apply this philosophy in addressing systems and structures. And I had to ensure I owned my own mistakes along the journey. At the institutions I have served, diversity and inclusion have lacked a presence in policy and actions, essentially living on the margins of our priorities. Historically, we have subscribed to a diversity and inclusion thinking that aligned with trying to not be seen as racist instead of engaging in being antiracist (DiAngelo, 2018; Kendi, 2019). To compound that philosophy, we have placed the heavy lifting of eradicating oppression on our minoritized employees and students, all of whom are the primary targets of the oppression occurring, and usually unpaid for their labor. Grasping this understanding and working to carry the weight of ending systems of oppression drives my approach in engaging in strategic diversity and inclusion work.

So far, the largest task I have had the honor of working on was leading the diversity, equity, and inclusion strategic planning at my first institution. The process of getting to the creation of a strategic plan included multiple points of intentional dialogue and development with key leaders across campus. I was serving in a mid-level diversity and inclusion position. Located in student affairs, my role reported to our vice president of student affairs, a cabinet-level member. Although I did not have the positional power to make cabinet-level members see the importance of this plan, I did have perceived expertise, referent power, and an understanding of leadership theory and practice (Bolman & Deal, 2013; Levi, 2014; Northouse, 2016). Developing an understanding of power, team dynamics, leadership theory, and organizational analysis have been key in becoming an effective diversity and inclusion leader

Levi (2014) discusses the use of personal power often being more effective than positional power. I have always been a social person and work to build strong relationships with others across the institutions, organizations, teams, and communities I have served. From my roles during my undergraduate studies, I have personally seen how leaders who work to build strong relationships from a team approach have a higher level of referent power (Bolman & Deal, 2013; Levi, 2014). These relationships become essential when addressing challenging situations and areas, such as deconstructing and reconstructing an educational institution on equity and inclusion, and centering minoritized communities. Those first two years of building strong relationships across campus were instrumental in getting a diversity, equity, and inclusion planning process off the ground.

Educating Others

Another skill that became essential in strategically leading toward a diversity, equity, and inclusion plan was educating others in moments when they were not seeking specific knowledge. I am not a parent but I do have many instances of observing family and friends with their parenting styles. Reflecting upon my own childhood experiences, I remember developmental moments from my mother and father and the modeling of their approach. The skill that I worked to most embody from all these instances was helping teach someone something they did not want to learn, at a time when they did not recognize they needed it. In addition, I wanted to help them lean into their growth as if it were their own discovery. This education style took time and practice to develop, and has yielded many moments of growth and development that most likely would not have occurred during those specific points of interaction.

Reflecting upon my career, I can think of multiple examples of educating others in moments they did not seek out that knowledge. Often we may think of the specific conversations of holding someone accountable for their language choices or their actions that are producing inequities. Those conversations are critical and necessary for diversity and inclusion leaders when holding others accountable, and are the instances of giving more than someone is asking. Practicing this skill in my one-on-ones with my supervisor and conversations with others while moving between meetings, events, and across campus became an essential skill in my toolbox.

Utilizing Bolman and Deal's (2013) work on reframing organizations has been pivotal in educating others and helping drive the institution toward implementing diversity, equity, and inclusion strategy. It was more so at my first institution but is still true today that I have worked to infuse educational moments with key organization members to lead us toward the direction of strategically thinking about diversity and inclusion. One way I have repeatedly done this was bringing in current examples of institutions who were experiencing a diversity and inclusion crisis. In most of these instances, I knew how the same crisis could easily occur on our campus, and was aware of the importance of being proactive, essentially less reactive. All of the times we feed information to other leaders across campus help build the referent power critical in driving diversity and inclusion principles (Bolman & Deal, 2013; Levi, 2014).

Looking Back and Moving Forward

Although becoming a diversity and inclusion leader was not the original plan, I am glad that my life journey has led me in this direction. We all have pivotal moments that drive us toward finding our calling and purpose. From noticing and not noticing my own biases and assumptions on the playground in elementary school to becoming more equipped with frameworks and knowledge throughout college and during the early years of my career, multiple learning moments and incredible people have shaped my leadership approach today. As a White person continuing to do diversity and inclusion work, it is my responsibility to carry the load and chip away at the multiple layers in our society, structures as well as within myself that are producing inequities and injustices. Although I hope I am never part of a "swing committee" again, I do hope I continue this journey of diversity and inclusion and doing my part to make structures and systems move toward being equitable and inclusive.

RECOMMENDATIONS FOR STUDENT AFFAIRS PRACTICE

Owning my story has been an essential foundation in my journey of diversity and inclusion leadership. We cannot move forward if we do not know where we have been at the individual, group, and system level. This section contains four recommendations from my experience geared toward supporting White folks who are working to develop diversity and inclusion leadership skills in student affairs practice. These four recommendations include doing your own self-work, understanding Whiteness, focusing on behavior, and staying grounded. I hope it helps you on your own journey and the critical work of eradicating the oppression and injustices from all layers of our institutions.

Do Your Own Self-Work

One way that continues to infuse White supremacy is expecting racially minoritized individuals to educate you about themselves and concepts of race. Instead of expecting others to teach you, do your own self-work. This philosophy applies to other identity groups along with how our identities intersect in creating who we are as individuals and members of groups. Doing self-work involves learning about yourself and how your actions and behaviors show up in relationships, structures, and systems.

We are fortunate that many great authors and researchers from minoritized identities have published work that can be easily accessible. From a few great authors, including the work of W.E.B. Du Bois, James Baldwin, and bell hooks, to recent publications from Beverly Tatum, Ibram X. Kendi, Ijeoma Oluo, and Crystal Fleming, these writings continue to be an essential piece in my own personal growth and development. We need to create space for advancing the work of authors and researchers from minoritized identities along with utilizing their work when approaching student affairs practice.

Self-work also involves understanding the foundation and historical perspective of exclusion and segregation in higher education institutions. Dafina Lazarus Stewart (2011) highlights how historical exclusion and privilege shape our campus environments today. From implementing assimilation policies for Indigenous people, prohibiting the education of enslaved Black people, and denying admission to other people of color, exclusion was intentionally built into our policies and practice (Stewart, 2011). Exclusion continues to show up racially and in other identities. Designed intentionally, exclusion maintains power and privilege within dominant identity groups (Levi, 2014; Stewart, 2011). Lean into this learning because much of the oppressive actions and behaviors of the past are present throughout our practices and policies today.

In doing self-work, we must continue to analyze our biases and the privileges we hold. When leading training and development sessions with student affairs practitioners, I relate the daily practice of thinking about how we think about exercising. Of all people, I would love to exercise one day in January and then be good to go for the rest of the year. Unfortunately, it does not work this way. Recognizing bias and privilege within yourself, like exercise, must be a daily practice. Too often we take the approach of doing a bias or privilege training once a year and then place ourselves in the "good White person" binary instead of continuing to incorporate antiracist and anti-oppressive actions (DiAngelo, 2018; Kendi, 2019). When we work to recognize bias and privilege daily, we continue to stay engaged with eradicating oppression and inequities from our policies and practice. Developing in these key areas highlighted on self-work make the challenge of eradicating structural and systemic oppression, primarily in the areas we hold privilege, easier to begin addressing.

Understanding Whiteness

Whiteness is the social construction and system of domination that gives privilege to White people over racially minoritized individuals and groups (Cabrera, 2014; Matias et al., 2014). Not until I was working on my dissertation did I thoroughly explore Whiteness through Helms' (1990) White Racial Identity Development Model. Looking back, this would have been the best place for me to begin in becoming a diversity and inclusion leader. I am thankful for this learning and continue to apply these concepts into my diversity and inclusion leadership.

In American higher education, we have normalized Whiteness throughout our policies, practices, and expectations of behavior from students and employees (Matias et al., 2014; Yoon, 2012). It is not easy for White student affairs practitioners to notice all the ways Whiteness is engrained in our daily professional practices until we make it a daily priority. We must include diverse identities in decision-making and exploring how each action will effect various identity groups. This concept, commonly referred to as a diversity impact analysis, is an essential component in striving for equity and inclusion in all of our decision-making within student affairs. Until we eradicate the normalization of Whiteness, Black, Indigenous and people of color will continue to experience the burden of representation.

Focus on Behavior

Northouse (2016) defines leadership as "a process whereby an individual influences a group of individuals to achieve a common goal" (p. 6). The words process, influence, and common goal all highlight that leadership involves specific behaviors. Northouse (2016) describes process as an interactive non-linear event, influence as the behavior in how one affects others, and common goal as a mutual purpose. Looking through a diversity and inclusion lens, focusing on behavior is critical in moving toward an inclusive and equitable campus community. Often we lose focus by looking at who we are and not focusing on the behaviors we are doing within our leadership role.

Brené Brown (2012) explains focus on behavior as essential to embracing vulnerability and moving from shame to guilt. Shame is an emotion experienced when focusing on oneself and guilt is an emotion experienced when focusing on behavior (Brown, 2012). Brown (2012) further explains that focusing on behavior allows a White person, when called out for doing something racist, the opportunity to change the behavior for the future, recognizing however that this will not change the impact for the racially minoritized individual affected by the actions of the White person. The White person will still experience guilt, which allows the White person the ability to correct this behavior for the future. Brown (2012) describes that when a White person goes to shame and focuses on self, they define themselves as racist instead of as someone who did something racist. This pattern, which happens frequently in White people who, when called out for racist actions and behaviors, stops their ability in making change for the future. Instead, the desire to show "I am not racist" occurs instead of leaning into growth and development.

Learning to focus on my own behaviors and actions and making corrections along the way has been instrumental in becoming a more effective diversity and inclusion leader. It is inherent that we will make mistakes at times and these mistakes will cause harm to others, even when done unintentionally. Following the research on vulnerability from Brené Brown (2012), we must notice and act on focusing on behavior; otherwise we will want to prove how we are a "good White person" and fall back into the negative binary previously discussed (DiAngelo, 2018). When called in on behavior, it is necessary to pause, reflect, and acknowledge the harm you caused. Take this moment to engage deeper in your own learning and deeper into eradicating oppressive thoughts and actions from yourself and from the work you are doing.

Staying Grounded

In being a leader in diversity and inclusion work from a privileged perspective, we must remind ourselves to avoid becoming what I refer to as a social justice elitist. Social justice elitists are people who continue to do self-work yet shame those of shared privilege identity for not having a similar level of diversity and inclusion knowledge. This concept is not the same as holding others accountable. Holding others accountable focuses on behaviors and calling in specific actions that are problematic. From my experience, social justice elitists utilize their own personal power in shaming others due to a focus on self. Maura Cullen (2008) explains we must move from "me" to "we" to build inclusive organizations. Becoming self-absorbed rarely creates connection or reaching the desired outcome of the interaction.

Besides moving from "me" to "we," staying grounded also involves continuing to approach the work from a place of knowing that we are an individual who holds multiple group memberships that makes up all the structures and systems currently producing inequities. Unintentionally, White diversity and inclusion leaders may try to remove themselves from the structures and systems continuously occurring around them or not engage until they feel fully competent. This statement defines multiple experiences early on in my career. Waiting for perfection or not seeing oneself as part of the problem are components in upholding White supremacy in our society.

CONCLUDING THOUGHTS

I am forever grateful to the people throughout my life who have challenged my thinking around diversity and inclusion, served as effective role models, and aided in my growth and development. Although this chapter does not include all layers of my journey in becoming a diversity and inclusion leader, it does highlight pivotal points that have led me to where I am today. I have learned a lot along the way and have a lot more to learn; through engaging in the four recommendations discussed, I will continue to lean in to becoming more effective while working to dismantle systems of oppression present in our higher education institutions.

We live on stolen land built by the unpaid labor of enslaved Black people. It is essential as White people we take on the responsibility of eradicating these systems of oppression within our institutions, systems, and the behaviors of White supremacy that are present in ourselves. It is beyond time that we, White leaders within student affairs and across our institutions, start carrying this load. Carrying the load does not mean taking on the lived experiences of racially minoritized individuals; it does mean we have a responsibility in rebuilding the inequitable and unjust system present today. Too often, we continue to rely on the unpaid labor of our racially minoritized colleagues. Do your own self-work, work to understand Whiteness, focus on behavior, and stay grounded. These recommendations can transform how we lead in doing diversity and inclusion work.

REFERENCES

Bolman, L. G., & Deal, T. E. (2013). *Reframing organizations: Artistry, choice, and leadership* (5th ed.). San Francisco, CA: Jossey-Bass.

Brown, B. (2012). *Daring greatly: How the courage to be vulnerable transforms the way we live, love, parent, and lead.* New York, NY: Penguin.

Cabrera, N. L. (2014). Exposing Whiteness in higher education: White male college students minimizing racism, claiming victimization, and recreating White supremacy. *Race Ethnicity and Education,* 17(1), 30–55.

Cullen, M. (2008). *35 dumb things well-intended people say: Surprising things we say that widen the diversity gap.* , Bloomington, IN: Wordclay.

DiAngelo, R. (2018). *White fragility: Why it's so hard for white people to talk about racism.* Beacon Press.

Helms, J. E. (1990). *Black and White racial identity: Theory, research, and practice.* Westport, CT: Greenwood Press.

Jensen, S. Q. (2011). Othering, identity formation and agency. *Qualitative Studies,* 2(2), 63–78.

Kendi, I. X. (2019). *How to be an antiracist.* One world.

Levi, D. (2014). *Group dynamics for teams* (4th ed.). Los Angeles, CA: Sage.

Matias, C. E., Viesca, K. M., Garrison-Wade, D. F., Tandon, M., & Galindo, R. (2014). "What is critical Whiteness doing in our nice field like critical race theory?" Applying CRT and CWS to understand the White imaginations of White teacher candidates. *Equity & Excellence in Education,* 47(3), 289–304.

Northouse, P. G. (2016). *Leadership: Theory and practice* (7th ed.). Thousand Oaks, CA: Sage.

Social Justice Training Institute. (2020). Retrieved from https://sjti.org/

Stewart, D. L. (Ed.). (2012). *Multicultural student services on campus: Building bridges, re-visioning community.* Stylus Publishing, LLC.

Yoon, I. H. (2012). The paradoxical nature of whiteness-at-work in the daily life of schools and teacher communities. *Race Ethnicity and Education,* 15(5), 587–613.

Chapter Five

Lead Self First

Leadership and Social Justice Self-Actualization from Within the System

Kelli A. Perkins and
Rafael A. Rodriguez

THE ORGANIZATIONAL DILEMMA IN HIGHER EDUCATION

Social justice is a core value in the field of student affairs, so much so that two of the largest professional organizations in the academy, NASPA (Student Affairs Professionals in Higher Education) and ACPA (College Student Educators International), have a shared professional competency in social justice and inclusion:

> For the purpose of the *Social Justice and Inclusion* competency area, social justice is defined as both a process and a goal that includes the knowledge, skills, and dispositions needed to foster equitable participation of all groups and seeks to address issues of oppression, privilege, and power.
>
> (ACPA & NASPA, 2015)

In [order to foster] this [process], every person serving in the academy has a professional responsibility to help facilitate the dialogues that move their respective institutions beyond diversity and inclusion models toward a social justice paradigm that challenges hegemony and removes barriers to ensure higher education and the world landscape are as accessible to students, specifically those whose marginalized identities have been kept at the lower echelons of society.

          DOI: 10.4324/9781003008521-7

Often in our conversations in higher education around diversity, equity, and inclusion efforts on our campuses, we frequently confuse proximity with commitment (Brown, 2016). That is to say, we think the work of creating collaborative, high-functioning, diverse, and inclusive environments in this realm begins and ends with our ability to bring people of color into the academy. When we merely focus on the presence of difference, "diversity," without consideration for the cultural, political, epistemological landscape of our institutions, we fail everybody, but especially leaders of color who often, to their dismay, become figureheads void of the ability to exercise any real change-making power within their positions on campus. In this, our current diversity landscape in higher education contributes to the continued marginalization of historically oppressed people instead of living up to the espoused values of dismantling the very system in which it is situated. While most efforts to diversify the academy are well intentioned, as Baldwin (1963) wrote, "... it is not permissible that the authors of devastation also be innocent. It is the innocence which constitutes the crime" (p. 5). Without radical, sustained efforts to foster real inclusion in the academy, leaders of color in the academy will continue to only serve as figureheads, adding structural diversity with their presence in the academy, but devoid of change-making authority to further inclusion efforts. Those in positions of power focusing strictly on the visible and representative diversity with little attention, resources, or commitment to address organizational and climate issues that inhibit and explicitly reinforces the oppressive isms experienced by staff of color and other marginalized identities. Institutional leaders who focus merely on visible and representative diversity are culpable in perpetuating trauma and bear responsibility in addressing organizational challenges faced by those they seek to recruit and plaster across various websites and marketing materials.

Our current diversity landscape in higher education is situated within a history of white supremacy. This history permeates and endures in all aspects of society and institutions, including the well-meaning liberal field of higher education. Our sole concentration on representation has resulted in a hyper focus on diversity and gross negligence in addressing the oppressive nature of the cultures framing our society and institutions (Dowd & Bensimon, 2015). This leaves leaders of color to engage often in cultural acrobatics balancing and enduring multiple, conflicting, and oppressive cultural norms rooted in white supremacy. Perfectionism, a continual sense of urgency, and dogmatic adherence to the concept of objectivity, individualism, and worship of the written word as defined by those in power are some of the most prominent cultural norms that impede and stifle the creativity and authentic ways of being and leading for many leaders of color.

The challenge is not merely the existence of these cultural norms, but rather how these norms are elevated and reinforced by those you lead, those you report to, and the institutional structure, functioning as a self-sustaining regulatory ecosystem. As a result of our shared history and socialization, we are all complicit in the proliferation and hurt by white supremacist cultural norms. For leaders of color, there exists a hypervigilance and regulation attached to their roles, and as such, their success and effectiveness is regularly assessed by a broad audience ... and with little hesitation. Within the context of higher education specifically, white cultural norms are at the core of measuring a leader's effectiveness, relying on a paradoxical scale which, depending on the individual, group, or organizational needs, rewards or punishes based on the capacity to uphold or refute white supremist cultural norms. These dynamics shape the everyday experiences of leaders of color.

According to Takacs (2002), we do not arrive at knowledge or ways of understanding without influence from our interactions in the world. Through self-reflection and examining the ways by which we know and have formed knowledge, we develop healthy skepticism and the ability to question even our own ways of knowing. However, because the diversity focus in higher education has turned away from the civil rights concerns of historically marginalized people in the academy to merely a game of percentages, leaders of color find themselves in a position where they are unable to shed light on the ideas, concepts, and philosophies that are incongruent with opposing marginalization and oppression, for fear of causing mass upset among well-meaning white colleagues who have the privilege of being indifferent toward societal ills that do not directly impact them (Jenlink, 2005).

White colleagues in the academy uphold an epistemological view of diversity in higher education that is highly skeptical of the experiences of people of color, especially those in leadership positions, because of the lack of accountability for exercising diversity beyond compositional and structural diversity, which simply focus on numbers of people represented as opposed to actual inclusion and equitable outcomes for historically marginalized people. There is little consequence for white colleagues (and frankly, our colleagues of color who have bought into the myth of being the magical minority) who are unwilling to engage in a continual process of self-discovery and assessment of one's own identity development, a process which is necessary for becoming an effective leader in advancing equity and inclusion efforts on our campuses (Nganga, 2011). This lack of accountability leads to an obstruction and defiance of leaders of color that has become commonplace in the higher education landscape. If healthy skepticism is fruitful for progression, then ruthlessly questioning those for whom we lack a frame for seeing in leadership positions makes sense. And in this, leaders of color in the academy tend to shoulder the greatest burden of the effects of navigating the lack of intercultural competence in the dearth of leadership from the margins in the academy. The personal, quite literally, becomes political for leaders of color.

This chapter focuses on the journey of a supervisor and supervisee, both Black, and how they have navigated leadership in advancing diversity initiatives in higher education, particularly when they both sit at the intersections of various dominant and subordinate, privileged and marginalized identities and how this has informed their approach to and understanding of diversity leadership in higher education. The chapter ends with recommendations for leaders of color to stay the course with advancing diversity efforts within their professional spheres that give consideration to intersectionality and the role that plays in a diversity leader's journey.

In the coming sections, you will explore the narratives of two staff members' individual and intersecting experiences within higher education. Our connections on this journey include a shared Black identity, supervisory relationship, formal and informal leadership responsibilities, and moments of deep impact as well as jubilation. What we share is our truth, experiences, and strategies we have developed as diverse leaders in navigating spaces, relationship, and dynamics. First, you will learn about the experience of an Afro-Latinx Man of Color progressing toward a senior leadership role and his process of moving beyond saliency in order to clearly identify the responsibility of unpacking and dismantling the privileges held while simultaneously navigating a culture of hyper-accountability and damaging frames that inform how individuals and organizations engage him. You will learn about the experiences of a Black woman holding marginalized salient identities, navigating the situational power held vis-à-vis her formal position within an institution, and how intersecting identities shape and limited frames for fully seeing a Black woman shapes her experience as a leader.

THE NEVER-ENDING RECEIVING LINE

Started from the Bottom, Now I'm Here?

My path toward becoming an Executive Director was unusually fast-paced and occurred within the same institution where I began my professional career. In addition to the learning curves and challenges inherent in a leadership role, overseeing a multi-generational and diverse team where some served for longer than I have been alive, I have established strong connections and relationships and introduced a unique set of challenges. However, due to the dominant and marginalized identities I simultaneously hold, these challenges did not exist apart from the realities of what it means to be an Afro-Latino cisgendered man holding positional power. As a non-passing Puerto Rican, claiming my African ancestry is a point of pride and responsibility given the erasure of our history rooted in the anti-Blackness rampant in our Latinx community.

Grounded in my core values and personal experiences, my commitment to the field of higher Education has been, as many things in life, equally rewarding and deleterious. Witnessing first-hand the paradoxical realities of race relations in the last decade, specifically as it relates to Black folx, has informed, challenged, and helped me evolve as a leader. My formal professional journey began during my graduate program at the same time President Obama was elected into office and has included significant moments, both collective and individual, of celebration and advancement as well as moments of fear and terror.

I entered the field of Higher Education firmly believing in the possibilities that exist. Specifically, the opportunities to amplify the voices and cement the undeniable awesomeness of marginalized peoples, and to push and work toward meaningful change that call us to question behaviors and practices that harm, silence, and erase those at the margins. In no way do I mean to imply that Higher Education is the most important place for this work to occur or even the perfect place. Yet it is because of the vast imperfections that exist and my experiences that made it the ideal space for me. At one point a high school dropout, notions of the vocational future I would hold was ambiguous at best, yet my commitment toward understanding and finding power in my truth was unwavering. When the time came to find my first work home after completing a Master's program, I entered the process clearly focused on my truth, which was the need to genuinely and honestly engage and make a change. For me this meant contributing to a place that was honest about its shortcomings and equally committed toward its improvements, acknowledging fully the ups and downs and living with the wins and losses until I decided I was no longer willing to do so. I found myself at a predominantly white institution in one of the whitest states in the country, where I would hold my first senior leadership role, which has included amazing learning opportunities and significant challenges. Given the identities I hold, moving beyond saliency, the hyper-accountability of men of color, and a deficit of trust are among the obstacles I have endured as a leader, far beyond the extent I thought I would endure when accepting the position.

Beyond Saliency

One of my biggest reckonings in an area of continual self-work and growth is the reality of my complex social identity positioning. The concept of complex social identity positioning refers "to one's ability to acknowledge and name both dominant and subordinate identities that most people hold" (Rodriguez, 2019, p. 94). Rooted in Black Feminist theory, intersectionality has become a field of study, method of understanding, and a foundational element of social justice work (Moradi & Grzanka, 2017). Importantly it has introduced complexities in understanding the lived experiences of folx with multiple and interconnected marginalized identities. As a first-generation cisgender Afro-Latino man with a terminal degree, whose lived and cultural class identity is different than my current class identity, intersectionality has allowed me to make sense of and honor my experiences while also ensuring I do not lose sight of my immense responsibility. Unpacking the fullness and complexities of my identities does not take away from the important work of exploring the impact of multiple marginalized identities, but in fac[t], as Moradi and Grzanka (2017) state, "encourage[s] full engagement of intersectionality, including critical analysis of privilege" (p. 504).

Through the lens of my marginalized identities, I believe it is my responsibility and self-work to reflect, honor, celebrate, pushback, and stand up for myself and [for] those who share similar marginalized identities given my leadership role. Simultaneously, I am responsible for fully understanding and unpacking the implications of the privilege identities I hold, including how these identities shape my perspective and impact those with whom I engage. Engaging intersectionality through this lens is a challenging process which stretches a leader. In my leadership capacity I often feel as if I am on a balance beam attempting to find my center of gravity and draw on my core in order to steady myself and get a read on difficult situations and interactions. When I first assumed my leadership role, I often asked the questions: what was happening in that interaction and why do I feel this way, was the interaction framed by my marginalized identity(ies) or is the fragility and inherent self-righteousness my privilege at play? My journey in navigating this work has been bumpy and continues to be a challenge.

Shifting and expanding and understanding who I was as an individual through the paradigm of intersectionality was and continues to be a work in progress. Early in my career and in my leadership, I was solidly in what Derald Wing (2019) refers to as the introspection stage where I was often reacting "against dominant culture," and I framed most of my interactions through the lens of race and class, two of my most salient marginalized identities. While understandable, I quickly realized, with the support of colleagues, I had areas of my own identity that required some focus and work. It was a personal interaction with a colleague and friend that completely solidified how harmful my approach was when they shared "we are often triggered or live our lives from our subordinated identities and respond out of our dominance" (J. Washington, personal communication, June 18, 2010). As I began to unpack the privilege I held, I was riddled with guilt and the strong desire not to cause harm which overcomes anyone who has truly engaged in the work of unpacking their privilege; and quickly my voice became absent from critical conversations. While safe at the time, my silence carried with it powerful implications and challenges. First, the implications of my silence in the name of making space for marginalized folks carried the assumption that this was enough and that this minimized any potential harm I could cause further; nothing could be further from the truth. Additionally, due to the multiple identities I held, it also meant my voice as a person of color was absent in spaces designed to exclude me. My focus on truly exploring intersectionality was propelled and heightened by my advancement into a formal leadership position. Based on the vastness of my role and sheer number of interactions with individuals across the institution, I could no longer rely on the trust developed through individual relationships. This is especially true, as leaders who hold marginalized identities are often, despite personal connections and charisma, caricaturized, and aspects of their identities either erased or hyper focused depending on the context. My commitment and pressing need were to engage in a praxis that honored and considered my identities fully within the context of my leadership. As Moradi and Grzanka (2017) state: "exploring the intersection of multiple minority statuses is a valuable focus and in need of continued attention. However, when this focus becomes an implicit prototype, the analysis of privilege as central to intersectional inquiry is neglected" (p. 504).

Exploring the intersection of my marginalized and privileged identities, specifically as a first-generation cisgender Afro-Latino man with a terminal degree, whose lived and cultural class identity is different than my current class identity, requires ongoing work, commitment, and strategies. First among them is acknowledging and becoming comfortable with the realities that your perspective, insight, and read on a situation is absolutely informed by both your marginalized and privileged identities which are inextricably linked. This requires a leader to then slow down and listen in order to understand the driving factors of your perspective. Often, I find it helpful to focus on core values and boundaries, provided [there has been] previous rigorous examination and deconstruction of values derived from internalized oppression or privilege. Additionally, it is critical for leaders to engage these and not simply retreat, a privilege afforded to those in positions of power. At my best moments, I role modeled and explicitly shared my struggle to reconcile multiple intersecting identities in a manner that positioned me as the learner and subject, being clear not to cause harm by focusing on the individual(s) or interactions at the center of an issue. These moments are rare; in fact, as I have mentioned several times, this is ongoing work.

I began this section discussing moving beyond saliency because I believe it is imperative that I highlight the complexity of leading and the responsibility that comes along with not only my positional power but some of the identities I hold. I will further discuss how a culture of hyper-accountability of Men of Color and damaging frameworks for understanding Men of Color in leadership roles perpetuates a deficit of trust, skepticism, and hostility for leaders who identify as such.

Hyper-Accountability and Damaging Frames That Inform How Men of Color in Leadership Roles Are Seen

Our society has and continues to pedal damaging portrayals and caricatures of Men of Color, specifically Black and Brown men, used to reinforce and justify the systemic regulation and policing of Black and Brown bodies. The regulation and policing are not limited to official law enforcement, but rather embedded within systems, institutions, and individuals both consciously and unconsciously. The damaging portrayals are embedded within our daily discourse and consumption of media, and policing begins at an early age and continues into the professional realm for those men still living or able to fully participate. What Men of Color, specifically Black men, in leadership often face on day one is skepticism, a lack of trust, and outright hostility.

When discussing challenges, we face as leaders with my counterparts that share some of my salient identities, hyper-accountability for leaders of color and other Men of Color is often at the center of our discussion. In an attempt to broaden my perspective in preparation for this chapter, I sought out scholarly research that discussed the experiences of Men of Color in Leadership roles; the lack of available sources was resounding. What followed was a search that yielded frightening results requiring me to retreat from writing for a few days. When searching accountability experience of Black men, the results focused exclusively on hypermasculinity, male violence, and rape and accountability for sexual violence. In contrast, a search for white male accountability yielded findings such as "ignorance and innocence" and "what is accountability?" While predictable, given the history of this country, the shock and hurt that proceeded was deepened, given the contents and focus of this chapter.

The internet is only one media platform propelling portrayals of Black men as dangerous and threatening. A study conducted by The Opportunity Agenda (2011) titled *Media Representations and Impact on the Lives of Black Men and Boys* explored the core of the problem related to distorted patterns and portrayal of Black men in the media and its causal links to public attitudes. The study found that the portrayal of Black masculinity, including portrayals of hypermasculinity and violence, caricaturizes Black men (The Opportunity Agenda, 2011). Furthermore, the study found causal links between these portrayals and an inability to identify with Black men, and furthermore outright antagonism toward Black men. At its most destructive the inability to identify and outright antagonism toward Black men perpetuates the violence and loss of life that has filled our history and informed how to maneuver and navigate society. These messages are perpetuated daily in the media, in our society, and places of work, including Higher Education.

Distorted portrayals, antagonism, and an inability to identify are at the core and inform a culture of hyper-accountability that begins in early childhood education. A study conducted by Cook et al. (2018) examines the root causes contributing to the disproportionate discrepancies in disciplinary actions between Black boys and their white counterparts. The study found the differences in disciplinary actions, two to three times the amount in comparison, to be rooted in (a) inadequate ability to proactively manage the classroom, (b) lack of recognition of implicit bias toward Black male students, and (c) insufficient training in progressive methods of responding to behavior (p. 141). This hyper-accountability of Black men, and to an extent other Men of Color, is also visible in policies and broad aspect of everyday life such as stop and frisk practices, racial profiling, and policies regulating hair length/styles in sports and at work, just to name a few. Hyper-accountability also frames the experiences of leaders of color. What I could not imagine when I stepped into my role was the ease by which individuals, b white (I assume this is a known phrase) and People of color, subordinates and colleagues alike, assume the role of regulator, often weighing in on matters of consequence and of little significance, to reinforce what they believe to be the appropriate boundaries and limitations I should observe. This is a constant tug-of-war that a Man of Color in leadership roles must contend with. The deference that exists for white colleagues holding similar or lesser positional power is not equally or similarly extended in any semblance.

In my experience, the climate a Man of Color enters when assuming a leadership position is often chilly, if not outright unwelcoming. Once the excitement dwindles and the honeymoon phase ends, leaders often begin to examine the landscape of an organization and attempt to understand and explore what needs to be done. Because organizations are complex and evolving, no one inherits a perfect organization or team; indeed, no such thing exists. The work is often expansive and good leaders approach it with a finely tuned ability to take in information and act when the time is right. However, the embeddedness of distorted portrayals and the culture of hyper-accountability which fuels outright antagonism and an inability to identify drastically impact the ability of Men of Color in leadership to execute their role to its fullest extent. Healthy skepticism of leaders is actually necessary, and I personally welcome it. It is necessary to ask questions to ensure leaders are as forthcoming as possible. For Men of Color in leadership position, even the most transparent leader will struggle to shake-off the inherent skepticism they face. While healthy skepticism leaves room for leaders to surprise and change perspective, the level of skepticism I discuss is often outright hostile and innate; so much so, individuals are unaware of how it permeates their interactions and engagement with Men of Color in leadership roles. Underpinning this dynamic is an inherent lack of trust in Men of Color serving as leaders, primarily fueled by an inability to identify. This sentiment, a lack of trust, is something staff have directly shared with me and my direct reports, even during moments and times in which decisions have been made with and in their favor.

Speaking Truth to Power

I often talk about leadership as a never-ending receiving line which requires a sense of purpose, a grounding in core values, and clear boundaries to ensure a sense of self-preservation. As a Man of Color, navigating this immense responsibility also requires that I move beyond my saliency in order to unpack my privilege and how it shows up, recognize and disrupt patterns of hyper-accountability that exist for Men of Color, and understand the obstacles rooted in a deficit of trust as a result of a collective socialization that perpetuates distorted portrayals. What I also have to navigate in my leadership is the ways in which I approach the work of advancing diversity efforts on campus when those doing the work with me are not only other people of color, who often hold less positional power than I do, but also colleagues for whom intersectionality means that they experience oppression in their work even more intensely.

A significant portion of the work is ensuring the ways in which I am unpacking my privilege also helps me better understand and interrupt the ways I am complicit in driving an oppressive environment for other people of color, especially women. My experiences on some instances either align or complexly differ from the experiences of my coauthor. The next narrative captures the experiences of a Black woman holding marginalized salient identities navigating positional power vis-à-vis her formal position, and the impact intersectionality and limited frames for fully seeing Black women have on her experience as a leader.

WHEN ALL OF THE (SALIENT) IDENTITIES ARE MARGINALIZED...BUT YOU HAVE POSITIONAL POWER

Oftentimes, being Black and woman in the academy means that you are good enough...until you are not. And this generally has nothing to do with your own doing. In my very first professional position in higher education, my supervisor, who was also a Black woman, would always say, "Everybody loves Kelli. You literally can do no wrong." She built me up in a way that has remained unmatched in my career in the academy. I was frequently rewarded for my merit – my hard work, my advocacy for students, my ability to be innovative and think outside the box, and my dedication to inclusion and speaking up for the least of us. If there was a new opportunity to collaborate outside of our department, my name was generally the first one thrown into the hat. I always had glowing evaluations and students and colleagues would go out of their way to stop by the office to sing my praises. I was confident in my professional abilities and took that confidence with me into my next position in a mid-level role. But it was not long before the academy would ensure I understood that everybody did not love Kelli, and in fact, was immensely threatened by my positional power as I climbed the ranks of the ivory tower. Even more, it seemed that the only people capable of seeing me in my fullness were other Black women.

Others only saw me in my mid-level capacity so far as to help push forward an initiative or say a word on their behalf in a space they did not have access to. In these times, I was hyper visible, which also meant that any decision I made, even as I ascended the ranks to a number two position in a department where I had an immense amount of support from my Black Latinx male department head, was subject to a level of scrutiny above and beyond what other leaders in the department were subject to. And any other time, I was invisible, not worthy of basic considerations, even with my elevated positionality. I had gone from pet to threat as the amount of positional power I amassed at work increased and as I began to exert my authority and influence in meaningful ways (Stallings, 2020).

Intersectionality

For Women of Color in the academy, there are not always differences between racism and sexism, and instead the two often work tangentially to keep Women of Color, especially Black women, at the fringes in our country and certainly in higher education (Patitu & Hinton, 2003). In some ways, they experience similar results as white women in the way that sexism affects their ability to progress in their careers, but also share similar experiences with Black men in regards to racism. However, intersectionality means that Black women have unique challenges all their own in how they navigate careers in higher education administration and that they are more often than not on the fringes of resource allocation, decision-making, and participation within institutions of higher education. For instance, when years of employment experience, employment status, and type of positions are controlled, Black women are much more likely than both white women and Black men to have terminal degrees at the senior administrator level, whether they are needed or not (Singh, Robinson, & Williams-Green, 1998).

There is one area of administration where Black women are not last. Bates (2007) purports that while the percentage of women college presidents hovers around 20 percent nationally, Black women were more likely to ascend to this role. This is largely due to the presence of historically black colleges and universities, where a third of college presidents are Black women. For predominately white institutions, the number of women at the helm is just 22 percent. Indeed, the level of marginalization that Black women feel in higher education administration is the direct result of how racism and sexism are inextricably intertwined in their everyday experiences and how they navigate their world (Patitu & Hinton, 2003). According to West (2015), the intersection of racism and sexism means that Black women not only have the physical experience underrepresentation, but also have their cognition, lived experiences, beliefs, and contributions in the workplace devalued on a regular basis.

Racism

Hinton (2001) claims that for Black women, race is a much more salient factor in the discrimination they face as they navigate higher education administration. Several participants in this specific study felt that their womanhood seemed to soften the perceived threat with which their white colleagues viewed them. Black women often experience marginalization due to cultural factors, which directly align with their racial background, as opposed to their gender. Because of this, Black women often express feeling isolated in their day-to-day work (Gardner, Barrett, & Pearson, 2014; West, 2015). These feelings of isolation often also fuel adjacent feelings of discontent, injustice, and intolerance (Jean-Marie & Normore, 2010).

Racism can also be attributed to how Black women are perceived in supervisory relationships. Culturally, Black people in the United States are more likely to communicate in a straightforward and direct manner. Specifically for Black women, truth is used as a means to push forward and serve as a support for others who may be feeling marginalized or if they cannot speak for themselves. This style of communication is often in direct conflict with the dominant culture, which can cause Black women to experience feelings, perceived or otherwise, of being ostracized (Chin et al., 2007). This ostracizing contributes to Black women being the group that has made the least forward progression in higher education leadership, as their modes of communicating are not regarded as esteemed leadership qualities (Henry, West, & Ferguson, 2013). More often than not, Black women who have achieved higher-level leadership positions within the academy are more heavily scrutinized and expected to assimilate in ways that are most likely afforded to racial disparity than gender (Richardson, 2002).

Sexism

While racism and sexism have many similarities, they can take on different forms in how they play out for Black women leaders in the academy. In many higher education institutions, women are completely excluded from senior-level administration (Patitu & Hinton, 2003). According to Waring (2003), when they are present, they more often than not have to deal with the historic factors that generally only affect women in the workforce: choosing between family and career. This often means that when women desire to move up, they have to choose.

This also means that women in many ways are left at the outer edges of senior leadership. For instance, according to Bates (2007), when it comes to presidencies, women are much more likely to obtain a president position at the community college level. Black women who desire to move into the presidency realm are most likely to experience success in achieving this professional goal at historically Black colleges and universities or Hispanic-serving institutions. However, unlike their white female counterparts, when Black women ascend to senior administrative roles, they are much more likely to report feeling unsupported (Crawley, 2006). These feelings of lack of support and isolation means that Black women are more likely than their white counterparts to experience feelings of inferiority and self-doubt and general feelings of imposter syndrome (Reid & Zalk, 2001). Because they feel that they are not receiving the necessary support from those on their same professional level or those whom they would report to, Black women report that most of their professional interactions on the consistent basis are with entry-level administrators (Clayborne & Hamrick, 2007).

Institutional Culture

Many factors influence the professional experiences of Black women who are leaders in higher education. A prime factor is their perception of the value their institution places on diversity. Gardner, Barrett, and Pearson (2014) purport that Black administrators specifically need to see institutions allocating monies to diversity initiatives. It is not enough for institutions to have functional diversity or the visual representation of diversity. Institutions need to move away from merely acknowledging racism, doing campus climate surveys, and thematic celebrations and really begin to tackle embracing diversity as a core institutional value (Wolfe & Dilworth, 2015). For Black women particularly, institutional climate is where racism and sexism collide. Poor institutional culture around intercultural competence and being intentional about creating an environment that supports and embraces diversity of person, thought, and approach mean that Black women who reach senior-level positions will feel isolation, but also alienation (Patitu & Hinton, 2003).

Lack of Frames to Fully See Black Women in Leadership

According to Crenshaw (2016), "when the frames don't fit, the facts don't matter." She goes on further to inform us that when the facts we are presented with do not fit the frames that we routinely utilize, then we have trouble incorporating new understandings into our ways of thinking about the world around us. It can stand to hold true then that without frames that allow us to fully see particular groups, they are relegated to the outer echelons of our understanding, our consideration, our respect. This is the experience of being a Black woman in leadership in the academy.

The fact of the matter is that despite the sound bites that tell us Black women seek out and complete higher education above and beyond any other American subgroup and are now the most educated segment of the United States, there are still no frames for the overwhelming majority of people to truly see us in the academy, even when we are in leadership positions and especially when we use our positional power to advance diversity, equity, and inclusion efforts on the campuses we serve. At the core, most people who have worked in higher education for any amount of time have a basic understanding of what racism and sexism are, but most fail to understand the particular brand of racialized sexualized oppression that Black women experience merely from existing.

This is the reason that in a search committee meeting of which I was the chair, with two white women and one white man, the white man repeated something I had just said verbatim and was wholly embarrassed when one of the white women called him out, but she could not understand why I was torn between being thankful for her willingness to call him out, but agitated by her inability to give me the chance to speak up for myself. This lack of understanding of my experiences as a Black woman in leadership in the academy is why, even in the last team I oversaw which was over 90 percent people of color (though I was the only Black woman), staff members had no issue being openly combative with any decision I made, even ones that worked in their favor, simply because they could manage to find something to critique about me at every turn. The lack of frames to see people who look like me and navigate the world in a similar way means that people will always attempt to go over my head or bypass me for decisions that are mine to make, even when we have had no negative interactions to make sense of understanding why they would attempt to navigate around me in that way.

The academy wants Black feminism in its course catalogs, but not at the top of the ivory tower. They want Black women in seats in class, but only as long as they are quiet about their truth. Higher education wants to be in proximity to the diversity Black women bring to their halls, but do not appreciate us enough to effectuate changes that make the environment of the academy suitable for our continued success. And so each day, we are left to make a decision of whether it is worth it to stay the course and correct, or as I have been forced to do several times over, look for a new employer (Stallings, 2020).

RECOMMENDATIONS

At the beginning of this chapter, we discussed the importance of examining the cultural, political, epistemological landscape of our institutions and the impact of white supremacist culture on leaders of color. The process of unlearning a lifetime of white supremacist socialization can seem equal parts overwhelming and necessary, and indeed it is. What we offer are collective strategies that have supported our journey toward becoming champions of our self-care. This list is not exhaustive nor is it perfect, yet we share our collective practices from our hearts and as a means of role modeling.

Radical Self-Care and Introspection

For people of color who are leaders in the academy, specifically those who view their work in higher education as a calling that is connected to both personal career choice and as means to break the chains of this hegemonic, heteronormative, xenophobic, patriarchal, racist society, the burden of self-care and constantly examining one's positionality is an increasingly daunting but important task. According to Sue et al. (1999), the increasing diversity in our society has been a particular point of challenge for institutions of higher education to address. Hopkins (2010) posits that there are four reasons for this:

1. Absence of a Diversity/Multicultural Framework;
2. Lack of Integrative practices;
3. Lack of skill and self-awareness of practitioners; and
4. Lack of awareness, competency, and attitude to confront systems of power and privilege (p. 158).

Of the four reasons Hopkins (2010) provides for why higher education struggles with diversity and inclusion initiatives, two of them deal with the lack of awareness, self-awareness, and competency of the practitioners, not the actual implementation of diversity and inclusion paradigms.

According to Ross (2016), the most abominable piece about this white supremacist system is that we are all complicit in upholding and maintaining it, white folks and people of color alike. Therefore, it is no surprise that higher education often upholds the system of oppression that it is believed the many administrators in the academy should be trying to dismantle (Gardner, Barrett, & Pearson, 2014). So how do people of color in leadership roles within the academy make sense of their lived experiences while also disrupting what are often one-dimensional narratives of people of color across the board in higher education? Doing the self-work of radical introspection allows for leaders of color to further develop empathy and attend to the personal biographies of colleagues, particularly in a manner that allows them to approach diversity, equity, and inclusion conversations in the academy from a courageous place (Hopkins, 2010).

As two leaders of color in higher education, we often feel obliged to help facilitate dialogue that moves our respective institutions beyond structural diversity and inclusion models toward a social justice paradigm that challenges hegemony and removes barriers that have kept historically marginalized people at the fringes of the academy. However, it is difficult to do the work of social justice effectively without examining our own positionality, especially in regards to our areas of privilege. This notion can be incredibly challenging, especially considering intersectionality and the interconnected nature of oppression, meaning that some leaders of color experience increased disadvantages within their scope in the academy for no other reason than because they exist.

Being a crusader of introspection and radical self-care allows us, as leaders of color, to fulfill our role as transformers and provocateurs by enabling us to check our biases in order to retain some sense of neutrality to produce a culture of sympathetic understanding (Williams, 2008). While leaders across the board cannot and should not divorce themselves from their own beliefs and thoughts on life and the world, especially those who deal as intimately with students as many higher education professionals do, it is critical to retain as much objectivity, in other words a healthy degree of separation, because you will ultimately hit a wall as a leader, but specifically as a leader of color, if you take on all the fullness of the various understandings and conclusions that many will draw about you and your approach as a leader sheerly based on your presence as a person of color (Williams, 2008).

Developing an Appetite for Imperfection

As Black leaders and socialized beings, we are in an all-out battle with a clear enemy that has permeated all fronts, white supremacist culture, and often perfectionism and individualism are the weapons of choice that lead to our demise. The unattainable myth of perfectionism, used by others and us to assess our effectiveness and the sense of rugged individualism that is reinforced by hierarchy and positionality, are ideals we internalize despite being contrary to our cultural and ancestral ways of being, further distancing us from ourselves. For us this means developing a healthy appetite for failure. We often fear and discuss openly the external repercussions of failure as a means of avoiding our own discomfort with departing from lessons we have mastered so well to get us where we are – performing perfectionism. Yet for us, our work toward unpacking perfectionism means getting clear and becoming comfortable about a number of things. First, it means recognizing the truth that we have less control regarding the external implications for being imperfect. At the same time, it is also empowering to recognize where we do have agency and control, choosing the type of leader we want to be. Becoming a true champion for your self-care is critical to explore the true short- and long-term cost of performative perfectionism on your body, your mental health, your community, and other people of color.

Developing a healthy appetite for imperfection has been a difficult concept for us and it can cause dissonance, given our internalized oppression and socialization. However, a healthy appetite for imperfection does not mean eliminating all standards, but rather rightsizing them to match our humanity rather than upholding the imposed superhuman standards many of us have learned to perform at a great cost.

Many of us know all too well the reality of these superhuman standards established in our quest and inevitable failure to achieve perfectionism, as it not only frames our professional lives but our personal world as well, including our parenting, relationships, and friendships. Yet many struggles alone, as white supremacist culture's other weapon, individualism, rears its ugly head. Unpacking perfectionism is not only an individual endeavor, but rather collective and organizational work. As leaders we seek out every opportunity to developing teams, friendships, and relationships that can embrace imperfection, debunk the myth of perfectionism, and allows us to be fully seen. This is an important strategy in becoming a champion for your self-care. As leaders, we play a role in deconstructing perfectionism and individualism for those we mentor and lead. As leaders, we leveraged our positionality by role modeling and continuously unpacking and deconstructing perfectionism as an anti-racists leadership framework. This includes resisting operationalizing the notion of people of color having to be twice as good, especially those among us for whom intersectionality means the ways in which they are oppressed in the academy will be compounded. Do not let perfectionism be the enemy of good enough.

Getting Clear on Refrigerator Rights

The concept of refrigerator rights was most notably conceptualized by authors Miller and Sparks's (2003) work aptly titled *Refrigerator Rights: Why We Need To Let People Into Our Hearts, Our Homes (and our refrigerators)*. As leaders who identify as Black, we broadly and with some nuanced and detailed distinctions believe establishing clear refrigerator rights is key in becoming a champion of your radical self-care. Simply put, establishing clear refrigerator rights refers to developing meaningful relationships of deep trust and significance with individuals beyond your immediate family and colleagues in the workplace. Such relationships have been our biggest saving grace as it offers us a space to simply be rather than being pigeonholed into a familial or institutional role which, no matter how much you attempt to avoid, will inevitably frame or influence a relationship. This can be particularly difficult and at the same time liberating. Realities like geography, age/generational identity, an increasingly polarized culture, and an overemphasis on cohorts that exists within higher education often make this a challenge. However, the ability to be build meaningful and trusting relationships that can equitably fill your cup and reciprocate when necessary is incredibly important for our balance as professionals and leaders of color with substantive responsibilities. We have found that such relationships allow us to completely move away from work and encourage to pause the constant need to either be on or produce.

As we transitioned into leadership roles, we realized our peers groups quickly changing, either by our choice or the inevitable boundary cast by hierarchical organization structures, and not reflecting a shared identity, purpose, or set of values either at or outside of work. We quickly began to experience the loneliness many leaders of color experience in their roles and realized the importance of developing meaningful relationships of deep trust and significance with individuals beyond your immediate family and colleagues in the workplace. Among other things, refrigerator rights relationships help ground us, enhance our perspectives which can sometimes be insular and steep in the privilege of the academy, and contribute to our overall well-being. This is perhaps one of the most important strategies we live by, yet the most under-discussed among leaders of color in higher education.

Reclaiming Our Time and Discretion in Battle

As a Black woman and an Afro-Latinx man in leadership roles, we are often leading diversity efforts on campuses, and for us the personal is professional. In order to stay grounded, it is incredibly important that we keep in mind that there are always things at play beyond your locus of control. Specifically, while leaders of color may be hired for their skillset and what they bring to the academy, your position will always be juxtaposed with your identities. This reality can feel particularly daunting when you are trying to balance wanting to effect change in a system that is slow to do so, while also resisting tokenization.

And there is the reality that in order to reclaim your time, you ultimately have to come to terms with the fact that sometimes tokenization is part of moving the conversation forward – that is, at times, your presence is the change that was expected in that particular place you are currently within the academy. While a weighty realization, largely because it makes little sense in relation to the espoused values of higher education, this is not a far stretch since there is little about this system of oppression and white supremacy that makes sense. This acknowledgment can make room for you to stand affirmed that you are doing good work, even when it feels as if the system is bogging you down. Being in a position to bring awareness to intersectionality that those in the room with you can begin, at a base level, to at the very least acknowledge and get grounded in the differences among us is a step unto itself.

But make no mistake about it, reclaiming your time does not mean merely settling for the reality that the academy is unrelenting in its fight against change, particularly change that interrupts privilege and means striving to move beyond structural diversity, but rather to redirect your energies to creating change from your specific level in the organization. It requires an immense amount of thoughtfulness to actually put the ideals of justice into practice, as opposed to turning your wheels theorizing around a conference room table with colleagues who would rather nuance the notion of justice and problematize oppression than to use their position as thought-leader to make a real difference (Salaita, 2020). Reclaiming your time means knowing that your worth is not confined to what happens from nine to five or within the walls of the academy. In this, it is important to find ways to contribute in meaningful ways beyond the confines of work and in spaces where you can be affirmed, especially in social justice and diversity work (Stallings, 2020).

CONCLUSION

As a leader of color, our inner voice, instincts, and most natural ways of being and leading are continuously stripped, questioned, or minimized by others. To lead self-first means to interrupt cycles and narratives that drive you to respond immediately and minimize the false sense of urgency embedded within most leadership roles in order to be grounded, clear, and authentically you in your leadership. Our self-work is grounded in a deep commitment for being crusaders in our self-care and introspection through unpacking and deconstructing white supremacist culture. We live this out by reclaiming our time and picking our battle wisely, understanding that while we strive to do good work within the halls of the academy, our experiences within higher education, for better or worse, are not major determinants of our value to the world.

REFERENCES

ACPA: College Student Educators International & NASPA—Student Affairs Administrators in Higher Education. (2015). *ACPA/NASPA professional competency areas for student affairs educators.* Washington, DC: Authors.

Baldwin, J. (1963). *The fire next time.* New York: Dial Press.

Bates, G. (2007). These hallowed halls: African American women college and university presidents. *Journal of Negro Education, 76*(3), 373–390.

Brown, N. (2017, January). All the lies are white. Lecture conducted at Illinois Wesleyan University MLK Teach-In, Bloomington, IL.

Chin, J. L., Lott, B., Rice, J. K., & Sanchez-Hucles, J. (2007). *Women and leadership: Transforming visions and diverse voices.* Malden, MA: Blackwell.

Clayborne, H. L., & Hamrick, F. A. (2007). Rearticulating the leadership experiences of African American women in midlevel student affairs administration. *NASPA Journal, 44*(1), 123–146.

Cook, C. R., Duong, M. T., McIntosh, K., Fiat, A. E., Larson, M., Pullmann, M. D., & McGinnis, J. (2018). Addressing discipline disparities for black male students: Linking malleable root causes to feasible and effective practices. *School Psychology Review, 47*(2), 135–152. ProQuest Central. https://doi.org/10.17105/SPR-2017-0026.V47-2

Crawley, R. (2006). Diversity and the marginalization of black women's issues. *Policy Futures in Education, 4*(2), 172–184.

Crenshaw, K. (2016, December). The urgency of intersectionality [Video file]. https://www.ted.com/talks/kimberle_crenshaw_the_urgency_of_intersectionality/up-next

Dowd, A. C., & Bensimon, E. M. (2015). *Engaging the "race question": Accountability and equity in U.S. higher education.* New York: Teachers College Press.

Gardner, Jr., L., Barrett, T. G., & Pearson, L. C. (2014). African American administrators at PWIs: Enablers of and barriers to career success. *The National Association of Diversity Officers in Higher Education, 7*(4), 235–251.

Henry, W. J., West, N., & Ferguson, D. (2013). Programs 'by us, for us'—Support black women. *Women in Higher Education, 22*(6), 11–12.

Hinton, K. G. (2001). *The experiences of African American women administrators at predominately white institutions of higher education* (Unpublished doctoral dissertation). Indiana University, Bloomington, IN.

Hopkins, P. (2010). Practitioner know thyself! Reflections on the importance of self-work for diversity and social justice practitioners. *Tamara Journal of Critical Organization Inquiry, 8*(4), 157–171.

Jean-Marie, G., & Normore, A. (2010). The impact of relational leadership, social justice and spirituality among female secondary school leaders. *International Journal of Urban Educational Leadership, 4*, 22–43.

Jenlink, P. M. (2005). Editorial: On bricolage and the intellectual work of the scholar-practitioner. *Scholar-Practitioner Quarterly, 3*(1), 3–12.

Miller, W., & Spark, G. (2003). *Refrigerator rights: Why we need to let people into our hearts, our homes (and our refrigerators)*. Exeter, England: Pedigee Books.

Moradi, B., & Grzanka, P. R. (2017). Using intersectionality responsibly: Toward critical epistemology, structural analysis, and social justice activism. *Journal of Counseling Psychology, 64*(5), 500–513. PsycARTICLES. https://doi.org/10.1037/cou0000203

Nganga, C. W. (2011). Emerging as a scholar practitioner: A reflective essay review. *Mentoring and Tutoring: Partnership in Learning, 19*(2), 239–251.

Patitu, C. L., & Hinton, K. G. (2003). The experiences of African American women faculty and administrators in higher education: Has anything changed? *New Directions for Student Services, 104*, 79–93.

Reid, P. T., & Zalk, S. R. (2001). Academic environments: Gender and ethnicity in U. S. higher education. In Worrell, J. (Ed.) *Encyclopedia of women and gender* (pp. 29–42). San Diego, CA: Academic Press.

Richardson, E. (2002). To protect and serve: African American female literacies. *College Composition and Communication, 53*(4), 675–704.

Rodriguez, R. A. (2019). Transformative preparation: Measuring the intercultural competence development of higher education and student affairs (hesa) students and exploring the intercultural learning experience across assistantship sites [Unpublished dissertation]. University of Vermont.

Ross, L. C. (2016). *Blackballed: The black and white politics of race on America's campuses*. New York: St. Martin's Press.

Salaita, S. (2020, February). *Off-the-record advice for graduate students*. Steve Salaita. www.stevesalaita.com.

Singh, K., Robinson, A., & Williams-Green, J. (1995). Differences in perceptions of African American women and men faculty & administrators. *The Journal of Negro Education, 64*(4), 401–408.

Stallings, E. (2020, January 16). *When Black women go from office pet to office threat*. Medium. https://zora.medium.com/when-black-women-go-from-office-pet-to-office-threat-83bde710332e

Sue, D. W., Bingham, R., Porche-Burke, L., & Vasquez, M. (1999). The diversification of psychology: A multicultural revolution. *American Psychologist, 54*, 1061–1069.

Sue, D. W., Alsaidi, S., Awad, M. N., Glaeser, E., Calle, C. Z., & Mendez, N. (2019). Disarming racial microaggressions: Microintervention strategies for targets, White allies, and bystanders. *American Psychologist*, 74(1), 128–142. http://dx.doi.org/10.1037/amp0000296.

Takacs, D. (2002). Positionality, epistemology, and social justice in the classroom. *Social Justice*, 29(4), 168–181.

The Opportunity Agenda (2011). *Social Science Literature Review: Media Representations and Impact on the Lives of Black Men and Boys.* San Francisco, CA: The Tide Center.

Waring, A. L. (2003). African-American female college presidents: Self conceptions of leadership. *Journal of Black Studies*, 30(3), 171–180.

Washington, J. (June 18, 2010). Personal communication.

West, N. M. (2015). In our own words: African American women student affairs professionals define their experiences in the academy. *Advancing Women in Leadership*, 35, 108–119.

Williams, D. R. (2008). At ease in between: The middle position of a scholar-practitioner. *Journal of Global Buddhism*, 9, 155–163.

Wolfe, B. L., & Dilworth, P. P. (2015). Transitioning normalcy: Organizational culture, African American administrators, and diversity leadership in higher education. *Review of Educational Research*, 85(4), 667–697. https://doi.org/10.3102/0034654314565667

Part Three

Doing

Chapter Six

Doing Diversity
Steps Toward the Impossible

Jennifer Hamer, Annie McBride, Kierstin McMichael, and Precious Porras

When we assumed new leadership of the Office of the Vice Provost for Diversity and Equity (D&E) for the University of Kansas (KU) in 2017, we were inspired to model a learning and workplace college community that, to our knowledge, had yet to be realized on a major U.S. campus. In our collective vision, we aspired to create this "ideal" campus as a place where those who identify as historically racialized minorities, queer and gender nonconforming, people with disabilities, and/or other structurally marginalized populations would be proportionately represented, fully participate as student leaders and heads of academic departments, fairly advance as staff and supervisors, and routinely lead systems as chancellors and presidents. This was our ideal then and it remains our model at this writing.

To be clear, when we began our collaborative leadership journey as Vice Provost, Assistant Vice Provost, Director of Projects and Policy Development, and Engagement Coordinator/Executive Associate from 2017 to 2019, we were optimists. We believed that our ideal of a model campus could be achieved via our determination, expertise, and hard work, even in the current conservative sociopolitical culture of higher education (Williams, 2006a,b). Upon assuming leadership, we publicly pronounced our commitment to the realization of this model because its promise, more than anything, is the underpinning of the field of diversity in higher education, moving diversity leaders to propose and implement meaningful reforms, and encouraging campus actors to support and accept these as interim steps toward transformational change.

DOI: 10.4324/9781003008521-9

In the pages that follow we reflect on our experience at the KU, pre the 2020 Covid-19 pandemic and surge in Black Lives Matter movement. Like so many other institutions at the time, Kansas was rocked by the 2015–2016 national and local student unrest which called for the removal of administrators as well as transformative change in practices and policies that perpetuated persistent inequalities in student, staff, and faculty demographics, experiences, advancement, and outcomes. The unrest resulted from what seemed the irrationality of universities like Kansas to amply address these real concerns despite demographic changes in constituencies and increasing demands from employers that demand logic to the contrary.

Kansas and its institutional peers increasingly turned to their established and new central offices of diversity, equity, and inclusion (DEI) to manage these problems and to respond to outcries for remedy. Yet, the profession and field of diversity in higher education remain in its formative years. The growing number of offices is characterized by varying organizational structures and designs, from central university-wide upper administration to smaller narrowly focused departments. Some are managed by a single staff person, while others consist of multitiered levels of reporting units and teams of personnel. These wide-ranging variations across the diversity profession also apply to operating budgets, which are often inadequate, may drastically fluctuate from one year to the next, or simply not exist. We attest that the formative stage of a 50-year-old diversity leadership field is actually a reflection of the unwillingness of higher education leadership to invest in the eradication of the social and economic differences in academia, which were the source of campus unrest.

Our task as new leaders focused on how best to manage our new administrative mantle in a relatively new field, with minimal resources, during a time of student unrest. Despite growing scholarship, there continues to be few written guidelines for "doing" DEI as part of a central university administration, particularly at a large predominantly white institution. Despite the growth of the field, few of those within it have offered a set of practical steps or guidelines that, based on their experiences, could inform the development of practical university diversity plans and their operationalization. Indeed, scholarship in the field has focused more on the role of Chief Diversity Officers rather than the work they and their teams actually perform. Documented experiences could serve as critical resources for a relatively new field and profession, especially for change agents tasked with the seemingly impossible task of realizing diversity. Thus, from the early months of our tenure, we sought to address this gap in the field.

From 2017 to 2019, the authors worked together as the leadership of the Office of the Vice Provost for D&E at the KU, a Midwestern Research

Institution with approximately 27,000 students. (Since 2019, two of the authors, Jennifer Hamer and Kierstin McMichael, have left the KU for Penn State University and Washington University, respectively.) In the pages that follow, we employ collaborative reflection and reflexivity to describe and understand our experiences as an administrative diversity leadership team. Our intersectional identity filters are as four first-generation college women, three of whom are women of color, all of whom have strong academic and professional experience in identity stratification in the U.S. and higher education, especially. We draw upon Cunliffe and Jun's (2005) call for organizations to go beyond ideas of "reflective" administration to "reflexive" administration to write about our collective experiences (Heidegger, 1966; Cunliffe & Jun, 2005). Reflexive administration are those practices that demonstrate ethics, responsibility, and decision-making that lay a foundation for institutional change.

As a leadership team, we routinely came together and actively shared and reflected on our thinking and actions. As we moved deeper into our work and met with the challenges of doing diversity, and even as we neared the end of our team journey, we questioned the assumptions that stationed our office as the mechanism for cultural transformation. From the start, we assumed that a cultural transformation of the University was a viable goal. We created a vision, mission, and guidelines framed by this belief, reorganized the Office of D&E, and advanced an urgent and aggressive set of tasks toward that goal.

Much had been accomplished in two years with a small staff, modest budget, and marginalized central administrative unit. However, as we reflected on those accomplishments, it was clear that our major intervention had been to bring calm and stabilize the disruption that began in 2015–2016 and, because of the illogic and instability it exposed, build meaningful reforms that could serve as a strong foundation for a transformative model campus. The model campus though was beyond our capacity. Our experiences evidence that a moderately staffed and funded central administrative office of DEI can effectively implement the foundations to cultivate change but, in the current climate higher education, cannot create it.

In the pages that follow, we highlight the context in which we began our work and some of the practical steps we took as a central upper administrative office to meaningfully "do" DEI. We developed a vision of a multicultural, multiracial, and multiethnic university to clarify the endpoint of DEI efforts. However, the culture of the institution was not one amenable to transformative change. Subsequently our accomplishments, though significant, primarily served to (1) clarify the illogic of maintaining an inequitable status quo, (2) re-envision and amplify the purpose, presence, and centrality of equity as a rational and stabilizing force in an unsteady university climate, and (3) build foundation shifting reforms that brought calm and hope but could not alone realize a model learning and workplace environment.

PUBLIC DEMAND FOR CULTURAL TRANSFORMATION: THE SET-UP

Student unrest, public protests, and disruptions have historically moved universities to give more meaningful attention to matters of learning and workplace inequities and outcomes. And so, it was a 2015 town hall titled "Race, Respect, Responsibility and Free Speech" that was the catalyst for change at the KU. The Chancellor- and Provost-led event was intended to get ahead of the campus protests that were loudly sweeping the nation. The disquiet outed the persistent racism that characterized university life and its underrepresentation of racial/ethnic minority students in particular; demanded greater diversity in faculty composition; and in some cases called for removal of administrators.

From the past to the present, KU inequalities had been most visible in its student body and workplace racial/ethnic demographics. The University had never witnessed a population composition that proportionately reflected its state or national constituencies. African Americans, Hispanics, Native American/Alaskan Native, and Native Hawaiian/Pacific Islanders have always experienced a disproportionately low presence on this flagship campus. This pattern had changed little in the early decades of the 21st century, either for Kansas or for other predominantly white institutions. Though an increasing percentage of underrepresented racial/ethnic minorities were enrolled in two- and four-year colleges and universities, relative to whites and Asian Americans, they were less likely to complete an associates or bachelor's degree, taking longer to complete, and leaving college with more debt, whether or not they graduated (Espinosa et al., 2019).

A snapshot of Kansas looked much like its institutional peers: American Indian/Alaskan Native, Black, Native Hawaiian/Pacific Islander, and Hispanic demographic groups were underrepresented among all categories of faculty, staff, administrators, and students. In 2016, these groups were only 258 of 1,111 tenure-track faculty and librarians, and only two of almost 50 faculty administrators (less than 10 percent) according to the University of Kansas Office of Analytics and Institutional Research (2016a). Among faculty, librarians, and faculty administrators, 11 identified as American Indian/Alaskan Native, 52 as Black and African American, and 52 Hispanic/Latinx. Among unclassified academic and professional staff, only 222 of approximately 3,500 (less than 10 percent) were historically underrepresented racial and ethnic minorities. Among these, 21 identified as American Indian/Alaskan Native, 93 Black/African American, and 108 Hispanic/Latinx (University of Kansas Office of Analytics and Institutional Research, 2016a). A similar pattern existed among our student body. In spring 2016, students on the flagship and Edwards Campus, located in the Kansas City, KS metropolitan area, who self-reported as part of historically underrepresented racial/ethnic minority categories, were approximately 10 percent of KU's student composition, less than 3,000 of 23,488 undergraduate and graduate students (University of Kansas Office of Analytics and Institutional Research, 2016b).

This demographic history, a lack of cultural competency among mostly white and cisgender faculty, staff, and students were complicated by a series of police killings of Black people which were at the forefront of the national and local news. Though only 2 percent of the U.S. population, young Black men between the ages of 15 and 34 were 15 percent of all those killed by policy in 2015, five times higher than their white male counterparts (Swaine et al., 2015). Twelve-year-old Tamir Rice, 18-year-old Michael Brown, and others stirred outrage across communities, including campuses.

Violence against other groups had also seen an uptick. In 2015, the U.S. Congress created a new task force to address bias as violence against transgender people and physical attacks on gender nonconforming people had seen a tripling since 2013 (Federal Bureau of Investigation, 2014). Sexual assault and violence on university campuses was also at issue. Findings from the American Association of Universities' *2015 Campus Climate Survey on Sexual Assault and Misconduct* (Cantor et al., 2015) indicated that among 27 participating universities, nearly 12 percent of students reported at least one experience of "nonconsensual sexual contact by physical force, threats of physical force, or incapacitation since they enrolled at their university" (para. 4). In addition, Facebook and other social media tools facilitated the ability of students to share apprehensions and negative experiences correlated to social identities within a network of online social media communities.

Demands for change were not just at KU. According to Jack Dickey of *Time Magazine* (2016), "at more than 50 schools in all, student protesters made demands to right what they see as historic wrongs—demands for greater faculty diversity, new courses, public apologies, administrators' ousting."

A Lackluster and Ill-Prepared Administrative Response

In fall 2015, the call for a town hall campus conversation by leaders of the KU's upper administration was a strategic misstep that signaled their underestimation of marginalized students' despair as well as their strong organizing skills. The proposed conversation was an attempt by administration to demonstrate care and avert a public student protest that they understood was likely to occur in the then current national climate. The well-publicized, live-streamed, and choreographed event did not go as planned. The stage set by administrators became a platform co-opted by a collective of students who presented an abridged summary of the inequities that affected student life and outcomes.

This multiracial/ethnic/cultural coalition of students with 15 demands for remedy quickly assumed control of the live-streaming town hall (Ritter & Korte, 2015). Administrators were caught unprepared, with little experience or expertise to offer a progressive response (Flinn, 2015; Korte & Ritter, 2015; Osei, 2015). In the weeks that followed, administrators turned instead to a well-practiced University set of counteractions: the creation of a Diversity, Equity, and Inclusion Advisory Group, charged with reviewing the campus climate and making recommendations for improvement to the Chancellor. They called upon the student facing unit, the OMA, and a marginalized student support-centered office, to expressly include trainings for faculty and staff. In response, the OMA hosted training for three professional schools, several departments in the College of Liberal Arts and Sciences, and a half-day training for the Chancellor, Provost, and all Academic Deans. Additionally, the OMA's annual Tunnel of Oppression, a community-wide diversity awareness event, occurred the following week. The event saw a record turnout of almost 2,000 people in a three-day period, a participation that far exceeded staff capacity.

During this same period, the Chancellor and Provost made the decision to hire an external consulting firm to develop and complete a University-wide Climate Survey (Rankin and Associates, 2017). These and other steps seemed like promising moves in the right direction (Kite & Mitchell, 2015; Korte, 2015). Expectations for campus cultural transformation from students, faculty, and staff were high (Flinn, 2015; Korte & Ritter, 2015; Osei, 2015). The Advisory Committee and the Climate Survey, each commissioned by the uppermost administrators, were to provide a strong basis for the budgetary support of our office and the implementation of a plan forward.

Advisory Committee Report

After a semester of deliberations, the April 2016 Diversity, Equity, and Inclusion Advisory Report was released (Lang et al., 2016). It described a history of pervasive inequities based on identities and backgrounds, and

110

painted a portrait of a campus where students, faculty, and staff of color and those marginalized by gender and sexual identity, abilities, and international status felt harmed and unwanted. It described the failure of KU to care for and support success for all community members. The report, delivered to the Chancellor, Provost, and community provided a list of over 30 recommendations, many of them calling on KU leaders to take responsibility for institutional problems and hold themselves accountable for solutions (Lang et al., 2016).

Climate Survey Report

The survey was created by the firm of Rankin and Associates (the process of which was contested by many participating marginalized students) and data was collected over the course of 2016. In spring 2017, Jennifer Hamer began an appointment as Vice Provost of D&E and worked with the consultants to report the results of the first and long-awaited climate survey to multiple campus constituencies. The organization and implementation meetings to share the report's findings was the first major public task for this new leadership.

The consultants reported a summary of findings in spring 2017 that affirmed findings outlined in the Diversity, Equity, and Inclusion Advisory Group Report (spring 2016), and offered some science and clarification for administrators about the real experiences and substance of relationships based on social identities and differences among KU students, faculty, and staff (Rankin and Associates, 2017).

In addition to demographic composition and past reports, the Campus Climate Survey suggested additional areas in desperate need of improvement (Rankin and Associates, 2017). There were issues of exclusionary behaviors, retention, and unwanted sexual conduct that demanded the attention of the University. Eighteen percent of those who participated in the survey personally experienced exclusionary conduct within the last year at KU. The types of behavior included being shunned or ignored, bullying and harassment, and intimidating or offensive words or behavior. Those students, faculty, and staff who experienced such behavior cited five characteristics that made them a target: gender/gender identity, position status, age, ethnicity, and race. Students were both the top target and the top source of the exclusionary behavior. Only a third of the respondents reported their experience to a KU resource; of those that did, the majority were dissatisfied with the institutional response (Rankin and Associates, 2017).

There were no surprises for those of us who were immersed in equity work as students and as members of the faculty and professional staff.

111

For those faculty and staff with marginalized identities, the detailed power point presentations and 600-page survey report were quantifiable summaries of our university life at Kansas and elsewhere. For the KU in 2016–2017, minoritized and marginalized undergraduate and graduate students especially reported feeling a lack of belonging at Kansas. They, relative to their peers, did not perceive themselves as being able to succeed at Kansas and were more likely to seriously consider leaving the University. They were particularly discouraged in the early months and years of their academic programs (Rankin and Associates, 2017). For these groups and for all students, it was clear that the University had to not only create a "sense" of belonging, but also purposely build practices and policies of inclusion that ensure not only that all feel welcome, but that all were meaningfully included at KU. These practices and policies would need to be incorporated into classrooms, communications, student leadership and extracurricular activities, and living and social environments.

Most unfamiliar to many were the reports from University staff, which as a group expressed a desire to leave the University at rates that surpassed similarly surveyed institutions. Low wages, a lack of professional development opportunities, and little promise of upward mobility seem to offer some explanation. However, those from historically underrepresented racial/ethnic groups, international staff, queer, trans and gender non-binary identities, and those with disabilities especially reported inhospitable or unfriendly work environments. Regardless of their identities, staff broadly reported that fear of job security and retaliation from supervisors enforced their silence and inhibited their ability to report concerns (Rankin and Associates, 2017). Fear of retaliation and exclusion are, of course, unacceptable in professional environments.

Similar patterns of exclusion were reported for historically underrepresented racial/ethnic minority, queer, trans and gender non-binary, and other marginalized faculty members. These groups described discomfort in classroom exchanges with students, within their academic units, and in the community due to their respective identities. They also described a need for greater support and clearer guidance in the balance of teaching, research, and service, principally as it regards preparation for promotion and tenure (Rankin and Associates, 2017).

Faculty broadly shared encounters involving conflict with colleagues. They expressed the need for program and department chairs to have managerial knowledge and skills, which are components of supervision that often are not a requirement for leadership in academic units. Faculty also reported that they were uncertain of what policies and protocols were currently in place to address problems or to support their interests in administrative advancement (Rankin and Associates, 2017).

Many students, faculty, and staff survey respondents said they had seriously considered leaving the University. The percentage of faculty and staff who reported such a consideration was high, with 64 percent of faculty respondents and 55 percent of staff respondents having pondered the option. The rates were even higher among respondents from certain racial and ethnic groups and among individuals with disabilities. Staff members reported low pay and limited opportunities for advancement as key reasons for their responses. Staff also report concerns about opportunities, and about transparency and fairness in evaluations. Faculty members indicated low pay and the prospect of positions at other institutions as the top reasons for their responses. Undergraduate students said their top three reasons for considering leaving were (in order): a lack of sense of belonging, a climate that was not welcoming, and financial concerns (Rankin and Associates, 2017).

A small but meaningful number of survey respondents experienced a range of unwanted sexual conduct while at the KU, and 2 percent, the majority of whom were students, reported unwanted sexual contact. The contact was most likely to occur during the fall semester of an undergraduate's first year. Regrettably, only 12 percent of individuals who said they experienced unwanted sexual contact reported it to University resources (Rankin and Associates, 2017).

These survey data allowed a predominantly white staff to see themselves as part of the population that could benefit from DEI work. It facilitated the active buy-in and interest in the Office of D&E from a range of University employees, including, for example, facilities and housekeeping staff, parking and mechanical repair staff as well as clerical and accounting professionals. We recognized the vulnerability of these positions and placed the burden of naming the problems of equity on ourselves, as diversity leaders. By doing so, we demonstrated our care for their personal welfare and a steadfast commitment to their professional development to include cultural competency and general managerial training for unit supervisors charged with the maintenance of fair work spaces.

The Illogic of Inequalities

Readers of this volume are likely familiar with research that tells us we can all benefit from a robust multicultural learning and work environment. Twenty years into the 21st century, we are witnessing increasingly multiracial, multiethnic, and multicultural global living and professional spaces. Today's graduates are best prepared for contemporary citizenship, careers, and leadership when their education affords them opportunities to learn from a diversity of others, engage with people of varied backgrounds, understand multiple ways of knowing, and respect a range of perspectives. Employers are increasingly demanding higher education workers, researchers, and leaders who have the knowledge and skills to work within socially diverse employment settings. Further, multicultural and inclusive learning and work environments enhance individual critical thinking, the development of innovative research, and resolutions to complex problems (U.S. Department of Education, 2013).

Proportionate demographic composition also affects the academic and overall success of students. Underrepresented and marginalized students on predominantly white and cisgender (defined as a person whose sense of personal identity and gender corresponds with their birth sex) campuses especially benefit from supportive identity-based campus communities (Cooper, 2009). Additionally, relative to peers, graduates exposed to diversity in public higher education institutions, are more engaged in their jobs and are more likely to view their degree as valuable (Marken, 2015).

These realities require universities, like the KU, to emphasize greater social diversity among its student body, faculty, and staff membership, and to actively cultivate climates where campus citizens can fully engage toward best possible outcomes. Yet, inclusive, equitable, and demographically representative learning and work spaces are uncharacteristic of most large predominantly white universities.

Reluctance and Resistance to Change

As a D&E team, we have always collectively contended that the KU was, like other institutions, neither exceptional nor *autonomous* entities. It was a part of a dynamic ecological system of politics, culture, economics, and the varied constituencies it served. In 2006, the U.S. Secretary of Education issued a report that urged institutions of higher education to more purposely broaden participation of the growing multiracial/ethnic/cultural spectrums of their national and global constituencies. The accomplishment of this goal would require that universities develop greater cultural competency, admission policy revisions, and other systemic efforts to recruit and retain U.S. historically marginalized students to successful outcomes in particular (U.S. Department of Education, 2013).

This was dated news to the industry of higher education. And yet, according to a 2006 op-ed by Robert Diamond, founder of the Institute for Change in Higher Education at Syracuse University, little had changed. He noted, as evidence, the rise in part-time and tenure-protected faculty members; that one-half of students entering two- and four-year institutions do not complete their degrees; the replacement of need-based scholarship by merit-based awards; and the declining interest in state political leaders in higher education investment (Diamond, 2006). Among other items, resistance to change, he asserted, was a logical response to a status quo (i.e., alumni and donors, long-time campus actors, trustees, legislators, etc.) that was more powerful than the forces for change; the ease with which administrators and faculty can choose to do nothing relative to the perceived risks they associate with change; and ill-prepared leadership, unknowledgeable of innovative ways of managing and leading institutions in need of change (Diamond, 2006). At Kansas, upon our tenure, it seemed that upper administrators, provosts, and chancellors had routinely met persistent calls for prompt, adequate response on matters of DEI as short-lived phases or fads through which they simply had to navigate for containment.

The KU, like many others, had often managed problems of diversity with invitations to student dissenters to meet for private discussions with upper administrators. Other strategies included the creation of ad hoc advisory committees and task forces. Still other mechanisms consisted of turns to an ever-growing menu of costly for-profit diversity industry options that targeted the attitudes of campus actors. Contractual services were paid to speakers, artists, consultants, workshops, and retreats, for example, hired to raise diversity awareness and nurture the social tolerance of faculty, staff, and students. Consultant services were not intended to target administrator-led institutional reform and change.

This collection of lackluster responses, which included the development and distribution of a Climate Survey, were employed in the 2015–2016 period of disruption. However, they were complicated by the mounting frustration from employees over extraordinary low salaries and stagnant wages compared to peer institutions, accompanied by multiple and near simultaneous transitions in University upper administrative leadership personnel. These are the circumstances the authors found themselves working in as we transitioned into leadership roles. What follows are detailed descriptions of the six steps employed in an effort to lead dynamic and sustainable institutional change at the KU.

STEP ONE: AGREEMENT ON THE PROBLEM AND THE SOLUTION

Our entry into leadership was met with heightened community awareness of multiple forms of local and national inequalities in the workplace, living communities, and campuses. There was also fear among faculty, staff, and administrators of continued protests. More narrowly, faculty and staff expressed to us serious anxieties about their own cultural competency gaps, and our weeks and months were spent in multiple interventions to protect students and faculty from the after-effects of racial/ethnic/gender microaggressions and other inappropriate behaviors that faculty presented in their advising and teaching roles. Yet, in general and at that time, demonstrated knowledge and ability to work well with a diversity of social identities was not a job requirement for most employment opportunities.

These concerns were intensified by a well-organized and funded conservative backlash against the supposed liberalism of university campuses. Conservative student (and faculty member) groups, with the support of external forces, tested the meaning of free speech by targeting "politically correct" language, safe spaces, reflection rooms, and gender-inclusive restrooms.

Patterns of experiences and perception summarized in the Climate Survey clarified for us how inequities presented for different sectors of the campus community. Indicators of problems could be found in many reporting University spaces and groups. The quantitative and qualitative data affirmed reports from past advisory committees, varied anecdotal accounts of problems in the classroom and workplace, and informal testimonies of violence and biases among and between faculty, staff, students, and varying levels of supervisors and administrators. People were hurting and many felt that the University, as an institution, cared little about their welfare as either students or employees (Lang et al., 2016; Rankin and Associates, 2017).

These findings, along with other events and actions of the previous year, also made clear the need for a centrally led action plan to rebuild trust, to deliver a sense of relief, and to show visible progress to those most anguished. Research tell us that attitudes are difficult to change and biased behavior can occur sans prejudicial points of view (Ziegert & Hanges, 2005). Further, workshops and speakers are often attended by those who are already accepting differences, or at least open to learning about other ways of knowing and experiencing the world. Instead, efforts had to focus on behavior expectations and our ability to foster equitable and inclusive conduct between and among students, between students and faculty, between and among faculty, between faculty and staff, and between and among staff colleagues and supervisors.

For us, the work of DEI was not impossible. However, it was not labor that could simply be contracted out to consultants or corrected through public talks and keynotes. These conventional tactics could be no substitute for a focus on policies and protocols that could directly guide and respond to inappropriate and offensive behaviors in the classroom, the lack of transparency in staff promotion decisions, bias in faculty and staff recruitment efforts, and an administration reluctant to risk the comfort of doing as little as possible.

From our vantage point, if there was ever a moment for University administrators to support a cultural transformation, it was this one. As a team in the Office of D&E with marginalized intersectional identities, we understood our own positions as peripheral to offices and office holders who held more traditional and accepted roles in the organization. We felt a strong connection to those most harmed by inequalities as well as to administrator colleagues. Relationships held with faculty, staff, and students brought us some broad degree of early good will across the University. We also knew that this benefit of the doubt would soon be spent without prompt leadership action on our parts. We immediately set about the work of "doing diversity" and advanced a way forward for an institution that, it seemed to us, was fraught with distrust and an ingrained need to maintain the status quo.

STEP TWO: COMMUNICATION, TRANSPARENCY, CALM, AND STABILITY

As new leadership of D&E, we felt it important that we communicate our command and ability to move the University forward following a past year of tumult. We were especially concerned about marginalized students, who continued to experience microaggressive behaviors in living and classroom spaces, and staff who felt they had little recourse when supervisors and colleagues behaved badly. As women and women of color, we also knew that respect and authority were not bestowed with the title of Vice Provost, as it typically is for white male counterparts. Given this, we were very conscious of our every interaction. We were exceptionally well-organized, always professionally attired, relied on research and data as evidence for our positions, and confident and firm in our expertise in one-on-one and larger meetings with others.

Our initial public introduction to the campus and surrounding community was to lead the report-back of Climate Survey findings, in collaboration with the visiting team of external consultants. The Climate Survey findings and the pending public report-backs created considerable apprehension among University deans, vice provosts, and uppermost leadership. Their angst was based in their fear and belief that students would respond to the survey findings with anger, protest, and calls to remove leadership, a response to which the institution was still ill-prepared. In anticipation, there were multiple meetings, reviews of the data, and consternation about what qualitative data could and should be reported to deans and vice provosts. However, leadership and "ownership" of the Climate Survey rested in the Office of the Vice Provost of D&E. It seemed clear to us that should disruption occur, our office would and could serve as a buffer to bear the brunt of blame and shield other leadership from responsibility.

As a team, we maintained open communication with students, faculty, and staff, and were perhaps more aware than other leadership of how tired marginalized students were of protests. In addition, many of those involved in making the demands in late 2015 had graduated or were no longer enrolled. We realized too that any anger or protests that presented were well-earned by the KU and our task was to be the office that prioritized resolutions to their legitimate concerns.

The report-back sessions were a well-publicized, live-streamed, and orchestrated series of events. Multiple assemblies were scheduled for separate presentations to the University's multiple constituencies – administrators, faculty and staff, and students. It was our opportunity to immediately establish ourselves as the new DEI team. As part of the administration, we did not dwell on the University's past errors, but rather cast our plan as one that built on its previous energies: diversity workshops, ad hoc advisory committees, administrator meetings with students, and the Climate Survey. Our communications with campus audiences focused on simple, straightforward logical steps that acknowledged the personal troubles presented over the past year, the responsibility of University administration to make corrections, and our ability to lead in this regard.

However, this was a formidable task for an Office of D&E that, structurally, was only superficially a part of University upper administrative decision-making. Until our presence, it had never had a strategic plan, budget, or infrastructure to maximize its promise.

STEP THREE: ARTICULATION OF A VISION

Our second step was to reimagine the University as one that met the ideals of those students, faculty, and staff who had voiced serious concerns about their classroom environments, workplace practices, and the lack of belonging so many felt in their everyday campus interactions. This was not an especially challenging task. We had multiple reports authored by student senates and varied advisory groups, regularly collected university data, the ability to compare ourselves to aspirational peers, and a growing scholarship on the experiences of marginalized populations in higher education to inform our thinking. Most recently, of course, we had the 600-page Climate Survey Report and the Diversity, Equity, and Inclusion

Advisory Group Report commissioned by the Chancellor in Spring 2016. In the interest of continuity and public trust in processes, we respected the value of each in our collective thought, especially as we considered our vision and purpose. According to the Report of the Diversity, Equity and Inclusion Advisory Committee (Lang et al, 2016):

> The public university ideally is a cornerstone of a humane social contract. Public institutions of higher education can (1) allow a society to ponder, discuss and explore the diversity and complexities of the human condition; (2) promote the flowering of individual capacities and potential (self-actualization); (3) provide pathways to economic opportunity and professional mobility; (4) foster a well-rounded, critically thinking citizenry of lifelong learners who are prepared to creatively address the social problems of the day; (5) engage in cultural, scholarly, pedagogical, and technological innovation; and (6) demonstrate the possibilities of perspective-taking and empathy, democratic decision-making, forward-looking institutional reform, and social justice.
>
> (p. 4)

Our Vision and Mission for a more diverse, equitable, and inclusive KU rested on this humane social contract and it was upon this that we drafted the office's first set of guiding principles:

Our Vision
We are to be a learning and professional environment where identities and differences are valued as primary sources of academic and professional excellence, innovation, and centered as part of our shared responsibility and care for the academic, professional, lifetime success, and fulfilment of all members of the KU community.

Our Mission
We are to move forward with urgency and purpose the creation and maintenance of a more representative, fair, and inclusive KU by integrating diversity, equity, and inclusion into our institutional policies, protocols, practices, and learning spaces; building a community of care, accountability, and collective responsibility; and meeting our obligation to prepare students for work, leadership, and informed engagement in an increasingly diverse and dynamic global society.

119

Guiding Principals

Diversity: We are committed to an environment where differences strengthen our entire community and provide the foundation for equitable opportunities and successful outcomes for all. Our definition of "diversity" encompasses acceptance and respect for each other as a multiracial, multiethnic, and multicultural community. We recognize that there are inequalities and privileges generated by those differences that include race, ethnicity, gender identities, gender expressions, sexual orientation, socio-economic status, age, abilities, religion, regions, Veteran status, citizenship status, and nationality. By affirming the complexities of our histories, cultures, and experiences, we move toward a fuller understanding of ourselves and each other.

Equity: We are committed and obligated to create and enforce policies, processes, practices, and programs that appreciate difference and create fair, safe, and just learning, working, and living environments for students, staff, and faculty.

Inclusion: We are committed and obligated to provide a context in which our students, staff, and faculty, receive respect and opportunity for intellectual growth and professional development for careers, service to the public, and democratic participation in a diverse society, regardless of social, cultural and economic background and experience.

(Hamer, 2016, 2018)

STEP FOUR: RESTRUCTURE FOR PRACTICAL SCOPE AND CAPACITY

Students, faculty, staff, and administrators expected the Office of D&E to provide comprehensive institutional leadership. Yet, as past literature makes clear (Smith, 2015), the pervasive issues of DEI at major institutions of higher education cannot be addressed by a single office or office holder. While the navigation of obstacles is part of higher education leadership, it is a particular burden for those tasked with D&E work. As we alluded to in an earlier section, these offices generally exist as marginal and supplemental to university operations rather than a critical part of all of its elements. Diversity officers are disproportionately scholars and professionals of color. Within this category, women of color are overrepresented and are among the historically minoritized demographic categories on U.S. university campuses, their administrations, and the U.S. more broadly (Williams & Wade-Golden, 2013).

At the start of this chapter, we mentioned that the profession and field of diversity remains in its formative phase. In 2007, Williams and Wade-Golden defined the role of the Chief Diversity Officer as one established as a senior or executive administrator that reported directly to a provost, president, or chancellor. As such, the role serves the entire campus (or system) and the office leads university-wide diversity efforts. In 2014, the National Association of Chief Diversity Officers in Higher Education introduced the "Standards of Professional Practice for Chief Diversity Officers" (Worthington et al., 2014). Their 12 points were created and identified to serve as:

> guideposts to help clarify and specify the scope and flexibility of the work of Chief Diversity Officers, and provide a set of guidelines to inform and assist individual administrators and institutions in aligning the work of CDOs on their campuses.
>
> (p. 227)

In this same issue of the *Journal of Diversity in Higher Education*, Leon (2014) reported findings on the range of diversity, equity, and/or inclusion organizational structures and common strategies used by diversity officers to perform diversity work. Leon argued that the type of organizational structure or how it was integrated into the university affected the effectiveness of the office. Three structures were identified. The Collaborative Model was characterized by a narrow scope of activities, small budget, minimal staff, no direct reports, and little meaningful engagement with practical diversity efforts. Relative to the "Unit-Based CDO Model" which has a larger staff, supervision of lower-ranked diversity officers, and direct collaboration with other campus units around diversity initiatives, the Collaborative Model is less effective. The most effective model and the one that most fits the KU was the "Portfolio Divisional CDO Model" characterized by a more generous operating budget, direct reporting units, supervision of lower-ranking diversity officers, and direct collaboration with other upper top administrative officers (Leon, 2014).

The Office of D&E at the KU was established as one of several direct reports to the provost and vice chancellor for academic affairs. Yet and still, it was not a structure that supported or encouraged far-reaching DEI plans or actions. Rather, it seems that it had been employed, in the most recent past, to mediate the problems presented by marginalized populations, host public engagements that centered on these populations, and tout these activities and its existence as evidence of the University's commitment to broadening participation. Its reporting units were the OMAs, a student-centered office that had historically served as a hub of academic and social support services for underrepresented racial/ethnic minority students; a women's center that had historically provided information and support to women undergraduate and graduate students; and as a host to two scholarship programs committed to underserved undergraduate student populations.

The complexities of the task, for us, were complicated by the decentralization of University units, their varied missions and objectives, and the size of the KU community. The Office of D&E managed four direct reporting units and, despite overlapping commitments to equity and inclusion for students and the campus community, each unit operated autonomously with minimal resources and no centrally coordinated long-term planning or assessment. Additionally, in fall 2016, there were approximately 10,000 faculty and staff members, almost 25,000 students, and 13 academic units, including the College of Liberal Arts and Sciences, with over 50 autonomous departments, professional schools, and Undergraduate Studies.

At the start of our leadership, the office had three core staff: Vice Provost, Project Manager, and Administrative Associate. The development of greater cultural competency, equity, and inclusion required that the office personnel work collaboratively with each of the University's 13 academic units as well as service units (e.g., Student Affairs, Undergraduate Studies, etc.) on its two campuses; lead the development of macro-level policies and protocols that create greater equity and an environment of belonging for students, faculty, and staff; communicate effectively and responsively to daily concerns and to issues of diversity and social justice that have historically challenged the quality of University life.

Our vision demanded that we purposely integrate constructs of equity thinking and practices into the everyday facets of recruitment, retention, teaching and learning, support services, development, administrative decision-making, and governance. The Office of the Vice Provost of D&E could lead some of this, but multilayered integration on a decentralized administrative campus would require real collaboration with other administrative units.

Given this, we categorized the scope of our office into two areas: (1) Primary Leadership, or rather efforts led by the Office of D&E; and (2) Collaborative Leadership, or efforts led by other administrative units to which our office provided guidance, consultation, and other forms of involvement on D&E matters. This division of responsibility and labor enabled us to better focus on our mission, maintain focus, and develop and track progression. This framework provided for two important facts: (1) it allowed us to move forward an aggressive agenda that did not wholly depend on the calendars of others and (2) it accounted for the organizationally marginal status of the Office, as one with no authority over lateral peers who might respond with resistance and/or reluctance to recommended initiatives.

Primary Leadership

Primary Leadership were those comprehensive institutional-level goals and related activities that would be developed and led by the Office of D&E to create a more representatively diverse, fair, and inclusive University. These activities would necessarily include collaboration with the Vice Provosts of Academic Affairs, Faculty Development, Human Resources, Integrity and Compliance, Undergraduate Studies, Student Affairs, and other administrative units as appropriate. However, the Office of the Vice Provost for D&E was responsible for implementation, progress, and goal outcomes.

We created two divisions within our Primary Leadership category to further clarify our purpose and capacities: Division I: Educational Enhancement Resources and Campus Community Learning and Engagement; and Division II: Policies, Protocols and Assessment. Division I efforts were those that centered social identities in their respective DEI missions, activities, and programs. At the start of our collective tenure, the Office of D&E managed the Multicultural Scholars Program, Emily Taylor Center for Women and Gender, OMAs, and the Haskell American Indian Nations University Liaison. Within the first three months, the Center for Sexuality and Gender Diversity was configured into the Office structure, followed one year later by the creation of Jayhawk Student One Stop, a crisis support service. We then placed each of these semi-autonomous offices under the leadership umbrella of the OMAs to ensure greater collaboration, sharing of limited resources, and enhanced attention to students' intersectionalities. Broadly, this collective work offered student-focused educational enhancement resources and campus community learning and engagement programs. Within these categories, the campus received micro-level interactive resources to support the successful academic outcomes of marginalized students, especially supplemental learning and support for all students; and public engagement programming that contributed directly to institutional cultural competency for all students, faculty, and staff.

Division II was created to specifically elevate the new focus of D&E on policies, protocols, and assessments as a primary purpose. Emphasis on policies, protocols, and assessment complemented the micro-level activities in Division I, and also encompassed the broader macro-level work of building greater institutional cultural competency. This focus positioned

D&E as the center for comprehensive institutional DEI leadership; and collaboration and guidance for conceptualization, planning, and actions so that we could more holistically integrate representation, equity, and inclusion in learning, work, living, and social university spaces.

Collaborative Leadership

Collaborative Leadership were efforts undertaken in partnership with the College of Liberal Arts and Sciences, professional schools, administrative offices, and KU governance bodies to center DEI in the respective goals and activities of these entities. In this category, deans, directors, governing bodies, and other leaders were responsible for implementation, progress, and goal outcomes. This category acknowledged the structural inability of the central office of D&E to directly mandate actions and plans from leaders outside of its reporting lines. Collaborative Leadership was a strategic tool used to expand responsibility for change across the University. Deans and directors were encouraged to use the central office as a resource for consultation and guidance. Several Schools, for example, sought support and guidance from the Vice Provost Office for D&E as they created diversity committees, strategic diversity plans, and recruitment efforts. These efforts, however, depended on the interest and will of individual leaders and were not tied to budgetary or other incentives beyond perhaps pressure from students, staff, and faculty. Some chose to make few if any efforts toward cultural change, decisions that were enabled by the then current organizational structure.

STEP FIVE: BUY-IN RESTS ON A PRACTICE OF INCLUSION

Each classification of effort, Primary and Collaborative, demanded buy-in as much as possible from lateral peers, faculty, students, and staff. Thus, we spent the first six months communicating with and enlisting commitments and actions from lateral colleagues and campus-wide representatives of varied constituencies. Our requests for support were minimal and generally required no budgetary commitment and they asked leaders, themselves, for very little time. This was important because we did not yet have a clarity on the level of interest or trust lateral leaders held in the office or its leadership and, given the experiences of others in our field, we could not assume that we had 100 percent support.

Yet and still, our conscious practice was to always assume good will and the best of intentions from all campus actors, though we accepted that some may be more culturally competent and informed of equity than others and engage with our work accordingly. We strove to make equity and inclusion a cornerstone of our campus community engagement practices. This orientation to working with others was critical, given that many students, faculty, and staff had expressed distrust in administration and felt of little value to the University.

Our asks from others were in keeping with this worldview. We set regular meetings with elected representatives of the staff, faculty, and student body, and requested that fellow vice provosts assign one delegate to serve as a member of a newly formed DEI advisory group that would meet monthly for one hour. These included Graduate Studies, Undergraduate Studies, Student Affairs, Admissions, Human Resources, Faculty Senate, Office of the Ombudsman, Compliance, and each academic College and School. In these meetings, we were, first and foremost, respectful of participants' time regardless of their rank and title. We also felt strongly that everyone, again regardless of rank and title, offered a significant contribution to our work. Meetings were designated spaces to communicate about our plans and receive invaluable feedback on initiatives and implementations. Members facilitated outreach across the University and participated as an expanded team of consultants, especially to liaisons and others who were spearheading unit-level diversity plans and advisory groups. This committee also allowed for participants to report to our office any significant efforts or issues of concern in their respective units, allowing us to then work with unit leadership to address these issues.

Enhanced Presence and Leadership of Faculty and Staff Identity Group Networks

One of our more critical interventions toward stability and progress focused on those marginalized populations that experienced identity-based harm in almost every sector of University life. These were the students represented by the 2015 multicultural, racial, and ethnic group protests for equity as well as minoritized faculty and staff. The latter were Black, Latina/o, Asian American, Native American, and the Sexuality and Gender Diversity Faculty-Staff Councils. Their purpose was to offer supportive professional and social networks for their respective and overlapping constituencies, a necessity for recruitment and retention within a University that failed to provide a more welcoming and bias-free workplace environment. The stability and activities of each group ebbed and flowed with membership numbers and dues. Up until our leadership, membership rested on dues, and all financial support for sustaining these communities rested on the ability of members to contribute. From our view, it was unfair that these minoritized employees had to assume the burden of (1) creating and organizing activities for a body that mediated the negative aspects of the University environment and (2) paying out of pocket for its existence. We committed to the elevation of these groups by bringing them together as a coalition, providing them with budgets and support for website development, and calling on their service as an advisory body.

STEP SIX: SWIFT, TRANSPARENT PLAN, AND SUCCESSFUL IMPLEMENTATION

Our ability to build and maintain trust and stability depended on our capacity to present a logical plan of action and implement visible steps toward our articulated vision. As a central office, our goals were institutional, though the related tasks were both primary and collaborative.

Our first priority focused on the proportional composition of KU, broken into strategies for faculty/staff and strategies for students. We aimed to establish our commitment to and accountability for growing a faculty, staff, and student composition that is more socially diverse and proportionally representative of U.S. demographics, with particular emphasis on the recruitment and retention of historically underrepresented racial and ethnic minority populations. We recognize that other demographic groups, though historically minoritized, have achieved numerical over-representation among students, faculty, and staff. Nonetheless, university efforts to build DEI will actively integrate the experiences and concerns of this broad range of KU student, faculty, and staff populations, as outlined in Tables 6.1–6.4.

The second priority acknowledged that meaningful progress must not stop at equitable demographic composition. The values of equity and inclusion must be translated into every facet of the campus community and campus operations. We aimed to advance the purposeful integration of social DEI in our workplace and learning policies and practices as well as our everyday campus interactions.

The third and final priority acknowledged that the increased diversity in the demographic composition of our students, faculty, and staff provides all students an opportunity for meaningful learning and engagement with a diversity of others, and with access to varied pedagogical techniques, experiences, and ways of understanding. We aimed to provide students with direct opportunities to enhance their respective undergraduate majors and graduate areas of study through meaningful engagement in DEI activities.

Table 6.1 Priority One: Faculty and Staff Demographic Composition

Strategy	Action Item
Center diversity, equity, and inclusion (DEI) in staff, faculty, and administrative external and internal hires.	1. Create guidelines that more purposefully consider and integrate DEI into hiring steps.
	2. Work collaboratively with Human Resources Management, Faculty Development, University Governance, and others to implement hiring steps into job approval, search, and decision-making processes.
	3. Request membership on University-wide search committees for Diversity & Equity (D&E) staff to serve as subject matter experts.
Foster an active community of expressed care and support for faculty and staff.	1. Create Support Pathway for Faculty and Staff Success and Retention to serve as a point of contact and guidance resource.
	2. Create the Council of Councils, a collaborative social and professional network for recruitment, advancement, and retention of marginalized faculty and staff.
	3. Support the creation of additional councils, including the Women of Color Support Network and International Council.
	4. Facilitate and enhance policies to support more transparent and equitable professional advancement opportunities for staff.
	5. Facilitate the development and enhancement of policies and practices that acknowledge and better support work/life balance.
	6. Collaboratively foster greater community and support for international faculty and staff.
	7. Collaboratively foster greater community and support for non-tenure track faculty.
	8. Collaboratively foster greater community and support for faculty and staff with disabilities.
	9. Establish a committee to address issues of gender inequity in the workplace.

127

Table 6.2 Priority One: Student Body Demographic Composition

Strategy	Action Item
Foster and support activities that enhance recruitment efforts in undergraduate admissions.	1. Foster collaboration and partnership with campus units and local entities to enhance recruitment for greater social diversity.
	2. Engagement with local and regional school districts and community organizations to enhance recruitment of traditionally underrepresented students.
Foster an Active Community of Care and Belonging for undergraduate and graduate students.	1. Develop office and web resource to better support undocumented students.
	2. Reorganize Office of Diversity & Equity (D&E) reporting units for greater collaboration, long-range planning, and enhanced ability to meet students' needs of multiple and intersecting identities.
	3. Reconfigure, expand, and enhance D&E administrative units to better acknowledge and serve the multidimensionality/intersectionality of student identities and experiences.
	4. Advance student opportunities to learn and participate in diversity, equity, and inclusion (DEI)-related events and activities.
	5. Establish a "point of contact" or "one stop" to support the retention and academic success of undergraduate and graduate students to offer guidance to students who are experiencing multiple and simultaneous concerns that, if inadequately addressed, may inhibit their academic degree completion.
	6. Enhance and work collaboratively to better support the successful transition, retention, and academic completion of nontraditional students, such as the following: parenting students, transfer students, students of nontraditional age, part-time students, and students with disabilities.
	7. Strengthen support for LGBTQIA+ students by implementing components of a student profile project. This includes revisions to student identification cards, collection of demographic data, creation of the technical capacity to update name and pronoun across multiple systems, expanding availability of gender-inclusive restrooms and more.
	8. Facilitate and advance campus- and University-wide events for DEI learning, including a focus on mental health and professional development.
	9. Support and advance student and unit-level activities that encourage multicultural student learning and engagement. This includes Graduate Student Social, Graduate Student Welcome, Community Table monthly lunch program, Martin Luther King, Jr. week of events, Indigenous Peoples' Day events, and more.
	10. Work with the University of Kansas Endowment Association to engage current donors and identify new donors to support retention efforts for students.

Table 6.3 Priority Two: Center Social Diversity, Equity, and Inclusion

Strategy	Action Item
Foster trust in the University of Kansas' commitment to greater diversity, equity, and inclusion (DEI)-related learning, understanding, practice, and implementation.	1. Produce and make available an annual report from the Office of Diversity & Equity (D&E). 2. Revise and maintain the D&E website with updated and transparent reports of progress. 3. Develop website clearinghouse of DEI-related activities. 4. Develop communications protocols for social media. 5. Provide clear and consistent communication with campus and leadership on matters of DEI as appropriate.
Build and expand accountability for actions to improve representation, equity, and inclusion in learning, living, and work environments.	1. Develop DEI-related job expectations template language for use in job advertisements/postings and annual reviews of faculty, staff, and administrators. 2. Facilitate and support the development of unit-level strategic plans with clear goals and measurable outcomes related to DEI. 3. Develop guidelines for more purposeful attention to diversity in hiring of faculty, staff, and administrators. 4. Develop unit-level DEI self-assessment tools and facilitate the development of policies that support the integration of these tools in course materials, promotion/tenure/annual reviews, and faculty and staff student evaluations of teaching and services. 5. Measure DEI-related progress at regular intervals by developing and implementing KU Campus Climate Self-Assessment Survey. 6. Create the Campus Equity Implementation Committee (CEIC) to work as part of the Office of D&E to support collaborative efforts, direction, and review of DEI progress. This will serve as a formal communication network to enhance overall communication strategies with campus.
Foster greater institutional cultural competency demonstrated by the ability and willingness of students, staff, faculty, and administrators to understand social differences and respectfully and effectively engage, interact, and support the success of others regardless of those differences.	1. Create an accessible base-line DEI learning/professional development resource for students, faculty, staff, and administrators that offers (a) shared understanding of DEI practices, (b) related expectations, and (c) ongoing resource for faculty/staff professional development. 2. Develop multiple supplemental opportunities to enhance DEI knowledge and skills. Cultural competency is a multilayered process. This step must build upon the previous step and will offer online professional development, workshops, and other opportunities that move University community members and units toward greater multicultural proficiencies.

Table 6.4 Priority Three: More Purposely Prepare Students for an Increasingly Diverse and Global Society

Strategy	Action Step
Direct supplemental student learning.	1. Develop, promote, and maintain a diversity, equity, and inclusion (DEI) clearinghouse calendar of activities that are open to the attendance and participation of students.
	2. Support and advance community building activities that encourage peer-to-peer engagement among a diversity of students. Examples include regular graduate student socials, graduate student cross-disciplinary professional development opportunities, the addition of a peer-to-peer connection component to the Multicultural Scholars Program, Community Table lunches, Martin Luther King, Jr. week of events, and more.
Foster academic curriculum and classroom learning.	1. Foster greater consideration and integration of diversity and inclusion in classroom materials.
	2. Foster greater consideration and integration of inclusive and equitable classroom practices that demonstrate expressed respect and appreciation for social diversity and varied backgrounds and experiences.
	3. Appoint a Director of Academic Inclusion. Establish partnership with the Center for Teaching Excellence to foster greater consideration and integration of diversity and inclusion in expectations of student learning.
	4. Affirm partnership with Haskell Indian Nations University through the Haskell Liaison position.
Create purposeful collaboration with community organizations and businesses to supplement student learning.	1. Create paid student internship program in partnership with the Lawrence Public Library for students who participate in the HawkLink program, which is a retention program for students of color, queer students, and undocumented students.
	2. Create partnership with Ramen Bowls, a local restaurant, to offer the Community Table program monthly, which fosters connections over a free lunch.
	3. Create partnership with the local school district to better serve LGBTQ+ youth in the community. The creation of a queer youth group also provides University of Kansas students with volunteer mentoring experience.

LOOKING BACK AND LOOKING FORWARD

Education remains the best means of social mobility within U.S. society. Movement upward and accessing the ability to realize one's potential is most critical for those most marginalized by low socioeconomic backgrounds, first-generation status, historically underrepresented racial/ethnic minority categories, disabilities, and other intersecting identities. While the demand for higher education learning and work environments swells, university administrators remain reluctant to change accordingly.

At the KU, our two-year set of accomplishments provided a strong foundation for change, but alone they were more a promise than a transformational moment. Much of what was accomplished was via our Primary Leadership efforts. Our ability to effectively and directly integrate equity and inclusion into the practices of lateral colleagues was a challenge that essentially functioned as an accepted understanding. Lateral colleagues did their best to manage their respective portfolios, but there was little budgetary impetus or other incentive to upset the status quo. Our domain, and that of others, was clear and, from our view, our Collaborative Approach in many ways supported the territoriality that sometimes defined how we were received by peer offices. At the same time, it protected us from significant backlash and gave us space to move forward and implement major initiatives with little public concern. In the end, we simply did not have the authority, funding, or leadership support to create the organization to which we strived.

Nonetheless, students, faculty, and staff could see and participate in activities that supported the ideal of DEI, but these activities did not create DEI. For this to happen, the University leadership team (in the case of Kansas, these are vice provosts) as a whole would need to work intentionally and collaboratively to incorporate and integrate what was offered. In terms of student demographics, for example, we could suggest that greater attention should be made by the leadership team of admissions to recruit broadly, with an expanded definition of student excellence, culturally competent recruiters, and the designation of a well-staffed office to follow underrepresented student applicants from middle school through the first year of college enrollment.

However, such an effort might fail regardless should the Office of Student Affairs fail to adequately orient and prepare a predominantly white, cisgender, male-accommodating student body for the social differences that they will encounter in residence halls, recreational facilities, and classrooms. Undergraduate and Graduate Studies, Faculty and Academic Affairs and Deans too, would need to hold advisors, unit heads and supervisors, staff, and faculty accountable for developing culturally competent literacies and pedagogical learning. Of course, provosts, chancellors, and presidents must be brave enough to demand cultural transformation from their cabinets and leadership teams, prioritize resources in this area, and meaningfully hold their employees accountable when they do not meet expectations, of which the successful outcome of students is the principal goal.

The "Me Too," "Black Lives Matter," and "Defund the Police" movements elevated attention to diversity on university campuses and calls for greater equity. Aspects of these movements made more glaring the disparate impact of the Covid-19 pandemic on the most vulnerable U.S. populations (Godoy & Wood, 2020), a health crisis further fueled by an incoherent and right-wing federal response. Months of racial protests in 2020, letters to the editor, and social media posts demonstrated the declining level of tolerance for racist, sexist, heterosexist, and other culturally incompetent and problematic behaviors performed by white men and women, in particular, regardless of their stature. In the wake of spring 2020 protests in opposition to police brutality against Black and Brown bodies, many private sector business and corporations such as Reebok, Nordstrom, Warner Media, the National Football League, NASCAR, Ben & Jerry's ice cream, and YouTube swiftly acted to adjust their images in solidarity (Cadeaux, 2020; Hsu, 2020; NASCAR, 2020). Universities responded in much the same way as they had prior to 2020, with an acknowledgment that racism exists and that more must be done to create equality (Hadden, 2020). In other words, there seems no genuine effort from university upper administrators to change the practices or policies that maintain predominantly white, cisgender, male-centered campuses as they are.

Almost two decades have passed since Williams (2006a) argued that there are seven "Brutal Facts" descriptive of university and college organizational cultures that impede the ability of these institutions to realize transformative change in the area of diversity, most of which characterized our experiences:

1. Failure to conceptualize diversity work in terms of organizational change and shifting the institutional culture;
2. Resistance to the logic that diversity is fundamental to institutional excellence;
3. Low levels of meaningful and consistent support from senior leadership;
4. Failure to allocate sufficient resources to the process of change;

5. Lack of a comprehensive and widely accepted framework to define diversity and track progress;
6. Lack of accountability systems and means of getting individuals engaged in the change process at all levels; and
7. Lack of leadership and infrastructure to guide and facilitate the change journey and provide leadership to campus diversity efforts at all levels of the institution (pp. 2–3).

What we have learned through our engagement with diversity professional colleagues at professional meetings and other gatherings is that many diversity leaders share many common experiences, regardless of the size of their operating budget or office staff. First among these are (1) matters of DEI are historical and pervasive on predominantly white campuses; there are few if any campus sites in which their negative consequences are not embedded, (2) a reluctance for meaningful change seems to best characterize the actions that university leaders, faculty, and staff are prepared to devote to transformation, and (3) we must continue to learn from one another toward this "ideal" we call DEI in higher education. To that, we as coauthors, hope that this chapter offers some support.

REFERENCES

Cadeaux, E. (2020, June 5). *Roger Goodell releases statement condemning racism, admits NFL was wrong not listening to players.* NBC Sports. https://www.nbcsports.com/washington/redskins/roger-goodell-releases-statement-condemning-racism-admits-nfl-was-wrong-not-listening

Cantor, D., Fisher, B., Chibnall, S., Townsend, R., Lee, H., Bruce, C., & Thomas, G. (2015). *Report on the AAU campus climate survey on sexual assault and sexual misconduct.* American Association of Universities. https://www.aau.edu/sites/default/files/%40%20Files/Climate%20Survey/AAU_Campus_Climate_Survey_12_14_15.pdf

Cooper, R. (2009). Constructing belonging in a diverse campus community. *Journal of College and Character*, 10(3), 1–10.

Cunliffe, A. L., & Jun, S. J. (2005). The need for reflexivity in public administration. *Administration & Society*, 37(2), 225–242.

Diamond, R. (2006, September 8). *Why colleges are so hard to change.* Inside Higher Ed. https://www.insidehighered.com/views/2006/09/08/why-colleges-are-so-hard-change

Dickey, J. (2016, May 31). The revolution on America's campuses. *Time*. https://time.com/4347099/college-campus-protests/

Espinosa, L. L., Turk, J. M., Taylor, M., & Chessman, H. M. (2019). *Race and ethnicity in higher education: A status report*. American Council on Education, The Andrew W. Mellon Foundation. https://www.acenet.edu/Research-Insights/Pages/Race-and-Ethnicity-in-Higher-Education.aspx

Federal Bureau of Investigation. (2014). *2014 hate crime statistics*. https://ucr.fbi.gov/hate-crime/2014/tables/table-1

Flinn, A. (2015, November 11). *After town hall meeting, student senate rights committee passes two resolutions in support of Rock Chalk Invisible Hawk demands*. University Daily Kansan. https://www.kansan.com/news/after-town-hall-meeting-student-senate-rights-committee-passes-two-resolutions-in-support-of-rock/article_7aa0a850-88f9-11e5-8745-b37aae692d93.html

Godoy, M., & Wood, D. (2020, May 30). *What do Coronavirus racial disparities look like by state?* NPR. https://www.npr.org/*sections*/health-shots/2020/05/30/865413079/what-do-coronavirus-racial-disparities-look-like-state-by-state

Hadden, J. (2020, June 25). *How the top 25 colleges and universities in the US are responding to the Black Lives Matter protests*. Business Insider. https://www.businessinsider.com/college-top-us-universities-respond-*black*-lives-matter-protests-2020-6

Hamer, J. (2016). *Taking leadership on who and what matters: The plan to build a more diverse, equitable, and inclusive College of Liberal Arts & Sciences*. University of Kansas College of Liberal Arts & Sciences. https://college.ku.edu/sites/college.ku.edu/files/docs/About/COLLEGE_DEI_PLAN_Fall_2016.pdf

Hamer, J. (2018). *Forward together: A plan for a more socially diverse, equitable, and inclusive KU*. University of Kansas Office of Diversity & Equity.

Heidegger, M. (1966). *Discourse on thinking*. Harper & Row.

Hsu, T. (2020, May 31). *Corporate voices get behind 'Black Lives Matter' cause*. New York Times. https://www.nytimes.com/2020/05/31/business/media/companies-marketing-*black*-lives-matter-george-floyd.html

Kite, A., & Mitchell, C. (2015, November 13). *KU chancellor, university departments, senate presidents and student groups respond to campus discussions of racism and discrimination*. University Daily Kansan. https://www.kansan.com/news/ku-chancellor-university-departments-senate-presidents-and-student-groups-respond-to-campus-discussions-of-racism/article_4a38b390-8a31-11e5-9703-fbdbf10b08fe.html

Korte, L. (2015, November 24). *KU announces creation of diversity, equity, and inclusion advisory group*. University Daily Kansan. https://www.kansan.com/news/ku-announces-creation-of-diversity-equity-and-inclusion-advisory-group/article_481e1dea-92ea-11e5-944e-c31ca52baaf4.html

Korte, L., & Ritter, C. (2015, November 11). *KU community, along with Rock Chalk Invisible Hawk, demands a better response to racism on campus at town hall meeting.* University Daily Kansan. https://www.kansan.com/news/ku-community-along-with-rock-chalk-invisible-hawk-demands-a-better-response-to-racism-on/article_9f353054-88ff-11e5-a759-839af21a7fa0.html

Lang, C., Zenger, S., Bendapudi, N., Childress, T., Gómez Montoya, M., Hampton, J., James, L., Ng, J., Portillo, S., Wadud, I., Williams, M., & Zabel, T. (2016). *Report of the diversity, equity and inclusion advisory committee.* University of Kansas Diversity, Equity and Inclusion Advisory Committee. https://splh.ku.edu/sites/splh.drupal.ku.edu/files/files/DEIAdvisory-2016FINAL.pdf

Leon, R. A. (2014). The Chief Diversity Officer: An examination of CDO models and strategies. *Journal of Diversity in Higher Education, 7*(2), 77–91.

Marken, S. (2015, October 28). *Graduates exposed to diversity believe degree more valuable.* Gallup News. https://news.gallup.com/poll/186257/graduates-exposed-diversity-believe-degree-valuable.aspx

NASCAR. (2020, June 10). *NASCAR statement on confederate flag.* NASCAR. https://www.nascar.com/news-media/2020/06/10/nascar-statement-on-confederate-flag/

Osei, C. (2015, November 12). Letter to the editor: Silence of administrators, faculty and staff at town hall meeting is disgraceful. *The University Daily Kansan.* https://www.kansan.com/opinion/letter-to-the-editor-silence-of-administrators-faculty-and-staff/article_695383e6-896d-11e5-9c4a-671e58aa6043.html

Rankin and Associates. (2017). *The University of Kansas Lawrence & Edwards campuses campus climate research study.* https://climatestudy.ku.edu

Ritter, C., & Korte, L. (2015, November 22). A breakdown of Rock Chalk Invisible Hawk's 15 demands for KU. *The University Daily Kansan.* http://www.kansan.com/news/a-breakdown-of-rock-chalkinvisible-hawk-s-demands-for/article_795a7ef4-9172-11e5-846d-635fdd9d5955.html

Smith, D. G. (2015). *Diversity's promise for higher education: Making it work.* Johns Hopkins University Press.

Swaine, J., Laughland, O., Lartey, J., & McCarthy, C. (2015, December 31). *Young black men killed by US police at highest rate in year of 1,134 deaths.* The Guardian. https://www.theguardian.com/us-news/2015/dec/31/the-counted-police-killings-2015-young-*black*-men

University of Kansas Office of Analytics and Institutional Research. (2016a). *Faculty and staff at a glance* [Interactive factbook]. https://air.ku.edu/interactive_factbook/faculty-and-staff

University of Kansas Office of Analytics and Institutional Research. (2016b). *Kansas Board of Regents enrollment reports spring 2016: University of*

Kansas, student demographics report. https://air.ku.edu/sites/air.ku.edu/files/files/EnrollmentReports/KBOR_Enrollment_Rpt_KULC_4162.pdf

U.S. Department of Education. (2013, September 27). *New guidance supports voluntary use of race to achieve diversity in higher education* [Press release]. https://www.ed.gov/news/press-releases/new-guidance-supports-voluntary-use-race-achieve-diversity-higher-education

Williams, D. (2006a). Overcoming the brutal facts: Building and implementing a relentless diversity change process. *The Diversity Factor*, 14(4), 10–18.

Williams, D. (2006b). *Strategic diversity leadership: Activating change and transformation in higher education.* Stylus Publications.

Williams, D. A., & Wade-Golden, K. C. (2013). *The chief diversity officer: Strategy structure, and change management.* Stylus Publishing.

Worthington, R. L., Stanley, C. A., & Lewis Sr., W. T. (2014). National association of diversity officers in higher education standards of professional practice for chief diversity officers. *Journal of Diversity in Higher Education*, 7(4), 227–234.

Ziegert, J. C., & Hanges, P. J. (2005). Employment discrimination: The role of implicit attitudes, motivation, and a climate for racial bias. *Journal of Applied Psychology*, 9(3), 553–562.

Chapter Seven

Navigating Social Location and Identity as Transformative Praxis for Higher Education Diversity Administrators

Which Hat Do I Wear Now?

Bennyce E. Hamilton and
Kelley C. Kimple

Diversity work is not for the faint of heart. At institutions of higher education, the challenge often becomes more about how we learn to navigate, across the institution, with our colleagues and with our students. Diversity administrators are expected to support the mission, vision, and values of the institution (administrator hat) while simultaneously responding to the needs of students who feel marginalized (diversity hat). Sometimes there is a lack of trust which creates a chasm, and the diversity administrator must be the bridge builder (diplomacy hat). This pleads the question, "Which hat do I wear as the diversity administrator?"

If you ask a group of higher education diversity administrators that question, the answers would vary. Some responses might be based on our experience in the field, our ability to navigate and negotiate, the institution's size, or whether the institution is public or private. Other responses might be more personalized, based on the administrator's gender, gender

DOI: 10.4324/9781003008521-10

identity, sexuality, race, and/or other indicators of acculturation. Based on discussions with and observations of Diversity Administrators, our lived experiences shape the ways in which we view the world and "the hat we wear." More importantly, our lived experiences structure our interactions with others.

This chapter looks at the lived experiences of two higher education diversity administrators as exemplified through our identities, social location, and praxis as a prelude to becoming transformative higher education diversity administrators.

BENNYCE'S STORY

I am a Black, female, Black feminist, American Association of Retired Persons (AARP) eligible, teacher, educator, and administrator. I have not always embraced the myriad facets of my identity equally, in part because I did not fully know who I was, in part because I have had the opportunity to try on a few "hats." At this stage of my development, that haberdashery is who I am now and how I go about my work as a higher education diversity administrator. At this stage, I get to share some of the experiences that have shaped my work. Nikki Giovanni (2012) says, "Once you know who you are, you don't have to worry anymore." There is so much power in that simple statement. However, knowing who you are is not so simple. Who I am as a higher education diversity administrator is the result of the many proverbial "forks in the road," or stories that I have lived, in preparation for this career.

I use my story to empower, revitalize, and bring to light my search for and acceptance of self and the growth necessary for such. My story is a story of evolving, of becoming, of transforming. It utilizes the tenets of autoethnography as the means to understand myself through identity, cultural relevance, and feminist epistemologies. Autoethnography places self at the center of cultural analysis and "transcends mere narration of self to engage in cultural analysis and interpretation" (Chang, 2008).

Rodriguez (2001) proclaims that when Black women are given the opportunity to express themselves and offer insight, it reinforces the notion of the value of Black women's lives. This belief in the inherent value of Black women's lives is a guiding principle of Black feminist thought. That principle is embodied in this chapter. Further, Hamilton (2008) says, "it is the sum of our own lived experiences, and how those experiences are utilized and shaped in our interactions with students, who have *their own* lived experiences, that determine our outcomes." Women of color (WOC) particularly and Black women specifically, who are higher education diversity administrators, must learn to recognize, understand, negotiate, incorporate, and navigate our identities and social location as an inherent component to our success.

My lived experiences have shaped my identity and the ways in which I work as a diversity administrator. Identity is more deeply rooted than just my name, my race, the people that I am associated with, or the groups to which I belong. It extends to my beliefs, morals, values, and behavior. Identity has been defined in a number of ways. It is viewed as the foundation for how we view ourselves, our future prospects, and how we make meaning of lived experiences (Swanson et al., 2009) or the thing that separates us as individuals (Steele, 2010). Our lived experiences, then, become the proverbial foundation upon which we are built. Below I organize my story by sharing a few pivotal "lived experiences" as a way of demonstrating factors that I bring to bear in how I function as a diversity administrator. From my community, I learned othermothering. From my grade school, I learned to strategize against those who would seek to undermine my progress. From my high school, I learned to shift my identity, to blend and fit in. From my early professional career, I learned to negotiate, validate, and accept my identities.

I grew up in a house with my grandmother, mother, and older sister. My parents divorced when I was about four years old. I was also surrounded by many women (othermothers) in my neighborhood. There was Mama Mae, Mama Minnie, Aunt Willa, Mama Taylor, Aunt Hazel (my Godmother), Aunt Mary, Grandmother Thompson, Aunt Necia, Aunt Jackee, and Aunt Wanda to name a few. Each of these women was significant in my upbringing. They were my "in loco parentis" or "othermothers." Guiffrida (2005) defines "othermothering" as accepting responsibility for a child or children that are not one's own, through a formal or informal arrangement. Othermothering is a key component of Black Feminist Thought. Little did I know that I was being groomed to become a Black feminist well before the term even existed. Othermothering is also germane to education and in this case, higher education, because it goes beyond academic skill acquisition (Hamilton, 2008). Othermothering influences how we, as higher education diversity administrators, interact with the students with whom we come in contact. On numerous occasions, a student in need has walked into my office to tell me about an issue that they were having with financial aid or registration. Sometimes students have complaints about professors that they cannot contact or that they feel have mistreated them in class. More often than not a student will come in to talk about a personal issue related to home. In each of these instances, I become the "othermother," imparting wisdom, or walking a student over to the financial aid office, or giving them advice about how to talk with a parent, a professor, or a significant other.

While I always knew that I was Black, I had to learn from school experiences that my Blackness was problematic for some. I grew up in Kentucky at a time when the Civil Rights Movement was in full swing. I was sheltered from most of the struggle, but its effects were omnipresent. I was surrounded by Black people. My neighborhood was predominately Black. I had attended an all-Black elementary school (except for a few teachers) until fifth grade. Prior to "mandatory" bussing in 1971, my mother had already decided to send me to a school in a predominantly white neighborhood so that I could have more educational opportunities. All of the students at my predominately Black school were given a choice to attend any other elementary school in my hometown. My mother and my best friend's mother decided to send us to the elementary school in the neighborhood adjacent to ours. There were five Black students in the entire school. My only problem in this new school was with the school bully. He was a tall, red-haired, freckle-faced white kid. He never called me racialized names, but out of view of the teacher, he would kick and punch me. After a few weeks of his abuse, I yelled out for him to stop and was punished by my teacher for being disruptive. He, however, was not punished. I did not recognize it at the time, but this was part of the unrecognized, racialized, hyper-criminalization of Black students.

He finally stopped picking on me when I proved to be a better playground athlete. I was surrounded by my classmates who all wanted me on their team. I also won the fifth grade spelling bees which made my teachers pay attention. I was adjusting to my circumstances and educational environment. As a fifth grader, athleticism became my bargaining chip – my currency. I was learning to navigate, negotiate, and strategize. These three tools are a necessity for the higher education diversity administrator. In a recent study of Chief Diversity Officers, Coopwood and Lewis (2017) found that Black Administrators "often find themselves perceived by things that they cannot control like age, race, gender, and ethnicity. When we enter a room, those detectable pieces enter along with us." Those who are new to the field of diversity administration face the challenge of fitting in to the existing campus culture as well as "the unwritten rules that surface after hiring that confound the administrator's progress" (p. 4). Coopwood and Lewis (2017) refer to this phenomenon as "shadow culture." Knowing who we are helps to combat the effects of this phenomenon.

By the time I got to high school, I better understood how my "Blackness" was a quality that caused me to be perceived as different. The first time I became aware of this was at my predominately white elementary school. The next two instances took place in high school. I had become very used to being in mostly white spaces. I had white friends and Black friends and was invited to the white kids' parties and the Black kids' parties. I played basketball in high school and our team was half Black and half white. After a scoring play, I reached up to give a white teammate a high five. Immediately afterward, she wiped her hand on her shorts. I began to pay attention after that. I realized that she only "wiped" after a Black player touched her hands. The third instance was during a conversation with a white classmate at the same high school. It was about the "n-word." I told her that I hated the word and that it was not used in my household. She could not understand why I did not use the word and thought it was funny to say it repeatedly as if it was a word that was used often in her home. The fourth instance was in college. I attended a historically Black college and during my freshman year, a Black classmate told me that she could not believe that I attended a historically Black college because she heard that I did not "hang out with Black people." I was taken aback by the comment. I thought that I would not have to worry about "my Blackness" at a Black College. What I recognized was this: I was never going to be white in white spaces but I was often not Black enough in Black spaces. Sue and Sue (2013) created a racial and cultural identity development (RCID) model that addresses this experience. RCID happens in five stages:

1. Conformity, in which individuals of color identify with white culture and internalize negative stereotypes about their own culture;
2. Dissonance, in which their experiences contradict their white worldview and they begin to question the dominant culture and explore their own;
3. Resistance and Immersion, in which individuals reject white culture and immerse themselves in their own culture;
4. Introspection, in which they struggle to find a balance between the dominant culture and their own; and
5. Synergistic Articulation and Awareness, in which they integrate their own cultural heritage and knowledge to form an identity based on self-acceptance that balances racial/cultural identity with other aspects of self (Sue & Sue, 2013, p. 297).

Our lived experiences teach us how to navigate spaces based upon race and exposure to a variety of different cultures (Collins, 2009). However, sociologists tell us that social location helps us establish and reveal our identity to others. It determines where individuals stand in their community. Navigating my social location in these spaces was often challenging and required some navigation. Jones and Shorter-Gooden (2003) refer to this behavior as "shifting." Shifting is the behavior(s) that Black women undertake when faced with bias, but it also occurs when we fight back. Throughout my four years of undergrad, shifting (resistance or "fighting back") for me meant learning to use my voice. I became a member of our theater group, I participated in national political campaigning, and spoke out more in my courses. Deciding how to express oneself and when it's even wise or safe to say anything is at the heart of shifting, because what you say and how you say it is often the first and most important way that other people size you up (p. 95).

Shifting was a skill that I learned to master after college. A few years after graduating, I worked for a major Midwestern city's fire department with about 750 professional firefighters. I spent the first ten years of my career learning the fire department's organizational culture and constructing my social location within it. In higher education, learning the organizational culture is one of many "rites of passage," according to Phyllis Green (1997). Green further explains that there are four values associated with an organization's culture that serve to help or hinder women (administrators) depending upon how they are used. They are collegiality, institutional memory, merit, and "a good fit." During years 10–15 on the fire department I gained a great deal of institutional memory and created some as well. There was collegiality with many of the women and some of the men that I worked with. What I found to be troubling was that after 15 years, I still had to prove my merit, and realized that perhaps the fire service was not such "a good fit" for me. I invested in my education and remained a firefighter until retirement at 25 years. "Shifting" became a coping mechanism while preparing me for what was next – higher education.

Higher education diversity administrators emerge from a variety of backgrounds. Some enter from faculty ranks while others come from business and industry. Significantly few come from non-traditional routes like teaching High School English, blue-collar employment, or post-retirement. I took a non-traditional route and was in this significant minority. I taught English at a Vocational High School for 11th and 12th grade students where many of my students came from marginalized backgrounds, including but not limited to race. My social location as a Black woman in a community of men (mostly white) made me sensitive to the politics of race, gender, and hyper-masculinity that were pervasive on the fire department. Both of these experiences – teaching and firefighting – would prove valuable and impact my leadership as a diversity administrator.

Teaching allowed me to work with students who came from marginalized backgrounds that included race, social class, and sexual identity. Firefighting gave me firsthand knowledge about organizational politics and organizational culture. Firefighting also made me hunger for knowledge about equity and inclusion.

In 2008, I earned my doctorate in education and tried, without success, to attain a teaching position in the academy. In 2012, I applied to be Director of Multicultural Affairs at a small, private institution in the Midwest. I got the job and remained there for three years. During that time, my supervisor was the Vice President of Student Affairs and Dean of Students who was also a Black woman. There were three Black administrators at this institution, including the two of us, and no faculty members of color. My job duties included a myriad of aspects of student affairs such as connecting with students of color, programming, and advising the Black student organization. I met key stakeholders across the institution, including the newly elected officers of the Black student organization, as well as my predecessor who had been in the position for 19 years before moving into another role. It did not take long to figure out the power brokers, including those who no longer worked at the institution. Every time I introduced a new program, my ideas were met with resistance and comments like "we don't do it that way" or "we like it the old way." I introduced a pre-graduation program that incorporated traditions from our African roots, a program which was both culturally enriching and culturally relevant. An hour before the ceremony, I was still chasing down students to participate. It was clear that I had not fully learned or understood the finer points of the campus culture, and I needed a mentor. This experience taught me more than anything that diversity work requires more than just a leadership approach steeped in activism. I came from an environment (public service) that taught me to speak up or be pushed aside. I wanted my students to be activists, taking charge of their own cultural, political, and social empowerment. Diversity administrators must have more than one approach ("hat") in their leadership closet to be effective and transformative.

I have been a higher education diversity administrator for nine years. This career path was not something that I considered prior to taking my first job in the field. I tried on many "hats," so to speak. My role in higher education gave me the opportunity to teach a number of courses related to diversity. I created and taught a course called Women and Social Change and I currently teach a course related to the strength of cultural diversity. Teaching gives you an interesting perspective. Inside the classroom, I am the diversity content expert. Outside the classroom, I become the educator, utilizing lessons from my experiences. I become the "othermother," the mentor, and the bridge builder.

I have learned to lead through the lessons of my lived experiences. Not only do I have my lived experiences of being a Black, female, Black feminist, AARP eligible, teacher, educator, and administrator, but I also have the capacity to prioritize, the bandwidth to dialogue with faculty, staff, students, and community stakeholders, and the experience, knowledge, and wisdom that comes from having mentors. It is important to point out here that the most seasoned diversity administrator is set to fail if she does not know the culture of the organization. One of my mentors gave me some sound advice during my first year at my current institution. She said, "The first year, you listen. The second year you formulate a plan of action. The third year you work your plan. Year four, you improve your plan, and year five, you start all over." I am in year five and that advice has been sound. I have learned the culture of the organization and in so doing, developed relationships with faculty and staff throughout the institutional hierarchy (including the physical facilities staff). I created a program that highlights our faculty and their interests. Often these are interests outside their academic discipline. Faculty, staff, and students participate weekly. Because I built the "bridge," faculty contacts me to participate. This is how I identify, support, and promote diversity across the campus and through the campus stakeholders.

Utilizing theory from my background as a teacher and educator, I wanted to model the campus multicultural center using the conceptual framework that recognizes the importance of including students' cultural backgrounds, interests, and lived experiences (Ladson-Billings, 2014; Milner, 2017; Gay, 2018). My Center exhibits art from a variety of cultures, my student associates welcome those who enter and offer pleasantries to those who leave. We are situated in a space that is a "cut through" space. Students, faculty, staff, and visitors cut through to get to other parts of the building or to ask for directions. There are various stations, including a cozy seating area where students can converse and relax, chairs and tables for studying, a resource room with computers, display cabinets for cultural artifacts, and an art gallery where student art is displayed. Culturally relevant education is regarded as critical in improving student engagement, achievement, college readiness, and success (Knight-Manuel & Marciano, 2018). My Center is inclusive of the students, faculty, staff, and community that I serve. The work necessary to become a transformative practitioner is ongoing.

Hamilton (2008) introduced us to "reflexive culturally relevant pedagogy." Reflexive culturally relevant pedagogy (RCRP), which focuses on the student, extends the work of Ladson-Billings and Milner. Hamilton's work focuses on the personal – who we are inside the work that we do. Reflection on our own perceptions, beliefs, experiences, and practices is a core activity for all teachers – pre-service and in-service, in schools and in universities. Outwardly challenging ideas that one holds dear is not always comfortable, but as a practice, this challenge serves to affirm as well as to confront existing perspectives (Walkington, 2005). RCRP then becomes a means of self-improvement, recognition, and affirmation of self and the nuanced privileges that come with said recognition.

Audre Lorde (1988) reminded us that acknowledging privilege is the first step in making it available for a person's wider use. Each one of us is blessed in some particular way, whether we recognize our blessings or not. And each one of us, somewhere in our lives must clear a space within that blessing where she can call upon whatever resources are available to her in the name of something that must be done. If one Black woman whom I do not know gains hope from my story, then it has been worth the difficulty of telling.

It is not just that I am a woman or Black or feminist, or an experienced diversity administrator. Instead, it is all of those identities coupled with my lived experiences that make my work as a higher education diversity administrator transformative praxis. In order for a Black woman diversity administrator to implement transformative praxis, she must have the requisite wisdom and knowledge about race, gender, and class. Most importantly, she must know who she is and how her social location affects power and privilege.

KELLEY'S STORY

I was a little Black girl growing up and attending school from first grade to eighth grade in a predominantly white neighborhood yet still spending a substantial amount of time with extended family and friends in predominantly Black neighborhoods. Similar to my co-author's experience in her primary school environment, in elementary school I was either the only Black person, one of two Black children, or one of two students of color in my grade level. Thankfully my parents intentionally made sure I had a Black community to connect with others who looked like me and learn from. They understood the importance of representation and how it would shape the way I saw myself. Dr. Beverly Tatum uses Cross's Nigrescence Model to discuss that Black children who don't have positive cultural images of those who look like them can start to believe and adopt the notion that the dominant white culture is the best (2017). I was fully aware I was Black, but it seemed my white classmates didn't realize it until the third grade when some of them started to treat me differently in a negative way due to my race.

Growing up, I received the good, bad, and ugly actions and behaviors from people of various races and ethnicities. The bulk of my community of Black people consisted of my large extended family and friends who lived in my maternal grandmother's inner city neighborhood. On one hand, I had Black people who questioned why I talked "white" and called me an "oreo" (Black on the outside and white on the inside). Then, however, I was thankful to have Black people who simply accepted me for who I was; they realized it wasn't their place to say whether or not someone is "Black enough." Why was my Blackness in question? Why is speaking proper English considered "talking white?" It was bad enough I had to deal with the racist mindset and attitude of the people in the neighborhood I lived in, but then it was even worse when the people within my same racial identity group, a group that was also considered my refuge, talked about me. It made me start to question, "Where do I fit in or belong?"

It's amazing how my co-author and I both, even with a ten+-year age gap, dealt with people questioning our Blackness because we were different from what they considered to be Black. Society must understand that while people are categorized within groups based on our skin color and culture, this does not mean we are a monolithic group of people. The diversity of our personalities, physical features, and upbringings enhances who we are, and it does not diminish us to whom others think we should be. One of the most important elements of being a diversity practitioner is understanding all aspects of your identity, as it makes it easier to assist people to understand their own and those around them.

Even as a child, I was someone who had the ability to get along with a diverse group of people because I accepted them for who they were, not who I believed they needed to be, because that's how I wanted to be treated. This mindset allowed me the opportunity to be exposed to a variety of experiences and people I might not otherwise have had the chance to enjoy and build relationships. In being open-minded, I found myself having the ability to serve as a bridge between different identity groups and communities I engaged with on a regular basis. While I had to endure some internal battle scars to get here, I believe it was all a part of the plan toward my destiny.

Once my older sister was born, my parents believed that in order to provide their children with good school options and a safe living environment they could afford, they needed to live in a predominantly white neighborhood because that's where most of the good schools, outside of private schools, were located and crime was low. I personally believe their willingness to take that chance influenced the trajectory of my life. Being present in what at times felt like completely different worlds, I learned how to observe and navigate those spaces hopefully to get the best results. For me, the best results consisted of seeking to understand before looking to be understood. I had been studying people to understand why they do what they do well before getting my degree in sociology. This is a key factor in the core of who I am, especially when it comes to being a diversity professional.

My grandparents, aunts, uncles, and cousins played a huge role in my upbringing. My aunts took turns watching each other's children, which meant I spent a lot of time with my cousins. I truly saw my aunts as an extension of my Mama. Our family embodied the notion that it takes a village to raise a child. Many of the students on our campuses view the Black faculty and staff who have shown they care for their well-being as an extension of their families. Once we have built a level of trust with them, they seek us out for advice and/or a shoulder to cry on about whatever is going on in their lives, from academics to personal issues.

Countless people within the Black community have historically taken on the role of *in loco parentis*, meaning in the place of a parent. Whether you are blood relative or not, you look out for each other as if you were. This mentality helped many of our communities to thrive and keep each other safe. Research on the structure of Black families attributes the village configuration to how African tribes heavily involved and revered the elders of their communities. Other researchers connect this practice to slavery when families were sold to different plantations and they created their own extended families among the other slaves to have a sense of community (Strmic-Pawl & Leffler, 2011). While I believe this role is truly beneficial and necessary to assist our Black students on campus, many in leadership as well as those from different racial and ethnic identities don't always see the value it brings to campuses, especially at predominantly white institutions. Therefore, if they don't value this cultural component of what many Black staff and faculty members bring to these campuses, then they also won't recognize the additional emotional labor we endure on top of our already demanding roles and positions. "Feelings of isolation for African American professionals on predominantly white campuses can be stressful. African Americans are often called on to work with students of color on campus which can prove to be both physically and emotionally demanding" (Gardner, Barrett, & Pearson, 2014, pp. 240–241).

Before the end of eighth grade, there was a racial fight between the white and Black juniors and seniors at my junior high/high school. This issue caused my Mama to seek out other high school opportunities for me and gave me information about new magnet high schools opening up in the city. I was excited about the new experience and eager to cut out as many potential encounters of racism I could. Another exciting component of this change is that I would actually be attending high school in the same building my Mama, Daddy, Godmother, and many of their friends attended as well.

My surroundings dramatically changed as I went from being at predominately white schools for the majority of my schooling up to the eighth grade, to attending a predominantly Black high school. This was the first time in my educational journey that the majority of my teachers and classmates were Black. Being Black in this space felt different from my predominantly white schools, because I didn't feel like I had to do as much code-switching. "Code-switching could be characterized as the ability to adapt one's behavior as a response to a change in social context much like bilingual speakers switch languages in response to a change in linguistic context" (Morton, 2014, p. 1). During high school, I truly started to understand the various aspects of my blackness and to own it with no apology. This portion of my life's journey was another pivotal moment in shaping my identity, a moment that I truly enjoyed.

Similar to many of my friends in high school, I wanted to attend one of the historically Black colleges and universities (HBCUs), and accomplish yet another thing my mother had done. However, I attended a medium-sized, predominantly white institution in the Midwest a few hours away from home. The upper-class Black students at my institution continued demonstrating the practice of creating community as they understood the importance of family, especially in a new space. When members of my freshman class and I joined the Coalition of Black Students, we were paired with one upper-class student with a similar major and they became our big sister/big brother. From these relationships, I was asked to serve on the Executive Board of the Coalition of Black Students as the Historian/Curator, a role I held until my junior year. I was heavily involved in student leadership in a few organizations and enjoyed building community with my friends and peers.

In college, I was also blessed to build relationships with some amazing staff and faculty members from various racial and ethnic backgrounds. When I was struggling in my genetics course, the professor helped me by reaching out to our Associate Provost expressing her concerns. My professor understood I needed someone I already had a relationship with and who looked like me to provide the empowerment I needed to make it over this hurdle. Our Associate Provost was a short Black woman, who was also an Alumna of our institution; she was sweet, intelligent, and did not play. She took time to help me map out the next steps I needed to take, even considering changing my major from biology to something more suitable for me, and she directed me to write out every hour of the day for a week to schedule time for everything I needed to do. The Associate Provost was one of the first staff members to help get me together. She called in the advisor of one of my student organization as reinforcement – the Director of Multicultural Activities. She was another Black woman who wasn't cutting us any slack and who expected excellence. While the Director of Multicultural Activities came at me with the tough love approach and the Associate Provost had a more gentle yet stern and loving approach, both were necessary to help me recognize I needed to make some changes in order to be successful in the classroom and graduate from college. This was the moment I knew I wanted to be able to do for future college students what they both did for me. I am especially committed to help those who represent historically underrepresented identities.

My journey through Student Affairs, from graduate school, where I worked full time as a Residence Hall Director while going to school part time, to my previous position as the Director of a diversity and inclusion center, provided me with different levels of power and authority. Through this process, I also had to recognize how, at times, the levels of power and authority were more related to intersecting identities, particularly race and gender, than to the actual job position.

> In 1986, Patricia Hill Collins "described the marginalized and isolated status of African American women in various professional and academic settings as the 'outsider-within'" (p. S14). Howard-Hamilton (2003) relied on the term coined by Collins and noted that African American women in higher education "have been invited into places where the dominant group has assembled, but they remain outsiders because they are still invisible and have no voice when dialogue commences. A sense of belonging can never exist because there is no personal or cultural fit between the experiences of African American women and the dominant group".
>
> (p. 21) (West, 2017, p. 1)

Therefore, regardless of the position an African American/Black woman holds at a higher education institution, there is always a dominant group with more cultural and positional power who outrank her and have a hard time relating to ideas she brings to the table, especially around diversity.

As an entry and/or mid-level professional and someone who is not among the official decision makers for the institution, you may not agree with some of the decisions and tactics used, especially regarding diversity.

I feel, as a Black woman, that you have to be more careful than your peers who represent different identities when you disagree with something the institution has done. In a field like Student Affairs where it feels like there are six degrees of separation between the person in leadership who knows the negative statement you made and a member of the search committee for your next potential job, it's advisable to be mindful of what you say and to whom you say it. Sometimes it poses a challenge when you speak up and correct other administrators and faculty members about foundational diversity knowledge as well as teach them how to use best practices regarding inclusion and equity to create change in the campus culture. It is essential to work with the leadership to be explicit about their commitment to diversity instead of using surface-level gimmicks to make it look like they care about diversity:

> Within the context of Black Feminist Thought, it is detrimental for a Black woman's identity to be defined by the highly charged sociopolitical environment which exists in contemporary society. Instead, Black feminists assert the need for Black women to define their own sense of self-identity based on their personal experiences, beliefs, and values.
>
> (Henry, 2010, p. 3)

As Black women, we have to figure out the best way to assert our presence in a non-threatening manner while staying true to ourselves.

The institution level/position on the organizational chart of the diversity position as well as the commitment of the leadership team and the university to impactful diversity practices will determine how influential you can actually be in making sure this happens. "Furthermore, the idea of diversity leadership in higher education may not be compatible with organizational culture at PWIs, because diversity challenges homogeneity in leadership rankings" (Wolfe & Dilworth, 2015, p. 685). On top of this, many Black women have the additional stressor of dealing with the imposter syndrome, feeling the need to have to prove they belong in roles of authority at institutions of higher education, especially at predominantly white institutions. Research has shown:

> the perceptions that African American women [must prove themselves due to the prevalent stereotypes that they] are incompetent pervades much of their careers forcing upon them the undeserved stress of providing a defense they should not need to give and fighting to prove merit when merit is unquestionably apparent.
>
> (Myers, 2002; Henry, 2010, p. 11)

150

While many people will see you as an expert regarding diversity, inclusion, and equity, it doesn't always mean they will listen to your suggestions to make sure the institution is following best practices.

One thing people should remember about colleges and universities is at the end of the day it's a business.

> Another common attempt at co-opting would be tokenism. In this instance, the dominant group would incorporate demographic diversity in their existing normative structure of authority as means of showing that the organization embodies diversity as a core value (Contreras, 1998). Superficially, their presence seems to be proof of minority advocacy and representation.
>
> (Wolfe & Dilworth, 2015, p. 679)

This means many institutional leaders are only willing to make decisions that will keep particular types of people happy, such as the wealthy and closed-minded individuals. Unfortunately, at times when that is the case, it may negatively affect the diverse student populations you serve and care for because you want them to feel seen and welcomed by their institution for simply being who they are. You also have the desire to educate the majority population about their role in dismantling the systems of oppression and discrimination. When you run into these types of situations, there is an internal battle that starts to take place. How do you fulfill your purpose and passion to positively enact diversity initiatives which enhance the lives of the students and the culture of the campus, when the leadership team's idea of diversity and inclusion is superficial? Serving as a diversity leader becomes even more challenging when you realize:

> the expression of leadership has become identified with and embedded in how white interpersonal relations are developed. Furthermore, the idea of diversity leadership in higher education may not be compatible with organizational culture at PWIs, because diversity challenges homogeneity in leadership rankings.
>
> (Wolfe & Dilworth, 2015, p. 685)

Institutions run into this type of issue when they lack diverse representation on the leadership team and those who are present lack cultural competence:

> If institutions are to remedy the disparity gap and poor representation of African American administrators at PWIs, in addition to

151

> other administrators of color, the organizational culture at these higher education institutions and its marginalizing effect on the minority administrators must be understood.
>
> (Wolfe & Dilworth, 2015, p. 670)

Many of them also have limited foundational knowledge about diversity, equity, inclusion, and the effects of the various components of systematic oppression. It is important to note that even people with historically underrepresented identities are also capable of not being culturally competent. For some, they may be one of few individuals who represent diverse backgrounds. In order to keep the so-called level of power they have received by way of their position, they don't want to ruffle feathers for fear of being labeled as a troublemaker or getting shunned for going against their white and/or male peers and/or supervisor. However, there are some people who fear losing their jobs if they go against the "norm" of how things are typically done at the institution:

> Despite their awareness and concern, many administrators are reluctant to publicly bring attention to marginalizing campus issues for fear of political backlash or job loss. Instead of raising concerns, they are more likely to work privately with students, feeling voiceless and powerless to raise issues to other administrators or to White colleagues.
>
> (Wolfe & Dilworth, 2015, p. 677)

No person should fear losing their job due to trying to make a difference in the cultural fabric of an institution, but when we work at institutions with leaders who fail to speak the truth about the systemic racism and oppression that exist, many people believe they must stay silent to keep a faulty idea of peace.

In each position I've held, I do my best to speak up for those not represented in the room as well as to educate people on cultural competency practices. I have learned the ability to affect change within the culture comes from building good relationships with those in leadership and in influential roles at the institution. When trust has been developed, people's guards are down and they are typically more open to learning about the various aspects of diversity, equity, and inclusion. A method I found helpful in building these relationships was getting involved with things across campus that didn't have diversity as the main focus. While this did put some additional work on my plate, it was important to make these connections to help people see me not just as the staff member who works with diverse students, only talking about diversity, but as a staff member who worked hard to fulfill the entire mission of the university. "African Americans are always being relegated to programs and activities that are of a multicultural perspective and nature as opposed to being fully embraced by the university" (Gardner, Barrett, & Pearson, 2014, p. 241).

RECOMMENDATIONS FOR PRACTITIONERS

There is no script or prescription for how a person becomes a higher education diversity administrator. Our stories illuminate two circuitous paths to higher education diversity leadership at predominately white institutions (PWIs). Based on our narratives, you know that both of us identify as Black, female, and administrators. We both have worked about four years at the same institution (one on the main campus, the other on the regional campuses). Both of us also earned terminal degrees from predominantly white institutions. At some point in our early schooling, we attended schools where we were the only Black child or one of few and experienced some dissonance around racial identity. Aside from these few commonalities, our paths to becoming transformative diversity practitioners in higher education diverge. There are a number of differences between us. For starters, there is an age difference which directly correlates to when we began our careers in higher education and our pathway to get there. One began in Student Affairs while the other began post-retirement from a 25-year firefighting career. One of us attended a historically Black college while the other attended a PWI for undergraduate work. One of us was raised in a household with both parents while the other was raised by a single parent. Our similarities and the ways in which we differ further emphasize that there is no monolithic way to become a transformational diversity practitioner.

This chapter began with these words: Diversity work is not for the faint of heart. That cannot be overemphasized. Often diversity practitioners are expected to be everything for everybody. There is an expectation from the institution related to a job description. There is an expectation from faculty and staff around equitable and inclusive practices and recruitment and retention efforts. And, there is an expectation from students who want to give voice to their concerns and have those concerns addressed. These expectations do not always overlap and intersect. Transformational change and practice are not simple. They result from "doing your work". The first recommendation is to know who you are: personally and professionally. Our lived experiences are key components in determining this notion. Steps in order to know yourself might include activities like the social identity wheel, privilege walk, or things like counseling to unpack any unresolved baggage.

Second, seek out mentors. A mentor may come from within the institution or be outside the institution. Mentors might include faculty, staff, students, and administrators. They may also be members of the community. A key element is that your mentor(s) should know where you want to go, how you plan to get there, and be capable of helping you formulate a plan to do so. Your mentor should also be in a position to act as a sponsor for you; that person who can advocate for you in your absence. Effective mentors go beyond race, gender, ethnicity, position, and gender identity.

Third, to become a transformative diversity administrator means participating in professional development. Professional development opportunities allow us to meet other practitioners outside our own institutions. They also allow us to create networks and capitalize on the expertise and experiences of others who are diversity administrators. Organizations like the National Association of Student Personnel Administrators (NASPA), National Association of Diversity Officers in Higher Education (NADOHE), CoopLew Chief Diversity Officers Bootcamp, National Conference On Race and Ethnicity (NCORE), and National Inclusive Excellence Leadership Academy (NIXLA) outline standards for professional practice and offer networking and mentoring opportunities for higher education diversity administrators.

A fourth recommendation to the higher education diversity administrator is to develop a succession plan. You have put in the work to know who you are, sought out mentors, and participated in professional development opportunities. It is time to give back to those who are coming along behind you. Consider mentoring a graduate student or undergraduate student who is invested or interested in doing diversity work at the college level. One crucial element about succession planning is that it is multidirectional. Know who you want to succeed and who you want to take your place when you move up or out.

Fifth, Sister Circles are important and necessary for women in higher education diversity administration. These gatherings allow women of the same racial identity to share knowledge and information about their successes and the challenges that they have endured because of the bodies they live in:

> It is in the company of other trusted African American women that the African American female student affairs administrator may experience a safe environment in which she can speak expressively and directly about issues and experiences that have the

potential to impact her emotional, psychological, and physical health (Howard-Hamilton, 2003b; Hughes & Howard-Hamilton, 2003; Jones, 2004; Williams, 2005).

(Henry, 2010, p. 13)

One final recommendation is to stay abreast of trends, research, and literature centered around diversity, equity, and inclusion. Here is a list of some of our favorite books:

1. *Black Feminism in Education: Black Women Speak Back, Up, and Out* (edited by Venus E. Evans-Winters and Bettina Love)
2. *Shifting: The Double Lives of Black Women in America* (Charisse Jones and Kumea Shorter-Gooden)
3. *The Chief Diversity Officer: Strategy, Structure and Change Management* (Damon A. Williams and Katrina Wade-Golden)
4. *Strategic Diversity Leadership: Activating Change and Transformation in Higher Education* (Damon A. Williams)
5. *Multicultural Competence in Student Affairs: Advancing Social Justice and Inclusion* (Raechele L. Pope, Amy L. Reynolds, & John A. Mueller)
6. *Critical Race Theory* (Richard Delgado & Jean Stefancic)
7. *Why Are All the Black Kids Sitting Together in the Cafeteria?* (Beverly Daniel Tatum)
8. *Creating Campus Cultures: Fostering Success among Racially Diverse Student Populations* (edited by Samuel D. Museus and Uma M. Jayakumar)

These are just some of the books we go back to time after time throughout our professional lives. Others may be added as the body of research expands or our needs as administrators require such.

CONCLUSION

Former First Lady Michelle Obama (2018) ends the preface in her book *Becoming* with these words: "And here I am in this new place, with a lot I want to say." She goes on to discuss her life in the chapters that follow titled: "Becoming Me"; "Becoming Us"; and "Becoming More." While this book chapter is certainly not about our trek to becoming First Lady, it is about our trek to becoming higher education diversity administrators – the kind of leaders who transform the lives of the students in our care and the colleagues on our teams. And we, too, have a great deal to say.

Each of us began our scripting journey by reflecting on our lived experiences and determining how those experiences contributed to our identities. Our identities accompanied us to college, carried us up and through doctoral completion, as they continued to develop. We were becoming ourselves. And as we grew professionally, we were in a sense "becoming us" – higher education diversity administrators. We continue to work in higher education with students who sometimes come from the most marginalized spaces. Our work as diversity administrators requires us to become more, constantly evolving to meet the changing and challenging demands of the job. We began this chapter by stating that diversity work is not for the faint of heart and we end it with the same. The "hat" that each of us wears as administrator, as diversity champion, and as bridge builder is ultimately determined by the strength we each garner from the distinctive features of our identities – personal characteristics, culture, character, legacy – and by how we wield implements for change in our arsenal. Which "hat" is determined by how we leverage the self-perception of who we are. It is only after we each learned to navigate our identity and social location that we have been able to become transformative higher education diversity practitioners.

REFERENCES

Chang, H. (2008). *Autoethnography as method*. Walnut Creek, CA: Left Coast Press.

Collins, P. H. (2008). *Black feminist thought: Knowledge, consciousness, and the politics of empowerment*. New York: Routledge.

Contreras, R. (1998). Leading from the margins in the ivory tower. In L. A. Valverde & L. A. Castenell Jr. (Eds.), *The multicultural campus: Strategies for transforming higher education* (pp. 137–166). Walnut Creek, CA: Alta Mira Press.

Coopwood, K., & Lewis, W. (2017). *From their mouths: The lived experiences of chief diversity officers in higher education*. February 2018. <https://static1.squarespace.com/static/5ab163bfda02bc14ee0f-847c/t/5ac260fd575d1f0d54fb4a38/1522688261334/CooplewReSer.pdf>

Gardner, Jr, L., Barrett, T. G., & Pearson, L. C. (2014). African American administrators at PWIs: Enablers of and barriers to career success. *Journal of Diversity in Higher Education*, 7(4), 235.

Gay, G. (2018). *Culturally responsive teaching: Theory, research, and practice* (3rd ed.). New York: Teachers College Press.

Giovanni, N. (2012). <https://www.azquotes.com/quote/823346>

Green, P. S. (1997). Rites of passage and rights of way: A woman administrator's experiences. In L. Benjamin (Ed.), *Black women in the academy: Perils and promises* (pp. 147–167). Gainesville, FL: University Press of Florida.

Guiffrida, D. (2005). "Othermothering as a framework for understanding African American students' definitions of student-centered faculty." *The Journal of Higher Education, 76*(6), 701–723.

Hamilton, B. E. (2008). The reflexive journey: One teacher's path to self in the footsteps of her students. *Ohio Link ETD Center* (ucin1218800146).

Henry, W. J. (2010). African American women in student affairs: Best practices for winning the game. *Advancing Women in Leadership, 30,* 1–18.

Howard-Hamilton, M. F. (2003a, Winter). Editor's notes. In M. F. Howard-Hamilton (Ed.), *New directions for student services.* Meeting the needs of African American women (Vol. 104, pp. 1–3). San Francisco: Jossey-Bass.

Howard-Hamilton, M.F. (2003b). Theoretical frameworks for African American women. *New directions for student services, 2003*(104), 19–27.

Hughes, R. L., & Howard-Hamilton, M. F. (2003). Insights: Emphasizing issues that affect African American women. *New directions for student services, 2003*(104), 95–104.

Jones, L. V. (2004). Enhancing psychosocial competence among Black women in college. *Social Work, 49*(1), 75–83.

Jones, C., & Shorter-Gooden, K. (2003). *Shifting: the double lives of Black women in America.* New York: HarperCollins Publishers.

Knight-Manuel, M. G., & Marciano, J. E. (2018). *Classroom cultures: Equitable schooling for racially diverse youth.* New York: Teachers College Press.

Ladson-Billings, G. (2014). Culturally relevant pedagogy 2.0: a.k.a. the remix. *Harvard Educational Review, 84,* 74–84.

Lorde, A. (1988). *A burst of light.* Ithaca, NY: Firebrand Books.

Milner, H. R. 2017. "Where Is the Race in Culturally Relevant Pedagogy?" *Teachers College Record, 119*(1): 1–31.

Morton, J. M. (2014). Cultural code-switching: Straddling the achievement gap. *Journal of Political Philosophy, 22*(3), 259–281.

Myers, L. W. (2002). *A broken silence: Voices of African American women in the academy.* Westport, CT: Greenwood Publishing Group.

Obama, M. (2018). *Becoming.* New York: Crown Publishing Group.

Rodriguez, C. (2001). A homegirl goes home. In I. McClaurin (Ed.), *Black Feminist Anthropology* (233–257). New Brunswick, NJ: Rutgers University Press.

Steele, C. (2010). *Whistling Vivaldi: How stereotypes affect us and what we can do.* New York: W. W. Norton & Company, Inc.

Strmic-Pawl, H. V., & Leffler, P. K. (2011). Black families and fostering of leadership. *Ethnicities*, *11*(2), 139–162.

Sue, D. W., & Sue, D. (2013). *Counseling the Culturally Diverse: Theory and practice*. Hoboken, NJ: Wiley.

Swanson, D. P., Cunningham, M., Youngblood, J., & Beal Spencer, M., (2009). Racial identity development during childhood. In H. A. Neville, B. M. Tynes, & S. O. Utsey (Eds.), *Handbook of African American psychology* (pp. 269–281). Newbury, CA: Sage.

Tatum, B. D. (2017). *Why are all the Black kids sitting together in the cafeteria?: And other conversations about race*. Basic Books, New York.

Walkington, J. (2005). Becoming a teacher: Encouraging development of teacher identity through reflective practice. *Asia-Pacific Journal of Teacher Education*, *33*(1), 53–64.

West, N. M. (2017). Withstanding our status as outsiders-within: Professional counterspaces for African American women student affairs administrators. *NASPA Journal About Women in Higher Education*, *10*(3), 281–300.

Wolfe, B. L., & Dilworth, P. P. (2015). Transitioning normalcy: Organizational culture, African American administrators, and diversity leadership in higher education. *Review of Educational Research*, *85*(4), 667–697.

Chapter Eight

Taking It Personally
The Personal is Political is Professional for Women of Color Diversity Leaders

Allison C. Roman, Precious Porras, Willette A. Capers, Bulaong Ramiz, and Shantel Martinez

Women of color are a force to be reckoned with, both inside and outside of higher education. As one of the largest formally educated groups in the USA, women of color continue to overcome structural barriers which results in being lauded by some and envied by others for our persistence, resistance, and leadership. As women of color take on more institutionalized leadership roles, specifically in equity and inclusion work, we trail blaze in ways only compound experiences of oppression can allow. Epitomizing colloquialisms like "Black Girl Magic," steeped in traditions of survival, creativity, and making a way out of no way, women of color leaders are changing academia and the world at large. Even with the triumph and successes, women of color are often living with the pain and burden of "doing the work," namely the work to promote diversity, equity, and inclusion (DEI), while at the same time negotiating white supremacy and patriarchy in their own lives. While we have unique racialized and gendered experiences based on our specific identities, privileges, and interlocking oppressions (e.g., classism, ageism, cissexism), utilizing "woman of color" as a political identity marker means working and existing in solidarity with Black, indigenous, Asian American and Pacific Islander, non-white Latina/x minoritized women (Ross, 2011).

The narratives and experiences of women of color higher education leaders are largely absent from the literature. Even more so, the experiences of

DOI: 10.4324/9781003008521-11

159

diversity leaders, specifically women of color, are missing. The stories of women of color in higher education are often focused on the experiences of those in academia (tenure-track faculty), while women of color staff and administrators are regularly left in what feels like precarious situations. In this chapter, we seek to highlight the narratives of women of color leaders whose identities uniquely shape the way DEI work is done, lived, and experienced in higher education. While we recognize that women of color do not have a monolithic experience, the systems of oppression that impress upon our lives do result in similar experiences of institutional disenfranchisement. For women of color higher education leaders, the motivations that drive us to lead and excel in the arenas of DEI are rooted in the desire to disrupt, dismantle, and transform these systems that marginalize and radicalize us. We tirelessly work in the hopes that one day our jobs and our offices will be obsolete because DEI will not only be institutionalized, but prioritized within university systems. Yet, this is a futuristic dream. As Ahmed (2012) highlights, "When your task is to remove the necessity of your existence, then your existence is necessary for the task" (p. 23). Thus, we are often the sacrificial lambs who are placed as offerings to the very systems that we frequently work to dismantle—and, adding even more salt to the wound, we are often sacrificed by the same people who say they have our backs.

There exists a dearth of publications surrounding the experiences and narratives of women of color leaders in higher education, specifically in the roles of administrators and staff. With that being said, we do acknowledge the steep increase of foundational texts highlighting the voices of women of color faculty being published in the last ten years (see Calafell, *Monstrosity, Performance, and Race in Contemporary Culture* (2015); Edwards & del Guadalupe Davidson, *College Curriculum at the Crossroads* (2018); Gutiérrez y Muhs, Flores Niemann, González, & Harris, *Presumed Incompetent* (2012); Holling, *You intimidate me* (2018); Latina Feminist Group, *Telling to Live*; Marrun, "Somos gente estudiada" (2018); Nguyen, *Asian american women faculty* (2016); and Turner, González, & Wong, *Faculty women of color* (2011)). Again, while we appreciate and acknowledge the surge of information concerning women of color faculty experiences, we assert that our experiences are different from those of faculty, and instead, exist within shadowy and forgotten borderlands of higher education. Due to these gaps, a holistic understanding of what women of color leaders experience in higher education truly does not exist, although there is some literature that addresses bits and pieces (please refer to Davis & Maldonado, "Shattering the glass ceiling"; Sanchez-Hucles & Davis, "Women and women of color in leadership"; Wardell, *Twice as Good*). Our hope is that

160

this chapter adds further to the conversation, knowing that it will continue to take time to fully paint the picture of our experiences.

This is a political project as much as it is an intellectual one, a project that demonstrates that narratives and *testimonios*, both past and present, are the great instructors of our time. They are the key to unlocking the traumas of our pasts and our guides for a liberated future. Our fight to survive, our fight to exist, our fight to be heard and listened to exist in every bone and word in our bodies. As we have been changed by our experiences in these institutions, so do we change them by sharing our stories, ourselves, and our visions for truly equitable higher education communities. We hope that in sharing our experiences, we are able to illuminate the unique challenges and strengths that ground our praxis as women of color diversity leaders. *We are ready to be heard.*

THEORETICAL FRAMEWORKS

We acknowledge that this chapter is risky and invokes reliving trauma in order to shed light on such complicated matters and issues. Requiring us to reopen wounds that many of us try to forget and/or erase, we place our vulnerabilities on display knowing that to do so is a political act of solidarity, resistance, and survival. As such, we believe that such a personal project requires personal methodologies and theoretical frameworks: *testimonios*, women of color, Black and indigenous feminisms, and Critical Race Theory.

Testimonios are imperative to the nature and aim of this project. As one may guess, *testimonios are similar, but are not the same* as testimonies (i.e., living testaments of interviews and of being interviewed). Rather, *testimonios* are both theoretical and methodological interventions rooted within social justice and activism. First used to convey the experiences and struggles of marginalized peoples in order to rally for a call of action to end sociopolitical, cultural, and historical oppressions (Behar, 1993; Bernal et al., 2012; Burgos-Debray, 1984; Lomas & Joysmith, 2005), *testimonios* are the practices and processes of articulating an urgency to which they bear witness and make public an intentional intervention. "At the forefront of a *testimonio* is the author—whether spoken or written— who controls and commands themselves as agents of knowledge, speaking from the margins of history and experience" (Martinez, 2019, p. 357). By allowing narrators to pry open a space to name themselves into existence and honor their traumas, a *testimonio* "provides a kind of active journey from torture, oppression, or marginalization that ultimately leads the speaker or writer to become the empowered survivor" (Reyes & Curry

Rodriguez, 2012, p. 527). "While speaking from your own tongue and body doesn't necessarily seem like a revolutionary act, for *testimonialistas,* it is a form of liberation – especially from the oppressive powers of the academy and of society" (Martinez, 2019, p. 359). By doing this, *testimonios* not only cultivate new bodies of knowledge, but also value the marginalized bodies in which this knowledge comes from. Thus, *testimonios* braid and weave together an unbreakable bond between knowledge, stories, bodies, and identities, or as Canaan, Anzaldúa and Moraga (1983) assert, a theory of the flesh: "a theory....where the physical realities of our lives—our skin color, the land or concrete we grew up on, and our sexual longings—all fuse to create a politic born out of necessity" (p. 23). As such, *testimonios* are the "refusal of an *easy* explanation to the conditions we live in" (Canaan, Moraga & Anzaldúa, 1983, p. 23) and illuminate the many contradictions that we encounter as people of color trying to survive and thrive. Because the personal is at the foreground of *testimonios,* it allows us to examine and critique cultural, social, and political practices and experiences not only in our work within higher education, but even more specifically, the field of DEI.

By foregrounding narratives, *testimonios* nuance and complicate previous and current research trends via honoring positionality and the power of intersectionality. With putting the personal at the forefront, these qualitative formations maneuver through experiences that are sometimes too painful, embarrassing, or traumatic to discuss in other research paradigms, or are observed as "too personal" or taboo to discuss in the academy. Nevertheless, when these narratives want to be shared there needs to be a space for them—and *testimonios* help to create this space, not only for the stories but also the storytellers. Thus, *testimonios* create affective landscapes that embrace the epiphanies, pain, power, risk, trauma, and vulnerability that we encounter in our everyday practices (Martinez, 2019) and lives as being women of color higher education leaders. In addition to the use of testimonios as a framework, our perspective is deeply influenced and supported by Black feminist frameworks, specifically with the focus on self-definition, the use and power of narratives and storytelling, and concepts such as othermothering.

Black Feminist Thought also serves as a crucial theoretical foundation to ground this chapter. Patricia Hill Collins wrote that "As long as Black women's subordination with intersecting oppressions of race, class, gender, sexuality, and nation persists, Black feminism as an activist response to that oppression will remain needed" (Collins, 2000). In Black Feminist Thought, the use of narrative and self-definition is essential in being able to name and make sense of one's own experience (Amoah, 1997; Collins,

2000) when white supremacy has sought to define us in a way that is contrary to our own self-definitions. Black women constantly have to navigate and negotiate these two worlds in contradiction of one another. Storytelling and narrative allows us to be seen and be affirmed in spaces that deems us less than (Roman, 2019). Narrative creates sites of resistance that allows us to push back on the definitions created by dominant society and make meaning of our experiences in our own language and in our own words.

As women of color leaders in higher education, one thing that we all know and agree upon is that none of us can escape our bodies. In fact, oftentimes it is our bodies that serve as sites and evidence of our precarious place within higher education. Knowing that we were never designed to exist within higher education compounded by systems of patriarchy and white supremacy, our bodies are ripe with experiences and stories of continual acts of violence. In doing so, we cannot help but utilize women of color and indigenous feminism as a lens to interrogate, deconstruct, and highlight the conditions in which we live, labor, and love in.

Since multiple subjectivities serve as one of the primary sites of inquiry for women of color and indigenous feminism, issues of the body are central to the field. How bodies are read, positioned, disciplined, configured, observed, or not observed in society frequently are discussed, revealing counternarratives naming their own struggles. By writing the body, both from and about, women of color and indigenous feminists such as Leslie Marmon Silko, bell hooks, Trinh Minh-ha, Gloria Anzaldúa, Cherrie Moraga, Maxine Hong Kingston, Angela Davis, Audre Lorde, Paula Gunn Allen, and others rearticulate theories of the flesh. With asserting our own theory and our own words, women of color and indigenous feminism trouble previous feminist, Latinx/Chicanx, Black, Asian, and indigenous constructions of our experiences and bodies, thus creating new tools to deconstruct and defy the master's house (Lorde, 1984). In doing so, women of color and indigenous feminism affirm a new space for coalition building and alliances across unlikely borders. Although coalition building occurred prior to the 1970s, women of color and indigenous feminism's politics of rearticulation help strengthen cross-community dialogues by positing difference not as a commodity, but as a site for organizing. As Trinh Minh-ha (1989) argues, "it is, indeed, much easier to dismiss or eliminate on the pretext of difference (destroy the other in our minds, in our word) than to live fearlessly with and within difference" (84). Similarly, Audre Lorde (1984) exclaims, "it is not difference which immobilizes us, but silence. And there are so many silences to be broken" (44). By embracing difference and not shying away or demonizing

163

it, difference becomes a site for transformative politics that move beyond identity politics, allowing for more inclusive social and political change. It acts as a creative power, sparking connections to one another that is merely more than tolerance of each other. Rather, difference is a force possessing the ability to break down binaries of good/bad, dominant/subordinate, oppressor/oppressed.

Moreover, women of color and indigenous feminism speak to the importance of writing—not only for our communities, but for ourselves. Writing is a political act (Bird, 1998) deeply tied to voice, memory, stories, and personal agency. Gloria Anzaldua, Trinh Minh-ha, Audre Lorde, and Paula Gunn Allen all remark in their work the critical role writing plays with mental and emotional health. *We write out of survival. We write as a means for sanity. We write to break the silence.* Many women of color feminists are aware of the creative and political power writing possesses. It is believed writing serves as a mirror (Minh-ha, 1989) of what we can represent—ourselves, our perspectives on society, our subjectivities, etc. Simply put, "writing reflects" (Minh-ha, 1989, 23). In the eyes of women of color and indigenous feminists, writing is intrinsically connected to the experiential and the body (Lorde, 1984; Minh-ha, 1989; Canaan, Moraga & Anzaldúa, 1983). Our stories, papers, essays, and books have emerged from violent legacies of rape, censorship, oppression, patriarchy—the list is never ending. Women of color and indigenous feminism also remind us that writing is not a commodity or service (Minh-ha, 1989)—that it is indeed a necessary process to express and name ourselves. Further, women of color and indigenous feminism illustrate that it is okay to break and disidentify within dominant writing prose. That in fact we must unlearn the colonial tongues imposed upon us: "to write 'clearly,' one must incessantly prune, eliminate, forbid, purge, purify" (Minh-ha, 1989, 17). Instead, writing should be an extension of the body. The body should not be forgotten in the writing process, but at the forefront of it. Subsequently, writing makes visible bodies that have traditionally been invisible, exploited, and marginalized in both society and in education. Giving voice to our experiences, naming our silences, naming ourselves allow for women of color and indigenous feminism and feminists to cultivate new systems of meaning and knowledge.

Critical Race Theory can be used to take a deeper look into the experiences of people of color in the academy. Chicana feminist theory supports the notion of "survival" in the academy due to systemic oppression and the experiences of Chicana and LatinX women. Because of the low representation of women of color at our institutions, their needs can easily go unmet. With this low representation, systems of power, privilege, and oppression can continue to operate. It is because of these systems that we find the voices of women of color being silenced when issues of white supremacy are unveiled due to the traditionally "unrecognized" and "invisible" instinctive essence of racism in higher education (McCoy & Rodricks, 2015). This silencing has encouraged Black women to not trust one another due to their fear of hostility, aggression, unwarranted judgment, and being invisible among their peers (hooks, 2007). In the experiences of people of color who have been able to share their plight in the academy, the use of *testimonios* is seen as "…'healing' work—it is what empowers Women of Color to recover from the trauma caused by oppression and move toward positive social change" (Anzaldúa, 2002).

The use of these frameworks coupled with the narratives we will share seeks to situate and provide "contextual grounding" for our experiences as a way to "locate ones-self" and "provide a foundation upon which our understanding of the world, and our place in it, is built" (Banks-Wallace, 1998). These theoretical frameworks provide language and cultural context which helps validate and contextualize our experiences, which at times feel isolating. Our hope is that by utilizing these frameworks as lenses, one could gain a better understanding of our collective experiences and of how white supremacy, patriarchy, and other isms come together to shape and mold not only how we view the challenges we face, but also the potential solutions to these challenges.

WHO WE ARE: AUTHORS' POSITIONALITIES

As the authors of this chapter, as women of color, it is imperative to name our positionalities and name the ways we are similar and the ways we are different. We must "devise ways to use each other's differences to enrich our visions and our joint struggles" (Lorde, 1984). We offer our introductions to provide additional personal and institutional contexts for our experiences. The naming of our identities serves to link our individual struggles to the broader struggle for liberation, both in and outside of higher education.

> **Allison (Alli) Roman** is a Black cisgender-heterosexual (or cis-het) woman of Dominican and Puerto Rican descent. She is a first-generation college graduate from a lower socioeconomic status. She has earned her bachelors in social welfare and her masters in social work, both from predominantly white institutions. Her racial and ethnic identity, gender, and socioeconomic status greatly influences how she experiences higher education, both personally and

professionally. Alli served as the inaugural Director for Diversity and Inclusion at a small private, liberal arts institution in Texas for two years. Prior to her time as a director, she has previously served as an assistant director in a multicultural affairs office, and later a women's center at a medium-sized public institution in the Midwest. In early 2020, she became the eighth Black women faculty/staff member to leave that institution in the span of three years.

Precious Porras is a black bi-racial cis-het woman. She grew up socialized white, with only her white family. She has had to unlearn a lot of that white socialization over the past 15 years as she navigates doing equity work in higher education. She is a first generation college student, who grew up very poor. She earned her bachelors, masters and her doctorate, all first in her family. She works at the University of Kansas, a large, public, Research One, PWI situated in northeast Kansas. She is the inaugural Assistant Vice Provost for Diversity and Equity and the Director of the Office of Multicultural Affairs, where she was the first woman to hold that position in over 30 years. Her student affairs background has all been at the same institution, but she has held multiple, progressive leadership positions. She is an emerging scholar, focused on critical, radical works to unlearn her tradition as a means of un/re-learning higher education and student affairs.

Willette A. Capers is a rural born, first-generation graduate, cisgender Black woman of Gullah/Geechie heritage. She is currently a Doctoral student at Northeastern University where her research focuses on the impact of value for Black Women and their persistence rates in the field of Student Affairs. Capers, a certified Diversity Advocate, and QA for the IDI Intercultural Development Inventory has dedicated her career to DEI. work. She specializes in Critical Race Theory, Intercultural Development, and DEI Curriculum Development. Willette currently serves as the Director of Diversity, Equity, & Inclusion at Augustana University in Sioux Falls, South Dakota.

Bulaong Ramiz-Hall is a queer Black (African-American) and Puerto Rican Muslim woman who has spent most of her life navigating predominately white wealthy heteropatriarchal institutions. She is working to center Black feminist thought in her praxis, using the experiences of those most marginalized to shift institutional culture and norms. Bulaong currently serves as the first woman of color in over 20 years to direct the Emily Taylor Center for Women and Gender Equity at the University Kansas and is working to complete her doctorate in Higher Education Administration.

Shantel Martinez is a queer Latinx woman who is also a first-generation college graduate. Coming from a family of story-tellers, Shantel defines herself as a testimoniolista, fully embracing the notion that "in listening to the story of one, we learn about the conditions of many" (Bernal et al., 2012, 368). Shantel grew up in a lower socioeconomic status and was frequently one of the only (if not only) students of color in her honors, AP courses, and doc-toral education. Through these experiences, Shantel is dedicated to building pipelines for college access, persistence, retention, and graduation, as well as entry to graduate and professional schools for marginalized student populations. She currently directs the Ot-ter Cross Cultural Center at California State University, Monterey Bay. Although the Center has existed for ten years, her role at her level is inaugural. Shantel is also an affiliate faculty member in the School of Humanities and Communications at CSUMB. She has a PhD in Communications and Media with an emphasis on Latinx Communication and Gender Studies from the University of Illi-nois, Urbana-Champaign.

As a collective of women of color DEI leaders, we recognize the ways in which our identities both provide some similarities, but subsequently there are also some gaps. We acknowledge that while several themes have emerged in this writing process such as most of us are first-generation college graduates as an example, we simply cannot speak for all women of color. We also recognize that we all are speaking from our experiences as cisgender women and cannot speak on the experiences of trans women of color. We also understand that due to our varied identities that intersect with race and gender, some of us may have been afforded greater access to resources in our lives. However, despite these differences, there are many similarities in the ways that white supremacy and patriarchy have im-pacted our lived experiences as women of color. Our next section will ex-plore how specifically microaggressions, stereotype threat, and imposter syndrome show up for us as women of color DEI leaders.

MICROAGGRESSIONS, STEREOTYPE THREAT, IMPOSTER SYNDROME

As women of color leaders, we have unfortunately grown accustomed to walking into many spaces wearing our armor. Many of us experience the daily barrages of microaggressions and grapple with the impact of these microaggressions: racial battle fatigue, imposter syndrome, and stereotype threat. Microaggressions are the "brief and commonplace daily verbal, behavioral, or environmental indignities, whether intentional or unintentional, that communicate hostile, de-rogatory, or negative racial slights and insults toward people of color" (Sue et al., 2007). As we have transitioned from the classroom as students to the conference room and boardroom as higher education leaders, the microaggressions remain. These microaggressions come in many forms and can be rooted in both the racism and sexism that women of color are constantly barraged with every day. Colleagues, supervisors, campus visitors, and students and their families can all be the source of microaggressions. Queer feminist scholar Moya Bailey coined the term misogynoir to specifically name the unique phenomenon of intersectional violence experienced by Black women as a result of both their race and perceived gender identity.

These microaggressions are also embedded in the environment, in the organizational structure and culture, all of which can be especially salient in historically white institutions. Manifestations of white supremacy culture (Okun, 2001) which is intimately connected to cisheteropatriarchal cultural norms, create both covert and overt aggressions at the intersections of both our racialized and gendered identities as well as our sexuality. The perpetuation of white supremacy embedded in our professions' norms further communicates to women of color that our way of existing does not "fit" in the field. From our narrative communication styles, rooted in many of our familial cultural traditions, to our understanding of nuance and subjectivity due to our embodied intersectional existence, our presence in higher education institutions directly counters normative white supremacist and patriarchal culture. From being left off of crucial emails to not being invited to important meetings, or from having our departments not represented at campus events to just simply being forgotten, many of the environments we enter communicate to us both subtly and not-so-subtly that we do not belong. Some environments can feel so violent that it feels like an attack on our personhood. Environments like these are the ones we are hired to disrupt but it feels challenging to sit in it. While some leaders of color enter the field to dismantle these hierarchical structures of oppressions, many participate and uphold white supremacy and patriarchy, acquiescing in order to find success, power, or simply safety.

By utilizing stereotype threat (Steele & Arnson, 1995) or the fear of confirming stereotypes associated with members of marginalized communities, as a theoretical lens to examine the experiences of women of color, we acknowledge the ways that we are both cognizant of the stereotypes that are tied to our identities as well as the challenges that exist in challenging those stereotypes. For example, Black women might be seen as angry, as a threat, or as the mammy, or as the oversexualized woman (Winfrey Harris, 2015), whereas Latina women might be seen as feisty, spicy, and like Black women, are oversexualized and fetishized. Women of color might be seen as difficult to work with, if they are even seen at all (Winfrey Harris, 2015). Women of color have to be constantly aware of our body language, the faces we make, the tone of our voice, the hours we put in, the strength we have to show. The burden of having to carry the weight of others' perceptions as well as the stereotypes we may have internalized can sometimes feel like it's all too much.

In these roles, we live in the throngs of a paradox. Of both being seen, yet rendered invisible, of "high rank and low resources, and recognition and tokenism can result in marginalization achieved not through sidelining or sweeping under the rug, but in essence by hiding the [us] in plain view" (Nixon, 2017). Women of color in higher education are invisible when they need support and resources, but become hypervisible when they are needed to address diversity issues (Sanchez-Hucles & Davis, 2010). For Black women, they are often praised for their ability to survive, seen as the mules of the world, with the expectation to be magic, and to make more with less.

We constantly have to negotiate whether we should speak up about the experiences we have or risk experiencing the further marginalization which works to minimize our already limited institutional power. Sometimes we have to bite our tongues and swallow the bitter injustices we personally experience in order to get our foot in the door, to get in the room, or have a seat at the proverbial table. But we constantly have to ask ourselves, "at what cost?"

The following narratives illuminate the ways that women of color experience microaggressions, stereotype threat, and imposter syndrome in their professional work. As a collective of women of color and despite holding different identities and working at different types of higher educational institutions, we find several themes emerge from our experiences.

Examples of Microaggressions

"Don't be a younger looking woman of color on a college campus and not expect to experience public harassment from young men, disregard from leadership, or assumptions about you and your capacity from fellow colleagues." In my short time as a professional on college campuses across the country, I have experienced all of that at each institution I have entered. These microaggressions occur at the intersection of my race, gender, perceived age/experience, and role on campus. As a person with compound marginalization doing identity-based work on college campuses, I would move beyond the double consciousness DuBois discussed (DuBois, 1903) and say that I hold a triple, maybe even quadruple consciousness. The deep understanding of socialization, systems, and manifestations of superiority rooted in identity make it such that every day, seemingly small interactions have the potential to carry the weight of historical dynamics that remind me of ways I am marginalized. Due to positionality, my opinions are often (intentionally or not) disregarded despite my experiential or intrinsic knowledge. My experiences of this dismissal or disregard is then not seen as oppressive because it is rooted in the hierarchical nature of higher education without critical analysis of higher education as inherently patriarchal and white supremacist. I am made to question or deny my own understanding of identity-based systems because of the false espousing of higher education as an identity-neutral space where we, women of color, do not experience harm because of our identities. The unconscious manifestations of internalized superiority or inferiority lead women of color to experience microaggression often without correction or apology. This interpersonal violence within structural oppression makes instances of microaggressions too frequent and "compoundly impactful" (Bulaong Ramiz).

I was on a zoom call and the 3rd person on the call. I said hello to the first two people when I entered. The white woman, leading the call, did not acknowledge me. She did however, say hello to every person who came on the call after me, all of whom were white women. Including someone who came into the call 30 minutes late (Precious Porras)

I remember having a 'woke' white woman colleague proceed to run her fingers through my hair when I ran into her on campus with another one of her colleagues. She then proceeded to laugh and say 'Oh my goodness, you know, I was just reading an article about how Black women are tired of white women touching their hair. It was such a good article' not even acknowledging what she had just done (Alli Roman).

One day, a colleague (Black woman) and I were walking across campus on a summer day. We ran into a white woman colleague who had decided to walk with us. Because it was summer, cicada season was in full swing. This colleague then began to say, 'Please don't take this the wrong way, this is gonna sound awful, but the sound of cicadas, don't they remind you of lynchings' (Alli Roman).

As part of my role, I was responsible for supporting students with their respective cultural graduation celebrations. When working with the Latinx students, they expressed their frustration with the administration, feeling that they didn't support and understand them. They then told me that I didn't fully understand why having large celebrations with lots of family members is important for the Latinx community. Although I am Dominican and Puerto Rican, I was not fully seen as a representative or part of their community (Alli Roman).

When I introduce myself in large gatherings, I tend to use my formal title of Dra. (the Spanish version of Dr.) Martinez. I have lost count of the times when I have to remind people to use my formal title, when they easily remember the titles of others in the room. This isn't just about white folks either – many men of color have 'accidentally or innocently forgotten' my official title while introducing me. This slight is no accident, but also a perfect example of sexism and microaggressions at play while being a younger woman of color in the room. The act of discrediting is constant and builds to the point where I want to scream my credentials, while simultaneously knowing it makes me look elitist for something I worked so hard to obtain as a Latinx woman (Shantel Martinez).

My supervisor at the time would frequently mention to me how important it was that in leadership meetings (with other directors) or in meetings with the president's cabinet, I show initiative by offering to take notes/ minutes. She then remarked 'I just loved when we were in meetings and [former director of housing and Black woman] would take notes for us.' It felt like such an odd thing to consistently bring up, especially because the person who was usually responsible to take minutes was always present (Alli Roman).

Examples of Stereotype Threat

Women of color make up less than 1% of doctorate holders. As one of only two people in my doctoral cohort, I was convinced I could not succeed in the program. I've always been a good student, so I wanted to do well and I did, with course work, but after failing my comprehensive exams the first time, I felt that I was not cut out for this program. I had proved so many people right, that a black girl from a poor neighborhood didn't deserve to be a doctor. A mentor, a black woman, who had completed the same program as me, called me and we cried together as she told me she had also failed her comps and that it would be ok, that I could make it through also. It took the support of another black woman to help me see that I was good enough to do this. That experience still shook me and my belief in myself. It took me six more years to finish my dissertation after that, because I did not think I could be successful because of the identities I held. When times were the hardest and I wanted to quit, I called her up to ask for advice and guidance and motivation (Precious Porras).

About six months after I began my role, the only other person of color in our leadership team was fired. A Black woman, a fierce advocate for all students, was suddenly ushered out of the institution without being told what happened. One day she was here, the next day, gone. In the months that followed, I took over advising the Black Student Union. In preparation for an annual dinner at the Dean's house, I met with the dean to discuss how to best support students who are feeling hurt and angry due to the firing of their mentor and advisor. In that meeting, the dean compared me to my former colleague and said to not be like her and that she was combative and put the students against the school. After the dinner, that did not go well, the dean had confronted me for "doing what [our former colleague] did" and for undermining him in front of the students, even though I was essentially doing my job and gently called him out for not listening to them. I also had suggested some resources for him to read about allyship (Alli Roman).

Examples of Imposter Syndrome

Constantly feeling the guilt of never being enough, as well as stereotype threat and imposter syndrome, I use to mask my insecurities with red lipstick, a killer sense of humor, and dedicated work ethic. *But this was never enough.* Stretched to the brink, each micro-aggression cut deeper and deeper, until one day I could not take it anymore. All of the moments of 'Oh, YOU'RE the director?,' 'Being labeled "feisty" is a good thing', 'You don't look old enough to have a PhD,' 'Latinx people aren't really people of color—like c'mon you're labeled as white,' 'No, where are you REALLY from…, all add up till the moment when you are looking at yourself in the mirror and start to question, 'is this actually worth it?' The personal is political and in this line of work, each backhanded compliment or microaggression can be taken personally (Shantel Martinez).

As the inaugural director for diversity and inclusion, I struggled at times with being taken seriously. As often the only woman of color (and person of color) in my division's leadership team, I often felt I had to prove that I was competent and experienced enough for this job. I sometimes felt this internal struggle with not feeling good enough or smart enough, even though I exceeded the requirements for the role (Alli Roman).

I am the first woman of color in over 20 years to direct the Women's Center on my campus. I understood that part of my being hired was both my identity and my ability to open that space beyond the white feminist framework that had been operating there for so long. With a background in race and ethnic studies, I felt immense imposter syndrome as I took on a role without the same level of content knowledge as my peers in the field. Though I know there is not a white woman in my role who is expected to 'know it all,' as a woman of color, I knew that I would never be given the same grace. My success in any role I hold is dependent upon my displayed knowledge, and upon my accomplishments toward the intended goals by the powers that be. While 'other duties as assigned' exists in almost every job description, the key word 'assigned' exists as a way to manage labor within the hierarchy. As a woman of color, I have many opinions based on my experience and the experiences of others who, like me, have to deal with policy, practices, and interactions that cause harm. It is my human responsibility to address these instances; at the same time, I know that my advocacy work can sometimes be seen as out of place or beyond my role and responsibility. The hierarchy of higher education contributes to the feelings of isolationism and tokenism leading me to conclude that my role is to make the institution look good, diverse, inclusive, and to keep students quiet, satisfied, and complaisant (Bulaong Ramiz).

Microaggression, stereotype threat, and imposter syndrome are all symptoms of a larger issue at hand – Racial Battle Fatigue. First coined by William A. Smith (2004) from the University of Utah, Racial Battle Fatigue is the onset of psychological, physiological, and behavioral stress and fatigue from experiencing constant covert and overt racialized incidents, exploitation, profiling, micro/macroaggressions, and oppression. It can manifest itself in shock, frustration, anger, disappointment, resentment, anxiety, helplessness, hopelessness, fear, problems concentrating, and headaches. Racial battle fatigue is a slow death. Slow death of spirit, of soul, and of living. Slowly taking pleasures out of life, racial battle fatigue does not only drain us of our careers and interactions in the workplace, but it creeps into all aspects of our lives as our bodies are the main site of interrogation, investigation, and oppression. It robs us of interactions with our loved ones and families when we come home from work as our minds and bodies are riddled with the wounds from previous battles. Our minds are often clouded with exhaustion; and although we may look like we are being present, we are in the midst of just trying to survive the rest of the day.

The collective toll in which racial battle fatigue can manifest itself is physical, physiological, and psychological. The stress from racism can impact women of color's mental health, physical health, and even maternal health. The effects of racialized stress have been linked to maternal and infant mortality, high blood pressure, depression, and anxiety. Higher Education Administration has been cited as one of the 12 most stressful professions (Charlesworth & Nathan, 1982). It is through a barrage of constant gaslighting that we find women of color facing racial battle fatigue due to "physiological, psychological, cultural, and emotional coping with racial microaggressions in less-than-ideal and racially hostile or unsupportive environments (campus or otherwise)" (Guthrie at al., 2005; Patton & Catching, 2009, p. 724). Added to that fatigue is the concept of Othermothering, where we find systemically non-dominant women of color serving as the campus "Mammy" due to the gaslighting and sabotage faced at the hands of not only their white colleagues, but their white students as well (Walkington, 2017; Wilson, 2012). These instances of fatigue are further exacerbated due to the limited number of systemically non-dominant women of color in administrative leadership roles in the academy at predominately white institutions, who have also experienced these situations and can understand the impact and implications they can cause.

Caught in the middle of the national backdrop of the #MeToo movement and #Blacklivesmatter movement, Black women and women of color are organizing, advocating, protesting, and surviving for themselves as their gender and racial identity simultaneously create a level of marginality for them and their families. Experiencing both invisibility and hypervisibility at the intersections of their identities, Black women in particular experience a compound trauma that does not disappear in the workplace. Ongoing statements about anti-Black racism released by institution leadership, various academic departments, faculty/staff senates, even student clubs and organizations only seek to assuage white power structures of their guilt, while Black folks endure the persistent reminders of their social position and the violence they experience:

> I am not sure there is any escape from racial battle fatigue while in predominantly white space, certainly not unconscious spaces rooted in whiteness. This reality requires an equity response that many white power structures are unable to engage in because higher education is still operating within an equality framework. I, a queer Black woman staff member at a predominately white institution leading the work on intersectional feminism, do not need equality. There is repair to be done. This repair might be in the form of money, opportunity, access to or even dismantling of certain structures. This repair requires a deep shift in the way our institutions, and those that lead them, operate: from recruiting, hiring, onboarding, and supervisory practices. Until then, our racial battle fatigue is quelled by our resilience and intimate (ancestral) knowledge of the operation of organizational white supremacy.
>
> (Bulaong Ramiz)

These narratives highlight the collective weight of being women of color in higher education spaces. A further complicating factor is that we are women of color engaging in DEI in higher education. Our experiences with microaggressions feel exacerbated as we seek to dismantle the root causes of these experiences. In the next section, we will discuss the unique experiences and circumstances that women of color experience while engaging in DEI work.

CAUGHT IN THE CROSSFIRE: DOING THE WORK WHILE LIVING IT

"Black women's lives are a series of negotiations that aim to reconcile the contradictions separating our own internally defined images of self as African-American women with our objectification as the Other" (Collins, 2000, p. 110).

As women of color leaders in DEI work in higher education, it is increasingly difficult and challenging in separating our "work" from our lived experiences. For us, the motivation to pursue DEI work has been rooted in our own experiences, both inside and outside of the academy. We have sought to create a world and educational experiences that are different from our own for the students that are coming up behind us. We recognized the inequities and marginalization in our stories and wanted to use our perceived power to "be the change." We bought into the idea that in order to effect change in higher education, we must be part of this system. But as women of color, we have quickly realized the ways that we get caught up in the crossfire, the ways we sit in the metaphorical borderlands, and the ways we try to dismantle the master's house while living in it. We will continue to feel stuck unless leaders in higher education understand the way women of color engage with diversity and inclusion as a field, as a practice, is fundamentally different. While those with privileged identities (white, cisgender, heterosexual, male, etc.) might approach DEI as a discipline, women of color cannot simply extricate themselves from this and apply an "objective" lens.

The following narratives illuminate the ways we often feel caught or stuck when doing diversity and inclusion work. Tensions might lie between ourselves and the students we serve and between ourselves and the institution:

> Being a first-generation, queer Latinx woman, I intimately know the self-imposed expectations that I must serve everyone—my family, friends, community, colleagues, etc.—before myself. Yet, what

175

served me in the past no longer serves me in the present or the future. Currently, I oversee and direct the only Cultural/Affinity Center on campus—a campus that of course, proudly brags about its commitment to diversity as we are a Hispanic Serving Institution (HSI) and have 67% first-generation students. Yet, what gets posted on websites and admissions brochures rarely reflects the reality of the University. With being the singular Center on campus that is simultaneously the Dream/LBGTQ/Black/Latinx/Women & Gender/ APIA Center, I tried to be everything to everyone....all the while burning myself out.

(Shantel Martinez)

The students I served were primarily students of color, LGBTQ students, first-generation students, and low-income students. Many of those aforementioned students sat in the intersections of those identities. My hiring signaled to the students that perhaps things were changing for the better at their institution, an institution that caused so much pain and trauma through the silencing, dismissal, and erasure of students. They were students whose identities mirrored my own. I soon would know the ways I would be silenced, dismissed and erased too.

(Alli Roman)

My prior position was at an institution on the East Coast rooted in white supremacy. When I interviewed for the job, I met another black woman who shared with me that she was excited to see another woman of color at the institution. She then pulled me in closer and said, 'so that you know, they are only interviewing you because you are black'... I knew my time would be short at that institution as I unintentionally made a white woman cry just for holding her accountable. I was her supervisor; it's what I was paid to do. She used her *whiteness as a property* against me. She gathered her troops and waged war on me. Just like that, I was gone.

(Willette Capers)

I recall one summer where another black person had been shot, it's sad that I can't recall who, there were so many deaths that year. I was mentally exhausted. I was tired. I was terrified. I had only been an OMA director for five months. I recall calling into work because I just physically, emotionally and mentally had nothing to offer my students or colleagues. I felt awful at that moment because

I wanted to be a strong leader and show up and keep fighting the good fight, but I just could not set aside my own identities as a black person and put a happy face on the situation. I needed time and space to process my own pain.

(Precious Porras)

In my role, I had developed strong relationships with students of color, many of them very active and vocal regarding the mistreatment they received at the hands of the administration. There were several situations where it was strongly implied that I had to essentially choose between supporting the students or siding with the administration. It felt like an impossible space to sit in, especially while holding my own identities.

(Alli Roman)

There are an abundance of experiences not captured in the narratives in the previous section. There exists a space where the simultaneous experience of holding our identities while doing DEI causes an immense amount of pain and trauma. This simultaneity provides a unique lens in which we examine issues of DEI as well, as we move forward toward transformative change. As women of color diversity leaders, we possess unique insider knowledge as well as the empathy to understand the necessity of creating substantial and sustainable change due to our status as an *outsider-within* (Collins, 2000). For as much as our fight is for our students, it also becomes a fight for us. The personal is political in this regard. We devote so much energy and labor in order to dismantle the oppression that exists in the academy, because we personally know what's at stake. Our collective liberation is intertwined with those we fight for.

The irony lies with the fact that although we, as women of color, often hold transformative solutions rooted in the knowledge gained through our own experiences, we often lack the institutional power necessary to drive change. What's worse is that while we are often hired and initially lauded for our perspectives and experiences, we later become relegated to the margins and silenced if we try to disrupt the status quo. It then becomes a tension of being hired to "do the work," but "doing the work" means disrupting and dismantling the systems of power, privilege, and oppression that so many people in higher education cling on to. And that is hard to not take personally:

When I departed my previous institution and my role as director for diversity and inclusion, I mourned what felt like a tremendous

177

personal loss. I literally put my body on the line, put countless extra hours in, and, as a result, my mental and physical health suffered. For a while, I felt that this sacrifice was worth it. I had to become part of the system in order to change it. I knew that my experiences fueled me to do things differently and to build a department from the ground up. I envisioned something that I hoped to be radical, and transformative, and to be what I saw was needed in higher education. My ideas, the excitement, the hope for something better kept me pushing, even though I should have walked away much sooner. I finally did when I realized that despite my fight, I would need to leave what essentially was my dream job because I was not feeling supported to do the work that needed to be done. Shortly after I left, I saw the institution quickly and with great urgency begin to implement some of the same projects and initiatives that they initially ignored or blocked.

(Alli Roman)

For myself, I have a unique approach that keeps my nose to the grind, head above water, and back as a bridge. This approach is rooted in *nagualismo* – a Nahuatl term for shapeshifter – as a transformative pedagogy that embraces borderlands performances and mestiza consciousness (Anzaldúa, 1990). Nepanlta is living *in-between*, living *ambiguously*, living as a *shapeshifter*. Robert Gutiérrez-Perez (2018) further illuminates this concept when he states, 'Nepantleras are monsters in everyday life that cross racial, gendered, sexual, spiritual, and classed borders as they mediate multiple worlds, which create understandings that are both feared and desired in cultural places and spaces. A nepantlera is a person who holds a positionality at the crossroads of several different identities and cultures' (347). As a womxn of color, I know that I am seen and labeled as a monster (Calafell, 2015; Holling, 2018). Yet, I use this to my advantage as it gives me the privilege to care less about what the institution thinks of me. By directing this energy away from trying to please an institution or people who neither support me nor believe I should have a seat at the table, I am afforded the ability to redirect this energy into students, issues, or systems where I know I can create positive change. Of course, this is not always the case, but I try to the best of my ability to place my monstrous energy into creating beauty and brilliance— because as we know, when labeled monstrous, cultivating acts of joy and laughter are forms of resistance. In doing so, I leverage my shapeshifter and monstrous ways as a strength and way to cultivate community when oppressive systems as well as the institution want me to remain the *only one*. So to all of my monstrous womxn of color in this line of work, I got you.

(Shantel Martinez)

Women of color diversity leaders must constantly and consistently balance themselves on the tightrope, being careful not to tip over one side or the other. This "balancing act" can become a source of stress that those with privileged identities might not have to contend with. Additionally, women of color leaders might be called to balance additional unspoken responsibilities such as mentoring (formally and informally) students of color as well as other marginalized students, serving on all the committees, and more. We are looked upon to solve all the problems and hundreds of years of injustice and inequity with limited resources and institutional power. It can be dismaying to feel like we are placed in these precarious positions.

OUR SISTERS' KEEPER (STRATEGIES FOR SUCCESS AND SUPPORT)

Nobody's going to save you.
No one's going to cut you down,
cut the thorns around you.
No one's going to storm
the castle walls nor
kiss awake your birth,
climb down your hair,
nor mount you
onto the white steed.
There is no one who
will feed the yearning.
Face it. You will have
to do, do it yourself
                    –Gloria Anzaldua

In this chapter, we have discussed the lived experiences as women of color leaders in DEI. As a collective, we have experienced setback after setback and been caught in between two feuding worlds, all while trying to do work that for many of us we genuinely love. We name the trauma, we name the pain. But we must also name the ways that some of the biggest sources of strength have been other women of color. In this section, we will highlight the ways that we have centered healing, joy, community, and love as a personal and collective practice:

> It took a year of intense therapy to begin the process of unlearning toxic behaviors and reclaiming my brilliance, my confidence, and myself in order to unleash my inner xhingon (or bad-ass woman). As a *testimonialista*, writing myself and my story into existence was the first step of taking back my power. I utilize writing not only to process the world in which I live in, but to seek clarity when chaos is the name of the diversity, equity, and inclusion game. Now, when our small, but mighty, team of three gets criticized for 'not doing enough' or 'being enough,' I can lead knowing that I am okay with that. You can criticize all you want, but at the end of the day, you will never know or understand all of the dirty work, messiness, or complexity we face on a daily basis. It takes strategy, patience, and skin as thick as an elephant in order to survive in this line of work. *Oh, and of course, a good therapist.*
>
> (Shantel Martinez)

> When I was initially offered my role, I knew I would need to be in community with other women of color. As a result, in 2017, I started the Women of Color Directors Network, a Facebook group that brings together women of color leaders engaged in DEI and social justice work in higher education. In three years we have grown to over 350 members, an active group chat, several convenings during national conferences, and even a weekly Zoom happy hour. It is healing to be in a space where people just get it. We don't have to fully explain what it means to be a woman of color doing DEI work. We can just exist, in all of complexities, and live with joy, community, and self-care at the center of our praxis. We have cheered each other on, provided advice, mentorship, and space to bring our whole selves to the group.
>
> (Alli Roman)

> There are many strategies I have employed over my career, some that have worked better than others, but all having one thing in common: community connection. I have been able to redefine success outside of the normative framework of the cishetero white supremacist patriarchy and the way it informs academia. My success is rooted in reestablishing collectivist ways of being amongst constituents, leaning into collaborative projects and resolutions,

180

and centering compassion and understanding in my interactions with colleagues and students alike. In 2017, when I was working at a small private liberal arts institution in New England, my student staff and I created community norms or ways of being that would inform our engagement with each other. One of the highlights of that list and experience was the uplifting of 'compassionate accountability' as the way we would be together, hold each other, and grow as individuals and as a unit. A sub pillar of compassionate accountability is truth-telling, something that is not historically received well by those positioned above me within the hierarchy.

As the title of this section alludes to, I believe in the idea of my Sister's Keeper in very specific and broad ways. One of the ways I practice protecting, loving, and supporting Black and brown women in higher education is speaking truth to power while, at the same time, trying to show compassion. I have found myself in many one-on-ones and around a myriad of tables where the actions (or inactions) of a person in power undoubtedly caused harm to me or to someone else even more vulnerable than I was. In many of these moments, I feel called into a practice of compassionate accountability, thinking that if, in connection and community, I can move someone in power to recognize and change behavior or a decision, it would create greater belonging for students. Unfortunately, unlike my amazing team of students who signed onto this way of being, many of my colleagues and peers receive, as aggressive, inappropriate, and out of my lane, my advocacy, truth telling, and attempt to hold them to account.

The dismissiveness and correction I have experienced within higher education workspaces further confirms that as a field, the subversive ways we exclude and harm women of color, and people of color more broadly, is deeply ingrained in the structure of the institutions and the socialization of those who lead them. Part of our duty as our sister's keeper is to combat these manifestations of violence against our humanity and ways of being so that others entering the institution can be seen, can be safe, and feel cared for holistically. The interpersonal caretaking of our fellow women of color colleagues and students that we take on is often a band aid on a wound constantly scratched opened by others. Until we change the larger system, women of color will continue to experience large scale marginalization as well as interpersonal violence.

(Bulaong Ramiz)

181

If it were not for my community, I would have burned out a long time ago. Doing this work is difficult. I need people to bounce ideas off, I need people to debrief with. I need people to be joyous with. I find, when I do not feel good, I know it's because I have turned inward (as an introvert this is a thing I do often). I need to engage with my people and my community to deal with the stress of this work.

(Precious Porras)

I also recognize the need to have an external community. This is my group of friends who work at other universities across the country that get it. These are the folks that I send emails to, to be looked over to ensure my point was getting across without coming across as argumentative or emotional. They are who I send the ridiculous things I hear day-to-day. They make me laugh when I want to cry. They push me when I want to quit. These are my people, and I couldn't do it without them.

(Willette A. Capers)

Women of color have served as lifelines and sources of affirmation and support for one another. We have found that being in community can create both formal and informal networks, both of which are crucial, especially in the field of higher education. These networks can connect women of color with job leads, professional development opportunities, leadership opportunities, and more. Moreover, these spaces provide the necessary affirmation and respite needed for many of us to be able to keep pushing on. These collective spaces also serve as sites of resistance through the centering of joy and rest.

CONCLUSION

We come to this work offering *our stories, offering ourselves*. Our *testimonios* of power and pain. *Testimonios* of courage and persistence. But most importantly, we offer our authentic *testimonios* of *survival*. Being women of color in this field is not for the thinned skin or faint of heart. We are expected to do twice the amount of work which often follows up with half the recognition – knowing that most of the time, there isn't even recognition of our labor, existence, or worth. Yet, we do not shy from offering our brilliance, our challenges, and our experiences. Rather, we offer our vulnerabilities as an invitation for others to do this work and get their hands dirty. For the women of color reading this, you are not alone.

We are here with you always in spirit. It not only takes a village to do this work, but more importantly, it takes a community full of ride or dies that intimately know and support the labor involved with this work and leadership. For you, here are our closing words:

> For women of color leaders in higher education I leave you these words: never forget your worth. One of my women of color mentors in my doctoral education reminded us daily to always protect our labor, protect our energy, and protect our worth. With that said, know what is your line in the sand and be ready to walk away if it gets crossed. *It is okay to walk away.* It is not okay for this work to steal your joy away from you. At the same time, know that this work is not a sprint, it is a marathon – so plan accordingly. Lastly, know that sometimes (and unfortunately) our biggest critics can come from our own communities. It doesn't take away the sting, but I wish I would have known this before going down this road.
>
> (Shantel Martinez)

Seek out and work to get to know your accomplices on campus and in the community immediately. Your accomplices are your folks who will use their power, privilege, talents, and skills to dismantle systems of oppression in their areas of influence; they differ from allies who traditionally only provide support. To encourage folks to attend my educational sessions, I needed leverage to get them in the door. To accomplish this, I created a ten-course certification program that would make them Certified Diversity Advocates after the completion of said program. Those who completed the program would be able to take part in a large graduation, receive a certificate, a t-shirt, and a customized stole to wear during commencement, convocation, and so much more. Prior to rollout, I met with the Vice President of Human Resources and our university's President to see if after a year with folks going through the program, if we required all search committees going forward to have at least one Certified Diversity Advocate sit on all search committees. They supported my request and passed the information down. I quickly saw who my accomplices were right away. They were excited. They were hungry. They shared that they were using knowledge gained in said sessions immediately. I knew once I developed a group of accomplices across campus, my thoughts and ideas would beat me in the room before I was even invited to the table. They were in their respective offices and departments cheering me on, supporting my decisions, and showing up when others didn't. This was my on-campus community, and I knew I could change the culture of the institution with them by my side.

(Willette A. Capers)

In order for women of color, particularly Black Women, to be successful in their role as diversity leaders, there are two recommendations I would share. I would first start by ensuring she has a seat at the table and that the words and knowledge she shares are valued and considered as deeply as the other voices at the table. While diverse issues are her specialty, these issues are interwoven into the entire fabric of the institution. She deserves a significant stake in the administrative functions of the institution when traditionally she has been used to clean up the mess that could have been avoided had she just been included in the first place. Next, pay her. Pay her in time, support, energy, and, most importantly, in money. Historically, women of color are paid 39% less than white men and 21% less than white women. In simpler terms, for every $1.00, a white man makes, women of color are paid $0.61 (leanin. org). We need to stop making women of color 'make a dollar out of fifteen cents.' Additionally, when budgets need to be reduced, stop immediately cutting funding towards diversity initiatives and or staffing needs. Institutions and humans cannot survive with diversity offices of one.

(Willette A. Capers)

For leaders of higher education institutions, we provide the following recommendations: Listen to the women of color leaders you hire to engage in this work, do your own self-work, and examine your institutional commitment to DEI and if it supports your women of color DEI leaders. As institutions undoubtedly engage with ways to enhance campus DEI efforts, it is important to assess the precarious landscape in which many DEI initiatives stand. With the added pressures and the sociopolitical landscape, many higher education institutions and organizations are responding to student unrest and protest with the creation of DEI positions. While a noble start, the creation of these positions alone should not, and cannot be the only solution to address the racism, sexism, homophobia, etc. that plague higher education institutions. The next section will outline and expand our recommendations for higher education institution leaders. These recommendations are based on our collective experiences as women of color and the experiences of other women of color DEI leaders.

184

Our first recommendation for higher education leaders is to listen to the women of color you hire to engage in this work. In our experiences, we have felt invisible and unheard, even in instances that demand our expertise. Because of our age (seen as relatively young and therefore assumed to be inexperienced and incompetent), our racial and ethnic identity, and our gender identity, we routinely experience roadblocks to our work as a result of the intentional and unintentional silencing and ignoring. As mentioned in a previous section, the straddling of both hypervisibility and invisibility creates an experience where many of us find it increasingly difficult to do the job we were hired to because we are not listened to. Consequentially, institutions lose out on innovative and creative solutions to campus issues.

In addition to listening to women of color DEI leaders as it refers to their job duties, it is important to build a relationship with trust as the foundation. Chances are, women of color have to negotiate and hide parts of themselves while engaging in their professional work. That means as the supervisors, colleagues, and leaders, it is imperative that *you* do the work and take ownership in creating an affirming and supportive environment for them where they can feel more comfortable in bringing their full selves. Women of color, across industries:

> receive less support from their managers, according to the McKinsey and Leanin.org study. They are less likely to have bosses who promote their work contributions to others, help them navigate organizational politics, or socialize with them outside of work. Thus, they're often left out of the informal networks that propel most high-potentials forward in their careers.
>
> (Washington & Roberts, 2019)

The implications for the lack of support that women of color experience in the workplace can exacerbate feelings of isolation, racial battle fatigue, and burnout. This then can contribute to high turnover rates for those in DEI leadership positions.

Our second recommendation for higher education leaders is to do your own self-work. For women of color DEI leaders to feel supported and have supervisors and colleagues that understand the work, it is important to take ownership of one's own learning and development as it relates to DEI. There is an abundance of resources, videos, literature, etc. that highlights the ways higher education replicates and maintains systems of oppression. The onus of building one's awareness of one's privilege and their role in maintaining systemic oppression falls on every institutional leader. Institutional leaders need to be honest with themselves and others regarding their willingness and commitment to do the hard work with the DEI leaders.

Because this work can be isolating and because many of us as DEI leaders have been situated as the only ones doing DEI work on their campuses (according to title and responsibilities). By having colleagues and supervisors who regularly engage with this work and their positionality within larger systemic issues of oppression, it can help create an environment where women of color feel less alone in this work. Again, it is the collective responsibility of institutional leaders to do their own self-work in order to make more equitable and inclusive campuses a reality.

Our final recommendation is to examine your commitment to DEI. There is a sense of collective urgency that is swirling around the higher education landscape that has seemed to accelerate the adoption of DEI language. Coupled with the mass creation of inaugural DEI positions and the establishing of DEI offices in the last ten years alone, it seems that institutions are trying to demonstrate their commitment to DEI. However, "when institutions acknowledge a commitment to diversity, that simply means they are open to, or are specifically recruiting, people of color" (Garrett & Turman, 2019) rather than grappling with and addressing "institutional whiteness" (Ahmed, 2012) and institutional racism. The use of the term "diversity," as both a starting point and sometimes an end, evokes a sense of comfort in those who believe terms like "equity" are too lofty, complicated, and unrealistic. As Ahmed (2012) suggests, "the word 'diversity' invokes difference but does not necessarily evoke commitment to action or redistributive justice" (p. 53). In fact, many institutional efforts seem to take on a cyclical process as part of their "action", in which a problem is identified, a committee is convened, recommendations are made, DEI positions are created and filled, the DEI leader, or if one is lucky, leaders, attempts to carry out the recommendations with little to no new budget, and then are burnt out after a few years. These leaders then leave, and the cycle begins again.

Unfortunately, while diversity and inclusion become espoused values and institutional "priorities", "not every institution is designed with or prepared to make such a commitment" (Garrett & Turman, 2019). As institutional leaders, ask yourself the following questions to assess whether the commitment to DEI is one of just language and appeasement or of action and justice (Stewart, 2017). Are your women of color DEI leaders figureheads or do they have the institutional power and capital to drive change? Do they have regular access to the president and to the president's cabinet? Who do they report to and does this reporting structure help or inhibit progress? Do they have the appropriate resources and staffing to do their job effectively? What barriers exist that prevent women of color DEI leaders from successfully doing their job? What structures of support exist to prevent burnout and the revolving door of DEI leaders?

These questions must be asked of institutional leaders. Many of the current environments that we have been situated in have led to our rapid burnout and to the rapid burnout of other women of color diversity leaders. It is unfortunate that, for many of us, we can come together and commiserate regarding our collective trauma and hurt. So many amazing women of color diversity leaders have even left the field or jobs that they loved, all because of the insurmountable hurdles they would have to jump. We love this work and will do so much to create change, but at what cost?

We hope that this chapter serves as a catalyst for substantial change in higher education, where our stories, strengths, and perspectives can not only be acknowledged but also our voices centered. There must be reckoning that we simply cannot divest our own experiences from the work that we do as DEI leaders. There must be an understanding that the personal is political and that it is through this understanding and intentional centering that we will see the transformative change we need in higher education.

REFERENCES

Ahmed, S. (2012). *On being included: Racism and diversity in institutional life.* Durham, NC: Duke University Press.

Amoah, J. (1997). Narrative: The road to black feminist theory. *Berkeley Women's Law Journal,* 12, 84–102.

Anzaldúa, G. (1990). *Making Face, making soul/haciendo caras: Creative and critical perspectives by women of color.* San Francisco: Aunt Lute Press.

Anzaldúa, G. E. (2002). Preface: Unnatural bridges, (un)safe spaces. In G. E. Anzaldúa & A. Keating (Eds.), This bridge we call home: Radical visions for transformation (pp. 1–5). New York, NY: Routledge.

Banks-Wallace, J. (1998). Emancipatory potential of storytelling in a group. *Journal of Nursing Scholarship,* 30, 17–21.

Behar, R. (1993). *Translated woman: Crossing the border with Esperanza's story.* Boston, MA: Beacon.

Bernal, D. D., Burciaga, R., & Carmona, J. F. (2012). Chicana/Latina testimonios: Mapping the methodological, pedagogical, and political. *Equity & Excellence in Education,* 45(3), 363–372. doi: 10.1080/10665684.2012.698149.

Bird, G. (1998). Breaking the silence. In S. J. Ortiz (Ed.), *Speaking for the generations: Native writers on writing.* Tucson: University of Arizona Press.

Burgos-Debray, E. (1984). *I Rigoberta Menchú, an Indian woman in Guatemala*. New York: Verso.

Calafell, B. M. (2015). *Monstrosity, performance, and race in contemporary culture*. New York: Peter Lang Publishing.

Canaan, A., Moraga, C., & Anzaldua, G. (1983). *Brownness*. This bridge called my back: Writings by radical women of color Albany, NY: SUNY Press.

Charlesworth, E. A., & Nathan, R. N. (1982). *Stress management: A comprehensive guide to wellness*. Houston, TX: Biobehavioral Press.

Collins, P. (2000). *Black feminist thought: Knowledge, consciousness, and the politics of empowerment*. New York: Routledge.

Du Bois, W. E. B. (1999). *The souls of black folk. Critical edition*. Gates, H. L., Oliver, T. H. (Eds.). New York: Norton (Original work published 1903).

Edwards, K., & del Guadalupe Davidson, M. (2018). *College curriculum at the crossroads: Women of color reflect and resist*. London: Routledge.

Garrett, S. D., & Turman, N. T. (2018, Nov.). Finding fit as an 'outsider within': A critical exploration of Black women navigating the workplace in higher education. In B. Reece, V. Tran, E. DeVore, & G. Porcaro (Eds.), *Debunking the myth of job fit in higher education*. Sterling, VA: Stylus Publishing.

Guthrie, V. L., Woods, E., Cusker, C., & Gregory, M. (2005). A portrait of balance: Personal and professional balance among student affairs educators. *College Student Affairs Journal*, 24(2), 110–127.

Gutierrez y Muhs, G., Flores Niemann, Y., Gonzales, C., & Harries, A. (2012). *Presumed incompetent: The intersections of race and class for women in academia*. Boulder: University of Colorado Press.

Harris, T.W. (2015). *The Sisters are alright: changing the broken narrative of Black women in America*. Oakland, CA: Berrett-Koehler Publishers, Inc.

Holling, M. (2018). "You intimidate me" as a microaggressive controlling image to discipline womyn of color faculty. *Southern Communication Journal*. doi: 10.1080/1041794X.2018.1511748

hooks, b. (2007). Writing for Reconciliation: A Musing. *The Journal of the Assembly for Expanded Perspectives on Learning*, 13(1), 3.

Latina Feminist Group. (2012). *Telling to live: Latina feminist testimonios*. Durham, NC: Duke University Press.

Lomas, C. & Joysmith, C. (eds) (2005). *One wound for another/ Una herida por otra: Testimonios de Latin@s in the U.S. through cyberspace (11 de septiembre de 2001–11 de marzo de 2002)*. Mexico, MX: Universidad Nacional Autonoma de Mexico.

Lorde, A. (1984). *Sister/outsider*. Berkeley, CA: Crossing Press.

Martinez, S. (2019). Lessons from my battle scars: Testimonios' transformative possibilities. In L. Hernandez, D. Bowen, S. De los Santos Upton, & A.

Martinez (eds.), *Latina/o/x communications studies: Theory, methods, and practice*. Lanham, MD: Lexington Books.

Marrun, N. (2018). Somos gente estudiada: Creating change within and outside the walls of academia. In K. Edwards, & M. del Guadalupe Davidson (eds.), *College curriculum at the crossroads: Women of color reflect and resist*. London: Routledge.

McCoy, D. L., & Rodricks, D. J. (2015). Critical Race Theory in Higher Education: 20 Years of Theoretical and Research Innovations: *ASHE Higher Education Report* (Volume 41, Number 3). Hoboken, NJ: John Wiley & Sons.

Minh-Ha, T. (1989). *Woman, native, other: Writing postcoloniality and feminism*. Bloomington: Indiana University Press.

Nguyen, C. (2016). Asian American women faculty: Stereotypes and triumphs. In Betty Taylor (ed.), *Listening to the voices: Multi-ethnic women in education*. San Francisco, CA: University of San Francisco.

Nixon, M. L. (2017). Experiences of women of color university chief diversity officers. *Journal of Diversity in Higher Education*, 10(4), 301–317. doi: 10.1037/dhe0000043

Okun, T. (2001). White supremacy culture in organizations, dismantling racism: A workbook for social change groups. https://www.whitesupremacyculture.info/uploads/4/3/5/7/43579015/okun_-_white_sup_culture.pdf

Patton, L. D., & Catching, C. (2009). 'Teaching while Black': Narratives of African American student affairs faculty. *International Journal of Qualitative Studies in Education*, 22(6), 713–728.

Reyes, K. B., & Rodríguez, J. E. C. (2012). Testimonio: Origins, terms, and resources. *Equity & Excellence in Education*, 45(3), 525–538.

Roman, A. (2019). The words that set us free: storytelling as praxis for student affairs professionals of color. In U. M Robinson-Nichols, M. Galloway Burke, & L. Hall (Eds.), *No ways tired: The journey for professionals of color in student affairs*.

Ross, L. [Western States Center] (2001, February 15). The origin of the phrase of "women of color" [Video]. YouTube. https://www.youtube.com/watch?v=82vl34mi4Iw

Sanchez-Hucles, J. V., & Davis, D. D. (2010). Women and women of color in leadership: Complexity, identity, and intersectionality. *American Psychologist*, 65(3), 171–181. https://doi.org/10.1037/a0017459

Smith, W., Hung, M., & Franklin, J. (2011). Racial battle fatigue and the miseducation of black men: Racial microaggressions, societal problems, and environmental stress. *The Journal of Negro Education*, 80(1), 63–82.

Stewart, D. L. (2017, March 30). Language of appeasement. Inside Higher Ed. https://www.insidehighered.com/views/2017/03/30/colleges-need-language-shift-not-one-you-think-essay

Steele, C. M., & Aronson, J. (1995). Stereotype threat and the intellectual test performance of African Americans. *Journal of Personality and Social Psychology, 69*(5), 797.

Sue, D. W., & Constantine, M. G. (2007). Racial microaggressions as instigators of difficult dialogues on race: Implications for student affairs educators and students. *College Student Affairs Journal, 26*(2), 136–143.

Turner, C. S. V., González, J. C., & Wong (Lau), K. (2011). Faculty women of color: The critical nexus of race and gender. *Journal of Diversity in Higher Education, 4*(4), 199–211.

Walkington, L. (2017). How far have we really come? Black women faculty and graduate students' experiences in higher education. *Humboldt Journal of Social Relations, 39*, 51–65.

Wardell, M. (2020). *Twice as good: Leadership and power for women of color.* New York: Morgan James Publishers.

Washington, Z., & Roberts, L. M. (2019). Women of color get less support at work. Here's how managers can change that. *Harvard Business Review.* 1–5.

Chapter Nine

Navigating Call-Out Culture

An Approach for Campus Transformation and Diversity Leader Resilience

Tony N. Tyler and Erin Lain

INTRO

It's 4 am and campus security gets a panicked phone call from a student in a first-year residence hall. The student just received a "canceled flyer" under their door that outs over a half-dozen men and one on-campus organization as predators of rape, sexual assault, and being physically and emotionally aggressive. The student's name is listed on the flyer for being emotionally aggressive and is now receiving threatening messages on social media. The student, Cedric, has engaged in a lot of equity and inclusion work throughout his time at his undergraduate institution, including planning educational events about the experiences of students of color on campus, lobbying his college to start an African diaspora concentration, and serving on multiple equity and inclusion committees.

Earlier that semester, the Equity and Inclusion office at the institution updated their website with more transparent data on the demographic diversity of the university, retention of faculty and staff of color, and information about the history of equity and inclusion initiatives the university has undertaken over the 150-year history. The data included how many students, faculty, and staff identified as lesbian, gay, or bisexual, because the most recent data they had only included those categories. Although the Senior Diversity Officer (SDO) was concerned about the lack of data on trans, nonbinary, or other gender identities, she decided to post the information to provide information on the demographics of the institution. The statistic listed the percentage of Lesbian, Bisexual, Gay, and Queer (LGBQ) community members, with an asterisk describing who was and was not included in the statistic. Two weeks after the unveiling of the website, students started to post on social media about the T missing within the LGBQ statistic and accused the Office of Equity and Inclusion of subscribing to Trans Exclusionary Radical Feminist (TERF) beliefs through these posts. The SDO received backlash on social media and students got local student organizations to call her out publicly through social media.

In the midst of election season, the university has hosted almost every candidate running for office, including Democrats, Republicans, and third-party candidates. A major news outlet hosts a debate on the campus with the Democratic candidates, and several prominent Republican figures come to the campus for town hall discussions. The university also hosts a political rally for President Trump in its stadium that brings approximately 9,000–10,000 supporters on campus. The College Republican group on campus wants to handout donuts to Trump supporters that have been waiting in line for days to get into the rally. A Student Affairs Administrator who directs multicultural programs and oversees all student organizations for the campus helps the College Republicans handout the donuts. A picture gets posted on social media of the donut distribution, which results in students, alumni, and community members condemning the Student Affairs Administrator. He later gets disinvited to other student of color activities, despite years of being an ally and huge supporter.

All three of these examples are true to life experiences, with slight changes in details to protect privacy. They illustrate the nature and nuance of call-out and cancelling on campuses, in relation to those who actively engage in equity and inclusion work on a routine basis. As campuses dig deeper into the work of equity and inclusion, various stakeholders have engaged in call-out culture as a means to express pain, gain power, and publicly shame others when they perceive wrongs. Due to the nature of our current cultural positioning, individuals feel empowered to speak out when people, practices, and structures perpetuate oppression. This speaking out often manifests itself as a 'call-out,' a contested practice that is manifest in various methods and motivations. Diversity leaders working in higher education are particularly vulnerable to call-outs because they participate in high stakes equity and inclusion work, engaging many marginalized communities. Often university communities engage in call-out culture when they feel that our allyship is disingenuous, out of a sense of guilt or discomfort, when they think we have misused or misunderstood knowledge or that we have not brokered knowledge or privilege in an appropriate way.

In our three examples, the student, SDO, and the Student Affairs Administrator are all involved in high stakes work. They are trying to push the campus to identify pockets of inequality and move the needle to make a more inclusive and equitable learning environment. The student is working to change curriculum, the SDO is working to change transparency, and the Student Affairs Administrator is working to support students from multicultural and underrepresented groups. For both the student and the Student Affairs Administrator, the call-out came from a perception of disingenuous allyship. Students perceived that the Student Affairs Administrator was not aware of, or would not acknowledge, the harm that the Trump administration has brought to marginalized groups. Those who called-out the student thought that the student used his privileged identities to oppress others, thus not being a true ally to marginalized groups that he is a part of. Finally, the community perceived that the SDO did not have knowledge of trans issues or was not a genuine ally. All these call-outs stem from pain and harm derived from oppression, but they also create pain and potential harm. Because those in diversity leadership positions are often from marginalized groups, the pain created by call-outs often compound years of trauma. In our examples, the student identified as a gay and gender-queer person of color, the SDO a woman of color, and the Student Affairs Administrator a queer person with disabilities. Navigating the call-outs was a complex process, as those called-out in certain respects do not come from a position of privilege, although in other ways are attributed privileges. This complexity of identity and role is an important nuance in navigating call-out and cancel culture.

WHAT IS A CALL-OUT?

The internet and social media have provided a new platform for individuals to express concerns with other people's actions, behaviors, and beliefs (Friedersdorf, 2017). Prior to the internet age, an individual could confront a person with concerns, but the audience that viewed the concern would be limited by location, access, and time. For example, in 1517 the monk and scholar Martin Luther penned a document of 95 theses that challenged and criticized the behaviors and beliefs of the Catholic Church and posted it on the Wittenberg Church door (Luther, Wengert, & Project Muse Content Provider, 2015). This early form of calling-out was quickly circulated through Germany and Rome, and served as a catalyst for the Protestant Reformation. Current day call-outs share many characteristics with Martin Luther's 95 theses. They critique individuals, institutions, and systems in a public way, with the purpose of informing both the individual and society at large about perceived wrongs (Ross, 2019).

A call-out is a public articulated critique or condemnation of another's actions, beliefs, or behaviors (Tatum, 2014). Typically, a call-out draws attention to a perceived problematic element of those actions, and generally surrounds issues of power, privilege, or oppression (Trần, 2013). These elements of oppression or privilege are often unseen by the offender, and the call-out acts as a catalyst for helping alter the sensitivities of the individual or systems. A typical call-out might traverse a range of actions, from an individual making a microaggressive comment and the recipient or bystander retorting that their comment was hurtful and had elements of racism, sexism, or homophobia to someone implementing or carrying out a policy or procedure that has oppressive implications. One of the primary goals of a call-out is to stop oppressive behavior and promote change. The call-out may also serve to give voice to those from marginalized groups that traditionally have had none. Often, both in the past and present, because of systems of power and oppression, the person from a marginalized identity could be subject to violence or other forms of punishment if they spoke up, such as being fired, being excluded, or subject to physical attack. The opportunity to call-out provides a means of reclaiming lost power and redeeming a sense of self-worth.

Call-outs can take a variety of forms, from in person dialogue to online posts, and can range in length from short tweets to lengthy articles published on websites (i.e., *Google's Ideological Echo Chamber*). All call-outs have a public element to them. A typical call-out enables multiple people to view the critique. A call-out that has no public dimension to it does not meet the definition, because the ability for the public, or at least a wide range of people, to consume the critique serves as a vital aspect of the call-out process. The ability for others to endorse the call-out uses elements of shame and public reprimand to help change the behavior of the recipient. A private criticism between two individuals is not the same as a call-out. Feedback on a paper from a teacher, a private write-up from a boss, or a lecture from a family member or friend does not operate in the same fashion as a call-out. Although all of these instances include critique or even the condemnation of a person's actions, beliefs, or behaviors, the lack of the public element precludes them from being a call-out. The call-out relies on the shame of public knowledge as a method of changing behavior.

WHAT IS CANCELING?

Canceling involves no longer supporting, engaging with, or working with a person because of their problematic action, behavior, or belief (Romano, 2019). Although canceling typically involves an individual with a public persona, the process can also be applied to other entities, products, institutions, or organizations. Cancellation is similar to call-outs, in the sense that it is a condemnation of the person in a public way, but cancelling escalates the condemnation because this public sanction, in order to correct the injustice, attempts to ruin the individual or group reputation and livelihood. For example, the public cancelled Harvey Weinstein in 2017, when stories of his years of rape and sexual assault surfaced. He lost his job, was condemned both in person and online, and generally became a pariah around the world. All of his potential projects or opportunities came to a halt, and people cut ties with him.

Cancelling, similar to calling-out, requires a public nature to the action (Yar & Bromwich, 2019). Without many people being able to appreciate the cancel, the action does not have the same effect. Although an individual can privately choose not to engage an individual or use a product, a private action will not have the same outcome as a public one, because it will not influence the person to change their behavior. Typically, cancelling begins with a person or many people declaring that they are "cancelling" an individual or declaring that they will not be supporting that individual anymore. Doing this on a social media platform allows many people to join in this effort. The movement grows until enough people have subscribed to the cancel to ruin the person's prospects of continuing in their position. Without the mass effort, the action will not achieve the intended effect.

THE NATURE OF CALL-OUT AND CANCEL CULTURE ON UNIVERSITY CAMPUSES

Culture has shifted in recent years to embrace call-outs as a common and expected way of dealing with perceived injustices (Waters, 2019). It has also become a way for people to take action. Social media provides a platform, with an unlimited audience, which enables people to easily express their critique or condemnation. In the past, to call-out someone you would have to write a letter to the editor, or find some other means of publication that was controlled by a third party who could edit or influence the message. Now, people can critique in a public way with no barriers, other than a complaint after the fact from an aggrieved party, which in rare instances might result in the post being taken down. The ease of the opportunity to critique and condemn has changed norms so that it is seen as an appropriate action in the face of injustice and oppression.

In wider society, call-outs and cancels typically occur between strangers. A citizen can call-out or cancel a politician or celebrity, or even call-out a high school classmate from the past who they rarely see in person. There is typically distance between the person who calls-out and the recipient, which creates some level of cushion. On college campuses, call-outs typically occur between those who inhabit the same space. Although a call-out transpires between people who have not been formally introduced, it may be a person they see in class, meetings, in the dining hall, or on the sidewalk. This proximity creates great anxiety (Friedersdorf, 2017). Those that condemn the actions are not distant screen names; they are fellow students or colleagues. The anxiety comes from being rejected by the person's community; the consequences can be real and long-lasting. Friedersdorf (2017) lists the types of call-outs that typically happen on a college campus, from condemning students for cultural appropriation for a Halloween costume to outing students on a Christian college campuses because they are gay. The result of the call-outs might be ridicule, loss of friends or social status, or the insistence that the person steps down.

HOW RECEIVING CALL-OUTS DIFFERS AMONGST CONSTITUENCIES

In our examples in the intro, we represented three different populations that experienced being called-out. The student, the SDO, and the Student Affairs Officer invariably will experience call-outs differently. For students, depending on the action or behavior for which they are being called-out, they can experience isolation from their peers; in the case of Cedric, the university initiated an investigation. Cedric felt so humiliated, scared, and traumatized that he did not leave his residence hall room for days, and he sought mental health counseling for an extended period of time to help him recover from the experience. For the SDO, the call-out about the LGBQ statistics resulted in spending hours defending and educating on the choice of the statistics. She also questioned whether she was really cut out for the job, or whether she had not fully explored her prejudices against trans people. Additionally, the SDO had to explain to her supervisor, the provost, and the marketing team, why the statistic was posted in the manner it was. For the Student Affairs Administrator, the call-out resulted in not being able to assist in student programming in which he would ordinarily participate. He lost a significant amount of sleep worrying about student and community perceptions, and felt like he was walking on thin ice, all examples of hypervigilance.

For each demographic which could experience being called-out, the repercussions can be different, depending on the person's social identities, status on campus, and reputation within the institution. Depending on the intersections of the identities of the person, being called-out will impact the perception of the public about the behavior or action that the person is being called-out for. For example, stereotypes about a certain group may enhance the believability. If a Black male is called-out for aggressive language toward women, the stereotypes about Black men are evoked and make the call-out believable (Ancis, Sedlacek, & Mohr, 2000; Fries-Britt & Griffin, 2007; Ghavami & Peplau, 2012; Omi, 2015; Solórzano, Ceja, & Yosso, 2000; Stone, Harrison, & Mottley, 2012). Additionally, certain communities with more power within the society may feel more entitled to call-out others because they have all enjoyed a sense of empowerment. For example, we often see white people calling-out others on behalf of communities of color. All of these dynamics mean that each individual will experience call-outs in different ways and may receive call-outs at different frequencies (Crenshaw, 1991). It also means that the repercussions for call-outs may be different. The SDO, who has received a lot of complaints and criticism for implementing aggressive hiring policies in order to diversify the faculty and staff of the university, may face harsh penalties if students call her out for an exclusionary tweet. The faculty who were complaining about the hiring policies behind closed doors may feel more empowered to take action against the SDO because of the student call-out. If the SDO is a queer woman of color, there will inevitably be biases that impact the situation. Whatever the call-out situation, the varied identities and power structures will impact the effect of the call-out.

CAUSES

While call-outs may be in response to oppressive behavior on the part of the recipient, they stem from a sense of lack of agency which leads to the use of oppressive methods to maintain and gain power (Johnson, 2016). It is important to remember that calling-out is not the only method of fighting injustice. For example, the alumni and students who called-out the Student Affairs Administrator could have made an appointment to talk to him individually to discuss what they thought was problematic behavior. Instead, individuals may use a call-out because they feel a lack of sense of agency.

Agency refers to a person's perception of their ability to control a situation or realize an outcome (Gallagher, 2000). When a student feels that they lack the capacity or importance to impact a situation of perceived oppression, the student may take to social media because they do not realize the power they might have to bring about consequences. This lack of a sense of agency likely comes from the daily toll of oppression that the student faces, if they come from one or more marginalized identities (Liebow, 2016).

The student may also take to social media to call-out a diversity leader because they are reproducing oppressive methods they witnessed their whole life. Young's (2014) five faces of oppression explains that oppression often manifests in exploitation, marginalization, cultural imperialism, powerlessness, and violence. The call-out and cancel mirrors elements of powerlessness, in the sense that the call-out silences the recipient and disallows them to frame the narrative about the action. Similarly, the call-out or cancel mirrors elements of violence, in the sense that the call-out effects harm to control the individual. Students may engage in this reproduction of oppression because they may never have seen non-oppressive ways of reacting, given that oppressive systems are so inherent in all aspects of our society.

EFFECTS

The effects of call-out culture manifest in various ways. We have observed, both in literature and in lived experience, the development of cultures of fear, leading to negative psychological and physiological impact, self-censoring, the reduplication of oppressive systems, deterioration in a sense of belonging, and decreased persistence in professional roles. The combination of these dynamics fashions a particularly negative impact of call-out and cancel culture. However, call-out culture can also provide a sense of agency and power to traditionally marginalized communities.

Call-out and cancel cultures have generated a culture of fear (Lee, 2019) for diversity leaders. Many leaders are hesitant to speak their full mind, to engage in complicated or nuanced forms of activism, or in any sort of social change that is not wholeheartedly embraced by those who would do the calling-out and canceling. This fear of messing up, of mis-navigating in such a way that it would raise the ire of the advocates of calling-out and cancelling, has resulted in a constant sense of fear for many diversity leaders. The diversity leader is by no means a position filled with perfectly developed or fully realized professionals. A culture of fear hinders risk-taking and opportunities for development for the diversity leader.

There is a pervasive fear that any diversity leader may at any time be the recipient of a mass calling-out to the level of canceling.

This constant awareness of avoiding mistakes creates a hypervigilance that often results in a wide array of symptoms (Dalgleish, Moradi, Taghavi, Neshat-Doost, & Yule, 2001; Healthline.com; Kimble et al., 2014; Medical News Today), including sweating, fast heart rate, fast shallow breathing, and even, over time, fatigue and exhaustion. It can also result in behavioral reactions such as jumpy reflexes and fast knee-jerk reactions to a person's environment. In an attempt to defend oneself, slight or minimal miscommunications from others can result in a diversity leader's disproportionately hostile reaction. It can also result in emotional reactions such as an increased sense of anxiety, fear, and panic. We have also observed a fear of judgment from others, or of judging others extremely harshly, which can develop into black-and-white thinking in which we find things either absolutely right or absolutely wrong. Diversity leaders can also become emotionally withdrawn, experiencing mood swings or outbursts of emotion or even an increased sense of paranoia as a rationalization to justify the hypervigilance as well as a lack of sleep. If you have severe social anxiety, you may rely on daydreaming or non-participation in events. These symptoms can result in social isolation and damaged relationships.

A high level of burnout and turnover often result from experiences of hypervigilance (Chatlani, 2018; Kollenberg, 2019; Prinster, 2015). It is easy for a diversity leader to become consumed with the heavy psychological, emotional, and physical effects of navigating the complexities of call-out culture. Burdensome expectations quickly contribute to a desire to leave the field of diversity leadership and not return. Anecdotally, we have noticed that SDOs typically have tenure of three years before leaving their position. With the emotional effects of the call-out culture, the diversity leader may seek other work that does not carry the high cost that exists in moving institutions toward equity and inclusion.

However, call-outs can cultivate a sense of empowerment for those engaging in the practice. By definition, marginalized communities have often been silenced (Young, 2014). By banding together and calling-out the perceived bad behavior of others, calling-out engages the collective voice of many who have often been robbed of that agency. This experience can be emboldening and can restore a sense of agency and power. Diversity leaders should be mindful that call-outs can serve as a powerful impact when navigating the critiques brought to their attention. Sometimes thanking the community for voicing their experience and concern is the best course of action.

VULNERABILITY

Institutions across the country have enhanced their commitment to diversity, equity, and inclusion by creating a high-level leadership position, often known as the Chief Diversity Officer or SDO (Arnold & Kowalski-Braun, 2012). Ideally, this role moves the institution forward in strategic progress regarding the climate of the institution (Williams & Wade-Golden, 2014). Although this role can be structured differently, the role has the potential to interface with academic affairs, student affairs, human resources, enrollment management, development, alumni relations, and the Board of Trustees (Williams & Wade-Golden, 2014). The SDO position can help the institution clarify, experience, and move forward in its commitment to diversity, equity, and inclusion; however, this can result in an overwhelming job that requires a wealth of skills and knowledge (Douglas & Little, 2017). Often the position is tasked with helping the institution increase access and equity in its enrollment and retention; this requires the SDO to work on recruitment, hiring, retention, and examining structural barriers that impede these efforts (Stanley, 2014; Williams & Wade-Golden, 2014).

SDOs face challenges on many fronts from a variety of stakeholders. The nature of their job to help lead institutional change results in the SDO experiencing stress and pressure from multiple areas. High expectations, coupled with the emotional nature of the work, and the resistance of a society that has not come to terms with privilege and oppression mean that the SDO sometimes has few tangible successes to show for all of their effort. The nature of the job puts the SDO at risk for burnout and fatigue that often result in a lack of retention (Williams & Wade-Golden, 2014). Burnout is broadly defined as "prolonged response to chronic emotional and interpersonal stressors on the job, determined by the dimensions of exhaustion, cynicism, and inefficacy" (Montero-Marin & Garcia-Campayo, 2010). One SDO characterized the work as "being on a battleground without bullets or the armor needed to be successful in the war for social inclusion" (Lam, 2018). This war analogy is particularly applicable when an SDO on a higher education campus is navigating call-outs directed at them or others, because the criticism can come from anywhere and often the SDO will not have allies to support them. Additionally, diversity leaders at entry-level or mid-level positions are often tasked with the day-to-day, face-to-face contact with students, faculty, and staff in affinity groups, and are directly affected by negative campus climates and hateful acts that occur while they are doing the work of supporting a positive campus climate and appropriate developmental opportunities. It is easy for the stress of call-out culture to lead to the type of exhaustion that results in the person not being able to provide effort to do the work, or to a cynical outlook that results in the SDO feeling that nothing can be done, or inefficacy where the SDO feels that they cannot perform the work necessary for change (Montero-Marin & Garcia- Campayo, 2010).

HIGH STAKES

Those who work in diversity leadership navigate high stakes situations every day. The nature of dismantling systems of oppression and creating more equity within an institution invariably means that high emotion will accompany the work (Williams & Wade-Golden, 2014). Often when individuals are confronted with their own privilege or the systems of power are unveiled to them, a sense of fragility emerges that brings out anger and fear. The SDO navigates this type of dynamic all day, every day. There is no way to increase the diversity of the faculty, or improve the retention rates of students of color, or create safe spaces for LGBTQ people without exposing and dismantling the systems of power that have created those situations in the first place.

Yet, the high stakes work does not just stem from the changing systems. It also comes from trying to supplant them with more equitable systems, something that has never really been done before. When the systems of oppression are identified on a higher education campus and then the SDO or other diversity leaders attempt to replace them, they have to try to replace them with a more equitable system. There will inevitably be missteps. The SDO can try their best to implement a system that does not oppress others and that acknowledges past and current harm, but it will not be perfect. In the attempt to diversify the faculty, there will be some groups that are overlooked or not supported enough. The SDO might create a mentorship program that includes content and structures to address issues that faculty of color face more routinely, but neglect to provide frameworks that support LGBTQ faculty. Thus, both the dismantling of the system and the attempt to replace it with something more equitable leaves the diversity leader vulnerable to call-outs and cancels because emotion is high for all groups.

HOW TO RESPOND

Responses to cancel culture and call-out culture require a nuanced and thoughtful approach. The cultural elements of both call-out and cancel cultures reflect a system of operation in which there are rules, expectations, and performative pieces. These "shared patterns of behaviors and inter-actions, cognitive constructs and understanding that are learned by so-cialization" (What Is Culture) operate to form a culture of calling-out and canceling perceived bad actors. The wide-ranging nature of culture requires a set of tools to holistically engage the phenomenon. Relying on simplistic or traditional engagement only serves as self-fulfilling prophecy for those who use the tools of the call-out and cancel culture. When di-versity leaders engage in both cancel and call-out culture we must do so in ways that neither reduplicate the systems of oppression that are being critiqued nor prove right the fears and harms raised by those who practice call-out and cancel culture. In developing a strategy for dealing with call-outs, we propose a three-part framework that engages traditional student development theory: critical social theories, elements of wellness, and a guiding ethic. Although the diversity leader's initial reaction might be to condemn, justify, and ignore when the call-out is directed at her or advise students to do the same when the call-out is directed at them, we need a nuanced and wholistic approach when navigating call-outs, and these frameworks and principles can help the diversity leader maintain bal-ance. The goal in navigating call-outs and cancels should be to maintain well-being, promote liberation, strengthen resilience, and halt systems of oppression.

Response Rooted in Theory

Theoretical frameworks can provide a helpful context and guide for ac-tion. We examine Sanford's (1962, 1967, 2006) theory of Challenge and Support, Critical Race Theory (CRT), and Queer Theory (QT) as infor-mative and guiding theories.

Challenge/Support for Each Stakeholder

Student development theory has equipped Student Affairs Professionals to do the work of supporting student development. Sanford's (1962, 1967) theory of Challenge and Support has long served as a foundational theory that provides clear direction for those often engaging students in direct relationships. King (2009) summarizes it well:

> When support is too high, there is no perceived need to change one's outlook or find a more adaptive stance. When challenge is too high, it is common to feel overwhelmed and be tempted to give up and not stay engaged with the problem at hand.
>
> (p. 614)

While this theory has been applied primarily to students, it has strong potential to be particularly helpful for diversity leaders as we engage minoritized and marginalized communities who face call-outs or cancels. Systemic and cultural oppressions require that we examine the student experience via a lens of *Challenge and Support*. Sanford's model ought not only be applied to students.

When being called-out as a diversity leader, operating through a *Challenge and Support* framework will help to make sense of the situation. Challenge requires that the diversity leader explore what types of actions they have taken that have furthered oppressive structures. For example, when the SDO mentioned in the introduction removed the T from the LGBQ statistic because trans individuals were not represented, she must ask herself if there was truth to the call-out that trans individuals were not recognized or valued. Yet, support means that the SDO must seek out support from others, so as not to feel overwhelmed by the task of trying to always get things "right" and to always conduct herself in a non-oppressive way. Support might come in the form of finding others who can be vulnerable and share times they conducted themselves in an oppressive way, or commiserating with those who work in diversity leader work.

Critical Race Theory
Critical theories assist us in understanding and navigating call-outs and cancels by bringing an intentional examination of power. Critical theories such as CRT and QT provide lenses to examine the fundamentally held beliefs and assumptions as well as the practical and emergent effects of actions. These frameworks help the diversity leader examine the context of the call-out or cancel they are experiencing, thus being able to understand the multiple realities and dynamics of what they are facing. CRT subscribes to several pillars such as critiquing liberalism, the centrality of race, racism, and intersecting oppressions (Hernandez, 2016, p. 170), whiteness as property (Delgado & Stefancic, 2010, p. 7), and valuing experience as knowledge (Hernandez, 2016, p. 170). These components of CRT help the diversity leader understand the reality of the people engaging in calling others out and their own positioning in the call-out.

Those engaging in call-outs are likely operating under a liberal framework with the belief that in general, all people are equal and that any inequality stems from personal responsibility. For example, when the Student Affairs Administrator was called-out for helping the College Republicans bring donuts and coffee to Trump supporters waiting in line, the critiquers were likely operating under an assumption that the action did not pain or bother the administrator. Liberalism suggests that the administrator would only act in his best interest, and because this belief is so pervasive in our society, those who called him out were likely operating under this belief. For the Administrator, understanding and evaluating his own actions and that of the people who engaged in calling him out through a CRT lens helps him think critically about the situation. He can understand the ways in which serving Trump supporters coffee and donuts fits within the systems of oppression in which he exists, particularly being a queer person. He can also understand the systems of oppression existing for those who called him out, with many of them coming from marginalized groups, with some having identities that historically have held positions of power.

CRT suggests that whiteness has been valued above color in our society (Delgado & Stefancic, 2010). White culture and identity have been seen as superior and as holding more capital within our society, portrayed in a culturally imperialistic way. Additionally, CRT provides for the same understanding with other types of power-laden identities, including male, heterosexual, and able bodied, to name a few. These identities and those who inhabit them have privileges in society and often act accordingly. This often means that individuals from privileged identities will be vocal in calling-out the diversity leader; while they may inhabit some marginalized identities, the action or behavior being called-out may involve an identity they inhabit. For the SDO who was called-out for the LGBQ label on the statistic published on the website, the most vocal student to call her out was not part of the LGBTQ community, and there were elements of his call-out that replicated the concept that certain identities have more value in society over others. Being a part of the community that may be impacted by the action being called-out is not a prerequisite, and certainly there are oppressive actions and behavior that take place on college campuses that need to be addressed. However, it is important to recognize that the privileged identities of some will prompt them to engage in calling-out, because their identities hold more value in society. Additionally, the identities of the diversity officer may play a role in the manner and mode of the call-out. Understanding these dynamics through a CRT framework helps the diversity leader navigate, make sense of, and evaluate the call-out.

Valuing experience as knowledge is a fundamental pillar of CRT. Specifically, the theory "recognize[s] the value of lived experiences of marginalized persons by giving them a voice to testify the consequences and effects of racism" (Hernandez, 2016, p. 170). Remembering that experience is a form of knowledge can help the diversity leader understand the context in which those engaging in the call-out are voicing their critique.

In order to move toward the goal of promoting liberation and not continuing systems of oppression, the diversity leader should be open to exploring when their actions may have furthered oppression. For example, when the SDO presented statistics on the website about the LGBQ community, in reality trans people may have felt silenced or not included in the community. The intention of the SDO does not change the lived experience of a trans person looking at that statistic. Recognizing that experience is knowledge as well as that individual's reality will help the diversity leader evaluate the call-out and change course.

Queer Theory

A critical examination of the intersections of identities and exploring the oppressive social constructions of sexual orientation and gender (Abes & Kasch, 2007) are hallmarks of QT. Post-structuralist in nature, QT resists definition (Patton, Renn, Guido-DiBrito, & Quaye, 2016); however, key elements do consistently rise to the surface. Liminality and Fluidity are concepts that comprise the theory and help explain our relationship to gender and sexuality. Liminality describes the "state of flux between two distinct stages of being" (Abes, 2009, p. 147). It refers to the threshold, living between two spaces or identities and roles, and can be applied to both concepts of gender and sexuality. Similarly, the concept of fluidity embraces ideas of movement, change, and "ambivalence and multiplicity, exceed[ing] the boundaries of what can be imagined" (Jones, Torres, & Arminio, 2006, p. 21). Fluidity suggests that gender and sexuality are not static and can flexibly change over time or from day to day. While the concepts certainly help diversity leaders understand their own sexuality and gender identity, it also can help give context to the fluidity and liminality of their roles of administrator, everyday citizen, and emotional being.

In both the examples with the SDO and the Student Affairs Administrator, their actions and reactions stem from not only their roles as leaders within the university, but also their identities and positionalities. They are administrators who through their work and actions, advance the mission of the university; they are also individuals with an activist mindset who come from marginalized identities. While the students and the community that critiqued their actions through call-outs viewed the individuals as administrators and therefore an extension of the institution themselves, the reality is that both leaders hold places somewhere in-between holding power and being vulnerable. Attempting such rigidity denies administrators their humanity and will likely lead to an increased chance of burnout. Diversity leaders should recognize that they can inhabit more than one role and that fluidity is in our nature as both administrators and humans.

Ethic of Activism

The Ethic of Activism framework helps diversity leaders navigate being called-out or helping others who are called-out. The framework looks toward valuing relationships in social justice work and tries to bring the community of those committed to dismantling oppression to a place of valuing people, love, and life-giving praxis. The framework includes knowing when to be hard and when to be soft, adopting a politics of imperfection and responsibility, and tapping into our shared humanity. Keeping these principles in mind when navigating call-outs and cancels or helping others to do the same will prioritize the relationships we all need in order to make progress toward equity and inclusion in our institutions.

Discerning how to respond and digest call-outs, particularly when they further oppression, can be difficult, but it is something the diversity leader needs to consider. Knowing when to be hard and when to be soft is essential within our communities. Lee (2019) suggests that sometimes hardness is necessary when confronting inequity and other times soft-ness is appropriate. Discerning which technique to use is challenging and may take a lifetime to perfect (Lee, 2019). Holding people accountable, even (perhaps, especially) ourselves, is a core part of moving any group of people toward justice. Sometimes those conversations require saying hard truths and honestly examining actions, beliefs, or attitudes that have harmed others. But when shedding light on how some have harmed others, a unilateral scorched-earth approach leaves no room for growth or change. Rather, one who is skilled in engaging offenders, in a manner that taps into how humans and institutions grow and change, will know that there are times when a word of encouragement, or forgiveness, or gentle prodding, while allowing someone to save face, will move a situation forward far more than will harshness. This is not to say that softness or gentleness should be used without reflection or as a cop-out. Just because a conversation or confrontation is difficult does not mean that it should be avoided. Systems are perfectly designed to perpetuate themselves, and at times those systems need to be confronted with clear, hard truth-telling. Developing our skills to ascertain when this should happen, how to do it, and doing it effectively will help to counter the effects of call-out culture.

To navigate call-outs and cancels, we must adopt a politics of imperfec-tion and responsibility (Shotwell, 2017). Realizing that purity politics is an ill-fated endeavor bound for mutual destruction, we must remember instead our potential for moving our institutions forward. Shotwell proposes:

> If we've failed to help in the past, if things we do are implicated in harm, if we benefit from something that harms others, or if we

accord only some people access to a podium, we can still be of benefit to this world. Even people who have harmed others or the world, whose ancestors owned slaves, whose current government is actively pursuing genocidal colonial policies, who regularly make mistakes—even we can be useful.

(2017)

Despite the criticism that we will inevitably endure as diversity leaders, focusing on our usefulness will help to put cancels and call-outs into perspective. Shotwell's assertions, coupled with a "politics of responsibility," where we must embrace our own responsibility to recognize our furtherance of oppression or how our roles might further oppression, helps us to evaluate and move forward from call-outs (Kinsman, 2009). Inevitably, we will sometimes get it wrong, which is okay as long as we have the perspective and reflection to recognize it and correct where we can. Adopting this recognition of imperfection is freeing and might help to relieve some of the guilt that many of us might feel as we are called-out. Those who get into diversity leadership desperately want to make progress, so being called-out for potential harmful actions hurts. But recognizing our imperfections and embracing responsibility and humility lessens the pressure to always get things right. Robin DiAngelo (2011) writes that guilt, white guilt in particular, is often coupled with other emotions, such as anger and fear, and leads to unhelpful behavior such as "argumentation, silence, and withdrawal from the stress-inducing situation" (p. 57). DiAngelo's analysis of white guilt is appropriately applied to feelings of guilt generally. A more productive and healthier stance of responsibility replaces frustrating feelings and actions with the possibility of forward movement. By taking responsibility, one (or a group) can both accept that harm has been done and that they play a role in repairing the harm. Taking responsibility is twofold – the responsibility for past harm done and the responsibility to make things as right as possible.

Adopting politics of imperfection and responsibility have strong echoes in practices of restorative justice. Restorative justice seeks simply to restore relationships and repair harm. For years, educators have worked to implement restorative justice practices to codes of student conduct and campus culture such as restorative justice conferences, circles, boards, administrative hearings, and circles of support and accountability (Karp & Frank, 2016). These practices seem so appealing because they emphasize needs of both restored relationship and repair to harm. As individuals, groups, and institutions move toward creating environments that make it permissible to admit imperfections, we move toward justice. When environments push toward perfection and accept purity as the only mode of existing, we push away from justice. Individuals, organizations, and institutions that instead focus on creating spaces that allow for imperfection – coupled with responsibility – are working toward justice. When we also embrace responsibility – both individual and institutional – paired with imperfection, a special opportunity develops. We are given an opportunity to grow and to get better. In communities where purity and perfection are expected, no one has the opportunity to speak up and seek out growth. In those communities, to admit that one needs support or that something should change necessarily implies that one is not operating according to community expectations, and will be called-out or even cancelled. As diversity leaders, a tangible step we can take is to model this, admitting when we fail and being proactive in communication with others – gently and overtly welcoming admission of imperfection and growth.

Finally, the ethics of activism requires that we tap into our shared humanity, particularly as we navigate call-outs or criticism of our work. Lee (2019) reminds us that oppressive systems seek to dehumanize us and, in service to the system, to debase both the oppressor and the oppressed to the most inhuman self. In other words, patriarchy, to varying degrees, harms all those along many gender spectrums as racism harms people of all races and ethnicities and so on. The ultimate beneficiary of any unjust system is ultimately the system itself – being perpetuated across cultures and for countless ages (Adams & Zúñiga, 2016). In many ways, Lee's call to embrace our shared humanity is reflected in Ross's (2019) *New York Times* Op-Ed which exhorts those in activist communities to "a much more effective way to build social justice movements" that happen both "in person" and "in real life." Mutual humanity is often more difficult to embrace when a simple retweet or share does not take into account complex human experiences, systems of both oppression or justice, or our own communities. As Ross notes, Khan-Cullors (2019), an organizer and activist, suggests that "people don't understand that organizing isn't going online and cussing people out, or going to a protest and calling something out." Diversity leaders do well to remember hallmarks of our work – that the deep, transformational, longitudinal work of transforming our institutions from machines of perpetuation to sites of justice work – requires engaging humans, real people, in face-to-face frank, loving, and justice-oriented work.

RESILIENCE IN RESPONSE TO PHYSICAL AND PSYCHOLOGICAL NEGATIVE EFFECTS

The stressors that come from both call-out and cancel cultures significantly affect those engaging in diversity leadership. Actions and mindsets that can lead to resilience include moral/spiritual support, flexible locus of control, an individual's ability to view adverse situations positively, autonomy, commitment, change, positive relationships, and viewing education as important (Polidore, 2004).

We have found that the development of supportive positive relationships is essential for the development of resilience and the successful navigation of call-outs and cancels. Some institutions have enough staff that peers in a diversity office can provide the opportunity to build camaraderie and friendships along shared experiences and like-mindedness; many, however, will find themselves being a staff of one. Both of us served in inaugural roles and were the first person at their institution to be tasked in their position description to undertake endeavors of diversity, equity, and inclusion; both of us operated as a staff of one. This has resulted in a need to intentionally form peer relationships based on shared commitment to equity and inclusion, shared experiences, and an eagerness to support each other.

Those who find themselves with a larger support staff may still need to branch out to other colleagues within the institution, diversity leaders at other institutions, community members, or family. Because of power balances, personalities, or a host of other reasons, it may not be feasible to rely on day-to-day colleagues for this type of positive relationship. Because much of the mindsets and actions that lead to resiliency come from such positive relationships, it is essential that intentional resources are dedicated to these relationships and this endeavor. Additionally, senior leaders such as the president or provost or others that may supervise the diversity leader should support and provide resources toward the development of such positive relationships; otherwise, they will face a continual revolving door of diversity leaders leaving their position, particularly if these leaders face call-outs and cancels due to the high stakes work they undertake.

Establishing clear boundaries with colleagues has proven invaluable to practice self-care. Often the diversity leader will be asked to attend every multicultural or diversity-related activity. If the diversity leader says yes, they will likely be on campus every weekend and most nights of the week. Similarly, the diversity leader is likely to be called whenever anyone on campus faces the slightest challenge. For example, we have been called by marketing during non-work hours to answer a wide variety of questions not in our functional areas. While it may seem to the diversity leader that they may be vulnerable to call-outs if they do not acquiesce to these requests, this feeling is actually a symptom of hypervigilance; thus, the diversity leader should work with their supervisor to ensure they will be protected if the community does not understand the boundaries they are setting.

Both of the writers have also found that consistently seeing a professional therapist has proven invaluable for processing the vicarious trauma that comes from supporting students and colleagues who are experiencing oppressive systems and experiencing call-outs. As diversity leaders who experience life in the margins, in addition to supporting students and colleagues, we are also navigating the world while processing the five faces of oppression: exploitation, marginalization, cultural imperialism, powerlessness, and violence (Young, 2014). When we engage a faculty member who is using racist language or engage a campus department that is embracing homophobia, not only are we educating and developing our campus community, we are also striving to survive the stressors of oppression for ourselves.

CONCLUSION

The role of a diversity leader is complex and requires a wide array of skills sets, personal awareness, and a willingness to engage in difficult topics while broaching challenging arenas. While call-out and cancel cultures are pervasive, diversity leaders are uniquely positioned and equipped to navigate these cultures in a thoughtful manner that leads their communities in paths of justice. Call-out and cancel cultures are ultimately an expression of people who are pushed to the margins while striving for justice. However, this attempt for justice often mimics the oppressive structures and systems enacted upon these communities. Diversity leaders are positioned to utilize developmental and transformative theories to lead communities in ways that are more emblematic of justice. Striving for personal well-being, building resilience to negative and harmful interactions, and embracing an Ethic of Activism are tangible and constructive means of navigating call-out and cancel cultures.

REFERENCES

Abes, E. S. (2009). Theoretical borderlands: Using multiple theoretical perspectives to challenge inequitable power structures in student development theory. *Journal of College Student Development, 50*(2), 141–156. doi:10.1353/csd.0.0059

Abes, E. S., & Kasch, D. (2007). Using queer theory to explore lesbian college students' multiple dimensions of identity. *Journal of College Student Development, 48*, 619–636.

Adams, M., & Zúñiga, X. (2016). Core concepts for social justice education. In Adams, M., Bell, L. A., Goodman, D. J., & Joshi, K. Y. (Eds.), *Teaching for diversity and social justice*. New York: Routledge.

Ancis, J. R., Sedlacek, W. E., & Mohr, J. J. (2000). Student perceptions of campus climate by race. *Journal of Counseling and Development, 78*, 180–186.

Arnold, J., & Kowalski-Braun, M. (2012). The journey to an inaugural chief diversity officer: Preparation, implementation and beyond. *Innovative Higher Education, 37*(1), 27–36. https://doi.org/10.1007/s10755-011-9185-9

Chatlani, S. (2018). Accessed February 2, 2020 from https://www.educationdive.com/news/burnout-how-can-higher-ed-leaders-survive-the-academy/518820/

Crenshaw, K. (1991). Mapping the margins: Intersectionality identity politics, and violence against women of color. *Stanford Law Review, 43*(6), 1241. doi: 10.2307/122903

Dalgleish, T., Moradi, A. R., Taghavi, M. R., Neshat-Doost, H. T., & Yule, W. (2001). *An experimental investigation of hypervigilance for threat in children and adolescents with post-traumatic stress disorder. Psychological Medicine, 31*(3), 541–547.

Delgado, R., & Stefancic, J. (Eds.). (2000). *Critical race theory: The cutting edge.* Philadelphia, PA: Temple University Press.

DiAngelo, R. (2011). White fragility. *International Journal of Critical Pedagogy, 3*(3), 57.

Douglas, T.-R. M. O., & Little, M. (2017). Voices from the field. *The Journal of Negro Education, 86*(3), 381. https://doi.org/10.7709/jnegroeducation.86.3.0381

Friedersdorf, C. (2017). The destructiveness of call-out culture on campus: Reflections from undergraduates of the social media era. Retrieved May 9, 2019 from The Atlantic: https://www.theatlantic.com/politics/archive/2017/05/call-out-culture-is-stressing-out-college-students/524679/

Fries-Britt, S., & Turner, B. (2002). Uneven stories: Successful Black collegians at a Black and a White campus. *Review of Higher Education, 25*, 315–330.

Gallagher, S. (2000). Philosophical conceptions of the self: implications for cognitive science. *Trends in Cognitive Sciences, 4*, 14–21.

Ghavami, N., & Peplau, L. A. (2012). An intersectional analysis of gender and ethnic stereotypes: Testing three hypotheses. *Psychology of Women Quarterly, 37*, 113–127.

Healthline.com, Accessed February 8, 2020; https://www.healthline.com/health/hypervigilance

Hernandez, E. (2016). Utilizing critical race theory to examine race/ethnicity, racism, and power in student development theory and research. *Journal of College Student Development, 57*(2), 168–180.

Johnson, M. (2016). 6 signs your call-out isn't actually about accountability. Retrieved May 9, 2019 from Everyday Feminism: https://everydayfeminism.com/2016/05/call-out-accountability/

211

Jones, S. R., Torres, V., & Arminio, J. (2006). *Negotiating the complexities of qualitative research in higher education: Fundamental elements and issues.* New York: Routledge.

Karp, D. R., & Frank, O. (2016). Restorative justice and student development in higher education: Expanding 'offender' horizons beyond punishment and rehabilitation to community engagement and personal growth. In Gavrielides, T. (Ed.), Offenders *no more: An interdisciplinary restorative justice dialogue* (pp. 141–164). New York: Nova Science Publishers.

Khan-Cullors, P., et al. (2019). Ge in formation. In Solomon, A., & Rankin, K. (Eds.), *How we fight white supremacy: A field guide to Black resistance.* New York: Bold Type Books.

Kimble, M., Boxwala, M., Bean, W., Maletsky, K., Halper, J., Spollen, K., & Fleming, K. (2014). The impact of hypervigilance: evidence for a forward feedback loop. *Journal of Anxiety Disorders, 28*(2), 241–245. doi:10.1016/j.janxdis.2013.12.006

King, P. M. (2009). Principles of Development and Developmental Change Underlying Theories of Cognitive and Moral Development. *Journal of College Student Development, 50*(6), 597–620. https://doi.org/10.1353/csd.0.0104

Kinsman, G. (2009). The politics of revolution: Learning from autonomist Marxism. Retrieved January 9, 2020, from Upping the ante a journal of theory and action: https://uppingtheanti.org/journal/article/01-the-politics-of-revolution/

Kollenberg, S. (2019). Accessed February 8, 2020 from https://www.educationdive.com/news/burnout-how-can-higher-ed-leaders-survive-the-academy/518820/

Lam, M. B. (2018, September 23). *Diversity fatigue is real.* The Chronicle of Higher Education. https://www.chronicle.com/article/diversity-fatigue-is-real/.

Lee, F. (2019). Why I've started to fear my fellow social justice activists. Retrieved May 9, 2019, from Yes Magazine website: https://www.yesmagazine.org/people-power/why-ive-started-to-fear-my-fellow-social-justice-activists-20171013

Liebow, N. (2016). Internalized oppression and its varied moral harms: Self-perceptions of reduced agency and criminality. *Hypatia, 31*(4), 713–729. doi: 10.1111/hypa.12265

Lorde, A. (1988). *A burst of light.* In Lorde, A., Byrd, R. P., Cole, J. B., & Guy-Sheftall, B. (Eds.), *I am your sister: Collected and unpublished writings of Audre Lorde.* New York: Oxford University Press.

Luther, M., Wengert, T., & Project Muse Content Provider. (2015). *Martin Luther's ninety-five theses with introduction, commentary, and study guide.* Minneapolis, MN: Fortress Press.

Medical News Today, Accessed February 8, 2020; https://www.medicalnewsto-day.com/articles/319289.php

Montero-Marín, J., García-Campayo, J. A newer and broader definition of burnout: Validation of the "Burnout Clinical Subtype Questionnaire (BCSQ-36)". *BMC Public Health* 10, 302 (2010). https://doi.org/10.1186/1471-2458-10-302

Omi, M. (2015). *Racial formation in the United States: From the 1960s to the 1990s* (2nd ed.). New York: Routledge.

Patton, L. D., Renn, K. A., Guido-DiBrito, F., & Quaye, S. J. (2016). *Student development in college: theory, research, and practice.* San Francisco, CA: Jossey-Bass, A Wiley Brand.

Polidore, E. (2004). The teaching experiences of Lucille Bradley, Maudester Hicks, and Algeno McPherson before, during, and after desegregation in the rural south: A theoretical model of adult resilience among three African American female educators (Doctoral dissertation, Sam Houston State University, 2004).

Prinster, R. (2015). Accessed February 8, 2020 from https://www.insightintodiversity.com/avoiding-burnout-how-10-cdos-balance-work-with-life/

Romano, A. (2019). Why we can't stop fighting about cancel culture. *VOX.* Retrieved from https://www.vox.com/culture/2019/12/30/20879720/what-is-cancel-culture-explained-history-debate

Ross, L. (2019, August 17). I'm a Black feminist. I think call-out culture is toxic. Retrieved January 25, 2020, from https://www.nytimes.com/2019/08/17/opinion/sunday/cancel-culture-call-out.html?smid=nytcore-ios-share&fbclid=IwAR0Y9K2y3-PqZJEOPDsV6OYzBvKLLEtFtBuN9Ii93v_nTX-OlX_chk4SxM98

Sanford, N. (Ed.). (1962). *The American college: A psychological and social interpretation of higher learning.* New York: Wiley.

Sanford, N. (1967). *Where colleges fail: A study of the student as a person.* San Francisco, CA: Jossey-Bass.

Sanford, N. (2006). *Self and society: Social change and individual development* (1st ed.). New York: Routledge.

Shotwell, A. (2017). There's strength in a politics of imperfection. Retrieved May 9, 2019, from University of Minnesota Press: http://www.uminnpress-blog.com/2017/02/theres-strength-in-politics-of.html

Solórzano, D. G., Ceja, M., & Yosso, T. J. (2000). Critical race theory, racial microaggressions, and campus racial climate: The experiences of African American college students. *Journal of Negro Education, 69,* 60–73.

Stanley, C. A. (2014). The chief diversity officer: An examination of CDO models and strategies. Journal of Diversity in Higher Education, 7(2), 101–108. https://doi.org/10.1037/a0036662

Stone, J., Harrison, C. K., & Mottley, J. (2012). "Don't call me an athlete": The effect of identity priming on stereotype threat for academically engaged African American college athletes. *Basic and Applied Social Psychology, 34*, 99–106.

Tatum, E. (2014). Getting called out: Why acknowledging oppression matters more than your hurt feelings. Accessed February, 8, 2020 from https://everydayfeminism.com/2014/09/called-out-acknowledging-oppression/

Trần, N. L. (2013). Calling IN: A less disposable way of holding each other accountable. Retrieved May 9, 2019, from BGD website: http://www.bgdblog.org/2013/12/calling-less-disposable-way-holding-accountable/ Waters, B. (2019, August 24). The rise of toxic call-out culture. *Psychology Today*. Retrieved from https://www.psychologytoday.com/us/blog/design-your-path/201908/the-rise-toxic-call-out-culture

What Is Culture. Accessed February 8, 2020 from http://carla.umn.edu/culture/definitions.html

Williams, D. A., & Wade-Golden, K. C. (2014). *The chief diversity officer: strategy, structure, and change management* (First). Sterling, VA: Stylus.

Yar, S., & Bromwich, J. E. (2019, October 31). Tales from the teenage cancel culture. *The New York Times*. Retrieved from https://www.nytimes.com/2019/10/31/style/cancel-culture.html

Young, I. M. (2014). Five faces of oppression. *Philosophical Forum, 19*, 270–290.

Contributors

steven p bryant, Ed.D. Eastern Michigan University, currently serves as the Director of Diversity and Community Involvement at Eastern Michigan University. He is responsible for leading campus-wide efforts in supporting and empowering minoritized students, providing intentional diverse learning experiences, and challenging systems and structures that perpetuate inequities. With over 14 years of higher education experience, he received his Ed.D. in Educational Leadership and Policy Analysis from the University of Missouri. His interests include creating belonging through holistic diversity, equity, and inclusion practices and policies.

LaTanya N. Buck, Ph.D. Princeton University, serves as the inaugural Dean for Diversity and Inclusion at Princeton University. She is responsible for providing a vision and integrated programs for diversity, equity, and inclusion to enhance Campus Life's mission and goals. LaTanya has spent her professional career supporting and advocating for students from traditionally underrepresented and marginalized populations and fostering collaborative relationships with campus and community partners to promote change in institutional policy, practice, and structure. LaTanya earned a Ph.D. in higher education administration from Saint Louis University, where she researched the cultural and structural shifts in race-conscious scholarship programs.

Willette A. Capers, Augustana University, holds a Bachelor of Arts degree from Claflin University in English Literature and Theatre and a Master of Science from Troy University in Educational

Leadership with a Higher Education Administration concentration. With over 16 years in higher education, Willette has worked at various institutions, including PWIs, HSIs, and HBCUs. She is currently a doctoral candidate at Northeastern University, where her research focuses on the impact of value for Black women and their persistence rates in the academy. She serves as the inaugural Assistant Dean of Students for Diversity, Equity & Inclusion at Augustana University in Sioux Falls, South Dakota, where she is responsible for supporting diversity strategic planning, the recruitment of systemically non-dominant faculty, staff, and students, and intercultural education for the campus community.

Brighid Dwyer, Ph.D. Princeton University, is Associate Dean for Diversity and Inclusion at Princeton University. Her research and practice focuses on intergroup dialogue facilitation practices, understanding student identity and organizational change at minority-serving institutions, and developing inclusive organizational cultures.

Erin Lain, J.D., Ph.D. Drake University, serves as the Associate Provost for Campus Equity and Inclusion and Associate Professor of Law at Drake University. She publishes in the area of diversity, equity, and inclusion, with a focus on diversifying the legal profession. Annually, she holds trainings and CLEs in the areas of mental health, substance abuse, diversity, and equity and inclusion.

Jennifer Hamer, Ph.D. Pennsylvania State University, has wide-ranging experience in higher education academic and administrative program creation and assessment, strategic planning, faculty development and mentoring, adult learning, and more. Her career spans 23 years in higher education as both a faculty member and administrator, including multiple appointments as academic unit department, associate dean, and director of student and faculty development programs. In her former role as Vice Provost of Diversity and Equity at the University of Kansas, she developed and successfully implemented a strategic plan for greater student, faculty and staff retention, academic and/or professional growth and advancement. Hamer is an accomplished author, researcher, and teacher with an academic focus on working-class and African American families, equity, qualitative methodologies, and higher education. Dr. Hamer recently joined Pennsylvania State

216

University as a Professor in the Department of African American Studies and as the first associate vice provost for faculty affairs-faculty development, and currently serves as one of two Senior Faculty Mentors for the university's 24 campuses. Dr. Hamer earned a bachelor's degree in sociology from the University of Texas at San Antonio, a master's degree in sociology from Texas A&M University, and a doctorate in sociology from the University of Texas at Austin.

Bennyce E. Hamilton, Ed.D. University of Cincinnati.

Kelley C. Kimple, Ed.D. Florida Memorial University, is the Assistant Vice President for Student Affairs/Dean of Students at Florida Memorial University where she supervises: Career Development Center, Cheer Program, Conduct Affairs, Housing & Residence Life, Student Engagement & Leadership, and University Counseling & Support Services. She has worked in the Student Affairs field for 19 years, amassing experience in Residence Life and Multicultural/Diversity Affairs. She's had the opportunity to work at various types of institutions: faith-based, private, small, PWIs, and HBCUs. Dr. Kimple is passionate about working with college students, primarily underrepresented and marginalized groups, in order to provide them with the type of support she was able to receive during her time attending predominantly White institutions. Dr. Kimple strives to create welcoming and culturally competent environments at institutions she has served.

Raul A. Leon, Ph.D. Eastern Michigan University, is a Professor of Higher Education and Student Affairs and Interim Department Head at Eastern Michigan University. Dr. Leon's scholarship focuses on strategic diversity management and student success. As a practitioner, Dr. Leon's experiences include serving in areas and units, including international student services, study abroad, residential life, living learning communities, pre-college programs, and diversity and inclusion units. He teaches courses in student affairs related to contemporary college students, student development theory, and diversity leadership.

Shantel Martinez, Ph.D. University of Colorado, Boulder, is currently the Director of First-Generation Programs and Enrichment at the University of Colorado, Boulder. Previously, she was at the California State University, Monterey Bay, where she was the

Director of the Otter Cross Cultural Center as well as affiliate faculty in the School of Humanities and Communication. She has a PhD in Communications and Media with an emphasis on Latinx Communication and Gender Studies from the University of Illinois, Urbana-Champaign. Her research explores testimonio as a form of ghost story—specifically in the form of reclaiming familial knowledge and oral histories to promote ancestral and community knowledge.

Annie McBride, City Colleges of Chicago, holds a Bachelor of Science in Journalism and a Master of Science in Higher Education Administration, both from the University of Kansas. She currently serves as the inaugural Project Manager of Equity Initiatives for City Colleges of Chicago. Annie has over ten years of higher education experience working in diversity, equity, and inclusion at various institution types, including a Hispanic Serving, small faith-based, and large predominantly White public research institutions. She spent the early portion of her career working in direct student support roles and educational programs. More recently, her focus has been on diversity, equity, and inclusion policies and project support, working directly with the Senior Diversity Officer on institutional initiatives.

Kierstin McMichael, Washington University in St. Louis, is a graduate student at the Brown School at Washington University in St. Louis. She will graduate with her Master of Social Work in Summer 2021, with a concentration in social and economic development and a specialization in policy. McMichael attended the Brown School on the Whitney M. Young Jr. full tuition scholarship and was a graduate of the Graduate Policy Scholars Program. McMichael worked at the University of Kansas in the Office of the Provost and Executive Vice Chancellor for three years. As an engagement coordinator and executive associate for the Office of Diversity and Equity, she managed programs, events, and community engagement opportunities for the Vice Provost's Office. McMichael is originally from Wichita, Kansas. She graduated from the University of Kansas in May 2016 with a bachelor's degree in English and a minor in sociology. A McNair Scholar, McMichael was also elected to Phi Beta Kappa upon graduation with her B.A., and later became a campus nominee for the Rhodes and Marshall Fellowships in 2017.

Eugene T. Parker III, Ph.D. University of Kansas, is a faculty member in the Department of Educational Leadership and Policy Studies at the University of Kansas. He is interested in matters of diversity, equity, and inclusion as it relates to college students and organizations. His research interests focus on organizational and institutional theories, governance, leadership, and structures. Recent research has centered on organizational leadership, diversity leadership, and leadership-centered theoretical perspectives. Dr. Parker received his B.A. from the University of Iowa, his MBA from the University of Illinois at Chicago, and his Ph.D. in Higher Education from the University of Iowa.

Kelli A. Perkins, Northeastern University, is an Ed.D. candidate at Northeastern University. Her research focuses on the experiences of Black women in executive level positions in higher education administration and identity-conscious supervision in the higher education workplace. She is also a student affairs administrator and over the last 13 years has served in roles in residential life, first year experience, orientation, and student leadership and engagement.

Precious Porras, Ed.D. Dominican University, is the Chief Diversity Officer at Dominican University. She has committed herself and focused on her career on issues of Justice, Equity, and Inclusion for over 16 years. She has served a variety of roles during her career, including working with student retention and advising, programming and advocacy within the DEI in higher education. She is a proud first-generation college student and TRiO alum. She earned her Ed.D. in Educational Leadership and Policy Studies from the University of Kansas. Her research interests include progression for women of color and Black women and student activism.

Bulaong Ramiz, University of Kansas, currently serves as the Director of the Emily Taylor Center for Women and Gender Equity at the University of Kansas where she is also completing her coursework for her Ed.D. in the Educational Leadership and Policy Program with a focus on Higher Education Administration. As a student, Bulaong is interested in exploring manifestations of White supremacy in diversity and equity spaces and initiatives. As a practitioner, Bulaong works to center those most marginalized and seeks to build communities where students of color, at their intersections, can thrive and where we can have more collectivist ways of being.

Rafael A. Rodriguez, Ed.D. University of Vermont, currently serves as the Executive Director of Residential Life in the Division of Student Affairs at the University of Vermont and is also an Associate with Consortium for Inclusion and Equity (CIE). Over the course of his career, he has built a solid reputation for successful organizational management, effective strategies for the recruitment, training, and retention of diverse staff, and the development of quality assessment programs and data gathering utilized for intentional and strategic growth.

Allison C. Roman, Van Andel Institute, MSW, better known as Alli, currently serves as the Director of Student Support Services at the Van Andel Institute. She attended the University of California, Berkeley, as a first-generation college student and graduated in 2009 with a bachelor's in social welfare. In 2012, she graduated with her Master of Social Work (MSW) with a concentration in community organization with children, youth, and families from the University of Michigan. Alli has held multiple positions in higher education focused on student support, retention, multicultural affairs, gender equity, and social justice work in higher education. In 2015, Alli launched Dear Sis, a virtual space for women of color by women of color. She has most recently served as Director for Diversity and Inclusion at Trinity University in San Antonio, Texas.

Tony N. Tyler, Drake University, M.Ed., is a PhD Candidate in Drake's School of Education where he researches critical theory and socially just environments. Throughout his career in Student Affairs, he has served as an Associate and Assistant Dean of Students, and in Residence Life, Student Organizations, Multicultural Organizations, and Equity and Inclusion initiatives, and has taught courses on topics ranging from LGBTQ health systems to introduction to #BlackLivesMatter.

Index

Note: **Bold** page numbers refer to tables.

action and equal opportunity track 33; budgetary considerations 22, 28, 31; and call-out culture 200–201; Collaborative Officer model 21, 121; collaborator role 27, 32; communicator role 24–25; configuration and positioning of 31–32; criticism of term 10; defining the role of 19–20; designing the role of 20–30; educator role 23–24; entrepreneur role of 27–28; executive–level position 20, 31; future of 30–34; line leadership track 33; persuader role of 25; Portfolio-Divisional model 21, 28, 121; professionalization of role 10; as public relations managers 25; recruiter role 29; reporting relationships 24, 25, 30, 31; research and assessment role of 29–30; research on the role of 18–19; role clarity, lack of 22; selection of 33–34; staff considerations 22; strategic diversity leadership track 33; strategic planner role 26–27, 31; symbolic role of 25–26; time in role 52; traditional leadership track 33; Unit-Based model 21, 121
Chubin, D. E. 25–26
civil rights movement 8–9
class xiv, 85
classroom practices **130**
cluster hiring 59
Coalition of Black Students 148
code-switching 148
cognitive gains 5
collaborative leadership 105, 122, 124, 131
Collaborative Officer CDO model 21, 121
collaborator role of CDOs 27, 32

collective responsibility 25–26
college presidents, Black women as 91, 92
collegiality 142
Collins, P. 149, 162, 175, 177
comfort, professional 53–54, 55, 56
commitment 184, 186–187, 209
committees: anti-racist lens 59; inclusive 59
communication 11, 42, 117–118; straightforward/direct, of Black people 92; *see also* language
communicator role of CDOs 24–25
compassionate accountability 181
competency 95; *see also* cultural competency
compositional diversity 3, 9, 82, 126
conformity 141
conservative groups 116
constructionist perspective on relational leadership 12
contextual factors xii, 5, 32–33, 34–35
Cook, C. R. 88
CoopLew Chief Diversity Officers Bootcamp 154
Coopwood, K. 140
COVID-19 pandemic 57, 59, 132
Crenshaw, K. 93
critical leadership 13; *see also* applied critical leadership
Critical Race Theory (CRT) 7, 164–165, 202, 203–205
Cross, W. E. 145
Cullen, M. 77
cultural centers 9
cultural competency 21, 109, 113, 114, 116, 122, 123, **129**, 131–132, 152, 153
cultural imperialism 198, 204, 210
cultural norms 81–82
cultural transformation *see* transformational change

transformative 6, 7, 58; *see also* diversity leadership; relational leadership
learning/education ix–x, 72–73; multicultural 113–114, **128**, **130**, 144; online 14
Lee, F. 206, 208
Lee, J. J. 50
Leon, R. A. xiii, 18–38
Levi, D. 72
Lewis, W. 140
LGBTQ+ community 14, 109, 112, **128**, **130**
liberalism 203–204
liminality 205
listening skills 11
listening to women of color 184, 185
literature: staying abreast of 155; on women of color leaders 160
locus of control 209
Lorde, A. 145, 163, 164, 165
Love, B. 155
low-income students 14
loyalties 34
Luther, M. 193–194

macroaggressions 34, 173
Maldonado, C. 160
marginalization 7, 80, 81, 82, 161, 198, 210; of Black women/women of color 48, 91, 92, 169
Marrun, N. 160
Martinez, S. 161, 162, 167, 171, 172, 175–176, 178–179, 180, 183
Maslow, A. 55
maternal health 173
McBride, A. 105–136
McCoy, D. L. 165
McMichael, K. 105–136
Me Too movement 132, 174
memory 164; institutional 142

men of color 83–90; distorted portrayals of 87, 88, 89; hyper-accountability of 84, 87, 88–89; lack of trust in 84, 87, 89; skepticism faced by 87, 89; *see also* Black men; Black (male) students
mental health 5, 97, **128**, 164, 173, 196, 199
mentors/mentoring 35, 97, 144, 154, 179, 201
merit 142
microaggressions 34, 48, 49, 67, 116, 117, 168, 169–171, 172, 173, 174, 175
Miller, W. 97
Milner, H. R. 144
Minh-ha, T. 163, 164
Minority Affairs offices/officers 9, 20, 29
minority-serving institutions (MSIs) 57
misogynoir 168
Montero-Marín, J. 200, 201
Moody, J. 57
Moradi, B. 85, 86
Moraga, C. 162, 163, 164
Morrill Acts 8
Morton, J. M. 148
Mueller, J. A. 155
multicultural education/learning 113–114, **128**, **130**, 144
multicultural programs 9
multiculturalism 4
Museus, S. D. 155
Myers, L. W. 150

nagualismo (shapefiter) concept 178–179
narratives 161, 162–163
NASCAR 132
NASPA *see* National Association of Student Personnel Administrators

supportive relationships 209
Sweeney, C. 11
symbolic role of CDOs 25–26
synergistic articulation and
awareness 141
systemic racism xiii, 67, 152

Takacs, D. 82
Tatum, B. D. 74, 145, 155
tenure review **129**; anti-racist 59
testimonios 161–162, 165, 180, 182
therapy 66, 71, 180, 210
Time Magazine 109
tokenism 98–99, 151, 169, 173
Torres, V. 205
transformational change ix, 6, 7,
11, 105, 107, 153; "Brutal Facts"
impeding 132–133; public demand
for 108–115
transformative leadership 6, 7, 58
transgender people 109, 112
transparency 113, 117–118, **127,
129**, 193
trends, staying abreast of 155
tribal communities, partnering
with 58
trust 11, 14, 34, 98, 152, 185; lack
of, faced by men of color 84,
87, 89
truth 55, 83, 84, 92, 181, 206
Turman, N. T. 186
Turner, C. S. V. 160
turnover rates 185, 199
Tyler, T. xiv, 191–214

Uhl-Bien, M. 12
Unit-Based CDO model 21, 121
University of Connecticut x
University of Kansas (KU) 105–133;
Campus Equity Implementation
Committee (CEIC) **129**; Climate
Survey 110, 111–113, 115, 116,
117–118, **129**; collaborative

leadership efforts 122, 124, 131;
demographic inequalities 108–109;
Diversity, Equity, and Inclusion
Advisory Group 110–111, 118–
119; faculty 108, 109, 112–113,
125–126, **127**; OMA (Office
of Multicultural Affairs) 110,
121–122, 123; primary leadership
by Office of D&E 122, 123–124,
131; "Race, Respect, Responsibility
and Free Speech" town hall (2015)
108, 109–110; resistance to
change 114–115; staff 108–109,
112, 113, 125–126, **127**; student
composition 108, 109, 126, **128**,
131; student unrest 108, 110;
Tunnel of Oppression diversity
awareness event 110
University of Kansas (KU), six
steps in effort for sustainable
institutional change 115–130;
1: agreement on the problem
and the solution 115–117; 2:
communication, transparency,
calm, and stability 117–118; 3:
articulation of a vision 118–120;
4: restructure for practical
scope and capacity 120–124;
5: buy–in rests on a practice
of inclusion 124–126; 6: swift,
transparent plan, and successful
implementation 126, **127–130**

values 7, 13, 43–44, 50, 86–87, 89,
139, 142, 150
veterans 14
violence 109, 116, 163, 170, 174,
181, 194, 198, 210; black male 87,
88; intersectional 168

Wade-Golden, K. 19, 20, 22, 25, 27,
28, 29, 33, 34, 121, 155
wages/pay 49, 112, 113, 115, 184